# On Modern Poetry
## Essays Presented to Donald Davie

# On Modern Poetry

Essays
Presented to
Donald Davie

*Edited by*
Vereen Bell
*and*
Laurence Lerner

VANDERBILT UNIVERSITY PRESS

*Nashville, 1988*

Library of Congress Cataloging-in-Publication Data

On modern poetry : essays presented to Donald Davie / edited by Vereen
  Bell and Laurence Lerner.
    p.   cm.
  ISBN 0-8265-1230-5 :
  1. English poetry—20th century—History and criticism.
2. American poetry—20th century—History and criticism.   3. Davie,
Donald.   I. Davie, Donald.   II. Bell, Vereen M., 1934-
III. Lerner, Laurence.
PR603.O48 1988
821'.91'09—dc19                                              88-244
                                                              CIP

*Printed in the United States of America*

# ACKNOWLEDGMENTS

The editors and publisher make grateful acknowledgment to the publishers of the following books for permission to reprint passages in this collection that first appeared in their publications:

Carcanet. "Love Songs," "Der Blinde," and "Junge" from *The Last Lunar Baedeker* by Mina Loy, 1985. "Or, Solitude" and "At Knaresborough" from *Collected Poems* by Donald Davie, 1983. "Ireland of the Bombers," "Advent," "July, 1964," "The Nonconformist," "Life Encompassed," "Oak Openings," and "In the Stopping Train" from *Selected Poems: 1970-1983* by Donald Davie, 1985. Used by permission of the author.

Collins. "Tel-El-Eisa" and "Sand" from *Poems* by John Jarmain, 1945.

USPB, Edinburgh. "First Elegy," "Second Elegy," "Seventh Elegy," "Ninth Elegy," "Opening of an Offensive," and "So Long" from *Elegies for the Dead Cyrenaica* by Hamish Henderson, 1977. Used by permission of the author.

Faber and Faber Ltd. "September 1, 1939" and "New Year Letter (January 1, 1940)" from *The English Auden: Poems, Essays and Dramatic Writings 1927-1939* by W. H. Auden, 1977.

Harcourt Brace Jovanovich. "Ash Wednesday," "The Wasteland," and "Four Quartets" from *Collected Poems: 1909-1962* by T. S. Eliot, 1970.

The Jargon Society. "Audubon," "Darwin," "Paean to Place," and "Wintergreen Ridge" from *From This Condensary: The Complete Writings of Lorine Niedecker*, 1985. "Love Songs," "Der Blinde," and "Junge" from *The Last Lunar Baedeker* by Mina Loy, 1985.

MacMillan. "Among School Children," "A Man Young and Old," "The Tower," "Blood and the Moon," and "Leda and the Swan" from *Collected Poems of W. B. Yeats*, 1956.

New Directions. "Cantos" from *The Cantos of Ezra Pound*, 1972. "Morning" and "Young Sycamore" from *The Collected Poems of William Carlos Williams*, 1951. "Workman" and "Travelogue" from *Collected Poems* by George Oppen, 1975. "John Sutter" from *Collected Poems* by Yvor Winters, 1960.

Oxford University Press. "Cairo Jag" and "How to Kill" from *The Complete Poems of Keith Douglas*, 1978. "Briggflats" from *Collected Poems* by Basil Bunting, 1978.

Random House. "September 1, 1939" and "New Year Letter (January 1, 1940)" from *The English Auden: Poems, Essays and Dramatic Writings 1927-1939* by W. H. Auden, 1977. "The Whitsun Weddings" from *The Whitsun Weddings* by Philip Larkin, 1964.

University of Notre Dame Press. "In the Stopping Train," "Ireland of the Bombers," "Advent," "July, 1964," "The Nonconformist," "Life Encompassed," "Oak Openings" from *Selected Poems: 1970-1983* by Donald Davie, 1985. "Or, Solitude" and "At Knaresborough" from *Collected Poems* by Donald Davie, 1983. Used by permission of the author.

Viking. "A Last World," "Two Scenes," "How Much Longer Will I Be Able to Inherit the Divine Sepulcher," "Glazunoviana," "Unctuous Platitudes," and "What is Poetry" from *Selected Poems* by John Ashbery, 1985.

A. P. Watt Ltd. "Among School Children," "A Man Young and Old," "The Tower," "Blood and the Moon," and "Leda and the Swan" from *Collected Poems of W. B. Yeats*, 1956.

# Editors' Preface

Donald Davie retires from the faculty of Vanderbilt University in 1988. The first half of his academic career was spent in Britain and Ireland, the second half in America. Vanderbilt, which was fortunate enough to have him for the last ten years, is able to act on behalf of Cambridge, Trinity College Dublin, Essex, and Stanford and commemorate his retirement by presenting him with this volume of essays.

We decided from the first that we wished to bring out a volume that would be not only a *Festschrift* but also a collection of intrinsic interest. We chose modern poetry, a subject that has always been at the centre of Davie's concerns, and invited a distinguished list of his friends and students to send articles. A gratifyingly large number responded, and the only way the volume differs from our original intention is that more people wrote on Davie's own work than we had expected. This seems to enhance the value of the collection, not only because it is appropriate to such a commemorative volume, but also because it gives Davie a deserved prominence in the history and discussion of modern poetry.

Vereen Bell
Laurence Lerner

*Nashville, Tennessee*
*December 1987*

# Contents

x            *Contents*

# On Modern Poetry

Essays Presented to Donald Davie

# Grace Dissolved in Place:
# A Reading of *Ash Wednesday*

## Vereen Bell

ELEN GARDNER describes *Ash Wednesday*'s structure as "less a
progress of thought than a circling round" a center which "is not
an idea of an experience so much as a certain state of mind which
is aspired to." This still leaves open the question of what that certain state
of mind is—to what extent it can be known and to what extent it is known
even by the poet himself. "The absence of clear structure is the formal
equivalent of this pecularity in the central subject." This essay is concerned with *Ash Wednesday*'s theme and eventually with its sources and
analogues in Dante and St. John of the Cross, these being relevant
because of the unusual way in which they are used. I wish to look at Eliot's
poem from the secular side and to consider how some of its psychological
implications impinge upon and modify our understanding of its spiritual
ones. For the sake of conciseness I wish to assume an acquaintance with
the traditional reading of the poem from which my own diverges. This
traditional reading is best represented by Leonard Unger's important
essay in *Southern Review* in 1939, "Notes on *Ash Wednesday*," and has been
subscribed to in one degree or the other by most students of Eliot since
then. It holds the influence of St. John of the Cross to be pervasive and
unambiguous. It takes the progress of the poem to be Dantesque, an
upward, Platonic one, directed by the Beatrice-like figure of the Lady, and
it takes the title to mean what it says: that this is a doctrinally orthodox
poem in which the poet expresses his commitment, though it wavers at
the end, to undertake the *via negativa* and, as he put it elsewhere, to
"divest himself of the love of created beings" in order that the soul might
aspire to achieve "divine union." It is this orthodoxy of *Ash Wednesday* that
I wish to interrogate and to interpret as being considerably more ambiguous than the title would have us believe.

It seems clear enough that the stairway in *Ash Wednesday* leads
eventually to God, to "The state of blessedness and divine love," but
whether, as Unger and others have argued, that is where both in his heart

and in his mind the poet is directed is another question. It does not follow necessarily that since the instruction of St. John of the Cross has been assimilated (as it clearly has) the poet has set himself in obedience to it. And to say, as Unger does, that the sexual impulse has been sublimated does not necessarily imply an issue of that experience in religious devotion, despite the classical precedents that would support such an inference. In fact by taking cryptographic liberties, we may construe the poem's title itself as a metaphor expressing an already existing state of spiritual and emotional deprivation: "Ash Wednesday" as a new version of the "Waste Land" within the self, the main subject of Eliot's poetry up to this point in his career and clearly the stipulated subject of *Ash Wednesday*'s opening section. Hence, it could be argued, the phrase "Ash Wednesday" denotes in a Christian idiom the same deprived state of being, a deadness within, that was expressed in mythic and pagan terms in the title of *The Waste Land*. "I will show you fear in a handful of dust," says the anonymous voice in "The Burial of the Dead"; "Dust thou art," says the celebrant of the Ash Wednesday Mass, "and unto dust thou shalt return." The change in the poet's attitude indicated by the image in the title from the Christian calendar seems not to be the quantum progression of religious conversion but instead that of a new and overlapping phase in an old and continuing conflict, the emergence of a new context or dispensation within which the struggle may be renewed.

The crisis for the Eliot persona before *Ash Wednesday* has been and remains not simply a separation from God but also a separation from nature within and without the self, and when *Ash Wednesday* is understood in that context, its relationship to the work before and after it in Eliot's career can be represented as logically continuous rather than oblique in the way that it must be if St. John of the Cross is understood to be the poem's principal spiritual instructor. The relationship becomes *logically* continuous in the sense that what happens or fails to happen in *The Waste Land* produces the experience of *Ash Wednesday,* and what happens or fails to happen in *Ash Wednesday* issues eventually in the disconsolate theological affirmations of the plays and the *Four Quartets*. It is the *Quartets* that express finally the poet's obedience to the instruction of St. John of the Cross: they express in retrospect the realization that the measures undertaken and described in *Ash Wednesday* to achieve an integration of flesh and spirit were ordained to fail.

> But to apprehend
> The point of intersection of the timeless
> With time, is an occupation for the saint—
> . . . . . . . . . . . . . . . . . . . . . . . . . . . . . . . . . .

For most of us, there is only the unattended
Moment, the moment in and out of time,
The distraction fit, lost in a shaft of sunlight
The wild thyme unseen, or the winter lightning
Or the waterfall, or music heard so deeply
That it is not heard at all, but you are the music
While the music lasts. These are only hints and
    guesses,
Hints followed by guesses; and the rest
Is prayer, observance, discipline, thought and action.

If the poet of *The Waste Land* may be said to have sought to recover nature in order to recover God, the poet of *Ash Wednesday* may be said to be seeking God in order to recover nature in order to be able to dwell in a time redeemed for consciousness by the revelation of the timeless within it—not the merely biological and phenomenal nature of atheism and philosophical materialism ("fear in a handful of dust") but nature as a formal immanence, the squared circle of perfected creation. The progression of the poem's speaker is arrested symbolically at a point that is the equivalent in *Ash Wednesday* of Dante's Earthly Paradise—the farthest point, spiritually, *toward* God (*Paradiso*) that is still *within* nature and within the world, "The desert in the garden the garden in the desert," the "Word within / The world" that Eliot's Pericles in "Marina," later, apprehends and describes precisely as "grace dissolved in place." "Grace dissolved in place" is another way of speaking of the intersection of the timeless with time, quite literally the best, for a while at least, of all worlds.

The poet's unwillingness to move beyond this median spiritual station would account for the silence of the Lady in *Ash Wednesday*, who though surrogate of Matilda and Beatrice in the *Commedia* does not proffer instruction. Instead she is empowered through the medium of her revealed presence to restore the years and "redeem the time" by redeeming "the unread vision in the higher dream." She makes "strong the fountains" and "fresh the springs," "cool the dry rock" and "firm the sand." That she becomes progressively identified with the Holy Virgin while remaining a creature of the earth, albeit remote and stylized, suggests that she herself is a formal analogue in human and sexual form of the physical creation. This perception of her role is reinforced by the fact that because of the simplicity of her presentation and her identification with the life of nature she bears a greater resemblance to the Matilda than to the Beatrice of the *Commedia*. Eliot's Lady, to fix a coordinate between all three, is identified by adapted phrasing with the figure in Baudelaire's "Bohemiens en Voyage" who "Fait couler le rocher et fleurir le desert"—except that this is

Cybele, the goddess of nature. The Lady of *Ash Wednesday* is secularized by such an association.

In this argument, I am considering that the stylization of *Ash Wednesday* expresses an effort to achieve access to the world (not to God) through a complicated process of sublimation; that the images and language express sublimated desire, but that desire has been sublimated in an effort to recover feeling. At the center of this arrangement is the Lady herself, the idealized womanhood of courtly love, of Cavalcanti, compassionate and remote, the veneration of whom is in itself a purifying and refining process. (In the Wall of Fire at the seventh cornice of Purgatory, beyond which is the Earthly Paradise, all souls are purged of lust, and love is refined.) Her attributes are obscure, but she is continuous with and commands a setting characterized by qualities of historical and artistic stylization—heraldic eagles and leopards, unicorns, gardens and fountains (nature subdued and arranged), baroque stairways, blue rocks, whispering yew trees—all of which represent a formal reconstitution of the otherwise obscured felicity of the temporal life. Like the Lady herself, this vision mediates between the flesh and the spirit—not simply the river and the sea, in other words, but the "*spirit* of the river" and the "*spirit* of the sea" (italics mine). The "thousand sordid images" of the street of "Preludes" of the Unreal City of *The Waste Land* have been purged. *Ash Wednesday*'s environment is the Unreal City's obscured essence, the Waste Land transubstantiated. The poem's liturgical idiom expresses the poet's endeavor to transcend the equivalent accidents of individual personality, but the tortuous and faltering syntax shows this to be more an earnest motivation than an achieved reality.

Without the grid of the metaphysical instruction of St. John of the Cross *Ash Wednesday* may be seen more clearly to express the spirit's struggle to achieve a form of homeostasis in relation to nature and time, not a transcendence of time altogether. At the end of *The Hollow Men* the inhabitants of that dead land seem to fade from reality, listlessly enacting two mutually exclusive religious rituals—the one pagan and sexual, going around the prickly pear (the "garden" so to speak, in *that* desert) and the other, imperfectly Christian, expressing humility before God: "*Thine is the Kingdom.*" Their ambivalence and division are pathological; their condition is that of being separated into their fleshly natures and their spiritual natures. "Suffer me not to be separated" is *Ash Wednesday*'s penultimate prayer, and at that point in the poem what it implies is, suffer me not to be separated again, as I was before, into flesh and spirit.

In an exchange of letters with Paul Elmer More in 1928 and 1929 Eliot

expressed privately what must have been the central crisis that the ritu-
alized experience of *Ash Wednesday* was intended to resolve.

> [There] seem to be certain persons for whom religion is wholly
> unnecessary. . . . They may be very good, or very happy; they
> simply seem to miss nothing, to be unconscious of any void—the
> void that I find in the middle of all human happiness and all
> human relations, and which there is only one thing to fill. I am one
> whom this sense of void tends to drive towards asceticism or
> sensuality, and only Christianity helps to reconcile me to life,
> which is otherwise disgusting.
>   What I should like to see is the creation of a new type of
> intellectual, combining the intellectual and the devotional—a new
> species which cannot be created hurriedly. I don't like either the
> purely intellectual Christian or the purely emotional Christian—
> both forms of snobism [sic]. The co-ordination of thought and
> feeling—without either debauchery or repression—seems to me
> what is needed.

In the paradoxical idiom of *Ash Wednesday* what Eliot describes in the first
paragraph is the experience of caring *or* not caring, the ambivalent fluc-
tuations of the hollow men, and caring or not caring not for God or salvation but for human life in the world. It is the separation and fluctuation
that is morally and psychologically intolerable. A synthesis achieved
within the framework of Christian belief would be the state of caring *and*
not caring, a sustained symbiosis of the flesh and the spirit. Hence Eliot's
comment in a letter to Boramy Dobrée eight years later:

> I don't think that ordinary human affections are capable of leading
> us to the love of God, but rather that the love of God is capable of
> informing, intensifying and elevating our human affections, which
> otherwise have little to distinguish them from the "natural"
> affections of animals.

In this view, a nature that is untransformed by grace is an affront to our
symbolic identity; it offers only bondage to the cycle of birth, copulation,
and death. "Teach [me] to care and not to care" thus finds in "Suffer me
not to be separated" a form of conceptual rhyme.

Perhaps the simplest way to focus this view of the poem is to draw
attention to the problematical lyrical passage at the opening of section VI:

> Wavering between the profit and the loss
> In this brief transit where the dreams cross
> The dreamcrossed twilight between birth and dying

(Bless me father) though I do not wish to wish these things
From the wide window towards the granite shore
The white sails still fly seaward, seaward flying
Unbroken wings

And the lost heart stiffens and rejoices
In the lost lilac and the lost sea voices
And the weak spirit quickens to rebel
For the bent golden-rod and the lost sea smell
Quickens to recover
The cry of quail and the whirling plover
And the blind eye creates
The empty forms between the ivory gates
And smell renews the salt savour of the sandy earth

If one reads the poem in the traditional way, this surprising development
toward its end is construed as a rebellion against the true way of St. John of
the Cross which requires the maturing soul to reject or pass beyond all
such sensual delight and all manifestations of the created world. If one
reads *Ash Wednesday* as I do, the passage may be construed to represent
the very revelation of the world, of the "grace dissolved in place," Word
within the world, which the poet has labored to achieve from the beginning. Because of the sails and wings flying seaward and the lost sea
voices, the passage recalls the forlorn separation of Prufrock from the
magical, female archetypes of *his* dispensation, the mermaids "riding
seaward on the waves" singing to each other but not to him. In the passage
in *Ash Wednesday*, however, a vision of the world is being recovered, not
lost, and the lyric emotion is elation rather than nostalgia. If this renewal is
compromised by reluctance and apprehension—"though I do not wish to
wish these things"—that would seem to be an effect not of austere,
spiritual resolve but of self-protection and a fear of exposure to emotional
jeopardy. This is, after all, the same poet for whom life in the physical
world has been a wrestling of hope and despair, for whom "April is the
cruellest month," and for whom minimal psychic survival is a matter of
"feeding a little life with dried tubers." Hence the parenthetical "Bless me
father" is not a confession of guilt but a plea to be sustained spiritually
through a crisis of regeneration and affirmation that the poet knows full
well to be potentially threatening and destructive. The lost heart stiffens
because it is recovering life, and the weak spirit rebels not against God but
against the pathological inertia of its own previous state, the condition
represented in the poem's opening section beyond which the poet has
painfully and gradually progressed. The heart and the spirit are "lost"

and "weak" because of the apathy that is now in process of being over-come; the eye is "blind" in the same sense for the same reason.

Though the argument has the logic of symbolic allusion on its side, it is difficult to see how, as Grover Smith and others have claimed, the presence of ivory gates in this image, coupled with "empty forms," can cause it to mean that the poet's eye is perceiving a false truth, a false world. The image, though cryptic in itself, is clearly parallel syntactically with the last line of the passage and therefore should be parallel in content and feeling; renewing the savour of the earth, by itself, could hardly be said to be associated with giving way to falsehood. Moreover, the emphasis in the last portion of this event is on a special transformation of the outer world, which is caused by the spiritual transformation within the believer: the blind eye does not perceive but *creates*, and the smell does not recover but *renews* the "salt savour of the sandy earth"; subject and object become united (as opposed to being separated), and this is a result of the re-awakening of the subject's spiritual imagination. Isolation has been over-come, and yet another separation has been bridged in the poem. Thus, it is said, this is a time of tension between the old being and the new ("dying and birth"), between sense and spirit, and also between subject and object—integrations, however, that the poet will eventually find to be humanly impossible to sustain.

One effect of this renewed synthesis with its associated way of seeing things is that the Lady is suddenly manifested in a clearer symbolic role. She is addressed as "Blessed Sister, holy Mother" and then more simply as "Sister, Mother": in the one case as the spirit of the fountain and the garden, and in the other as the spirit of the river and of the sea. In the first role she is the regenerating agent—"blessed" and "holy"—of the divine immanence in time and nature, of which the fountain and the garden in this context are the formal outward signs; in the other role she is of nature, of the river and the sea as opposed to fountain and garden, and thus closer to the poet, who remains a creature of time; but she still serves to affirm that nature is no longer merely phenomenal and instead the form on earth of the invisible Logos: in short, time redeemed. Nature as both form and energy is in vital equilibrium with divine presence, as in "Burnt Norton," "the pool . . . filled with water out of sunlight." Falsehood is the opposite of this; falsehood mocks and demoralizes the believer because it predicates a world without divine presence and the condition of being within it as a creaturely existence only, the ultimate end of which is the ultimate materialistic condition, the handful of dust.

The juniper tree beneath which the bones sing in section II in the cool of the day is at least partially a paradigm of "the Garden / Where all love ends." The transition from the one to the other is elliptical but suggestive. That Garden is where the torment of the hyacinth garden of *The Waste Land*—falsehood—"of love unsatisfied" and "of love satisfied" is purified and refined, as Dante's lust is refined by the Wall of Fire at the entrance to the Earthly Paradise. In the sense that this is our original spiritual home, beyond real time but alive within memory, this is the inheritance that we must strive to be worthy of, even before we may be worthy of revelation before God. There appears, then, to be an explicit point made of not uttering at the end of section IV and at the very end of the poem the full prayers: "And after this our exile *show us into the fruit of thy womb Jesus*" and "Suffer me not to be separated *from thee.*"

There are two "here's" in *Ash Wednesday*, separate and distinct from each other; but since they are not clearly differentiated in the text, they confuse interpretation regardless of which way one reads the poem. The one "here" is the temporarily achieved destination of the poet's spiritual journey, the place of tension where the dreams cross, and real perhaps in some subjective sense only—the realm of potential time first revealed, however opaquely, in section IV after the ascent of the stairway. The other "here" is the opposed realm of human society—where the disaffected "walk in darkness," where "what is actual is actual only for one time / And only for one place." This second setting represents an impediment to spiritual renewal and the vulgar antithesis of the time redeemed in the partial revelation of section IV. The sequence of sections or episodes prepares for a revealed synthesis of the two in section VI—a zone that is like section V in being particular in texture and located recognizably in present time (although the experience of time in VI is more immediate and personal) and like the environment of section IV in being transfigured in a way that the realm of section V is not. Again, then, synthesis appears to be the objective rather than absolute transcendence.

Section V remains problematical, however, because Eliot at that point transposes the poem's idiom to that of a subtly different mode or voice, and in this transaction the poet who has already been "dissembled" and then partially restored to affirmation, who has achieved three stations of his purgatorical stair, who has experienced at least in dream-vision ("through a bright cloud of tears") the years restored, now relapses, for a passage of thirty-five lines, into a choral identification with the masses of the unvisited and unredeemed. The identification is not complete. It is still *those*, rather than *we*, "who walk in darkness," and that distinction is carefully sustained throughout the passage; there is

No place of grace for *those* who avoid the face
No time to rejoice for *those* who walk among noise
    and deny the voice.

The effect of this interpolated section—pointedly a digression against the flow (imagine it omitted)—is to indicate that the supplicant in the time of the poem has turned his attention back to the fallen world and to the unredeemed within it who are stranded there between affirmation and disaffection, between hope and despair, in the dispensation of the hollow men—stranded, one might say, as the poet himself has been and is likely to be once more at any instant should the will falter or intercession lapse. So although he has partially overcome his own apathy, he is· yet in the presence of mortality and therefore of sin. Not the created world itself, but the clamor of the recusant souls within it prevails in this form of time and threatens to dissipate spiritual awareness.

    Both in the day time and in the night time
    The right time and the right place are not here
    No place of grace for those who avoid the face
    No time to rejoice for those who walk among noise
        and deny the voice

"[The] Word within / The world and for the world" is constant and remains, though the unstilled human world whirls against it. Remaining, against all the apparent signs, it is always accessible to the appealing spirit. There is the suggestion in the mannered theological word-play opening this section that the word is being understood idiosyncratically, in this context and throughout the poem, as having two manifestations: the "Word," which is absolute and beyond human revelation, and the "word," which is mediated, continuous with nature and within the world.

As this full section moves toward its resolution, the symbols and ambience of section IV—the veiled sister, the yew trees, the blue rocks, the garden in the desert—begin to reemerge, and with them, in a subtle drama of syntactical ambiguity, so does the individual petitioning persona of the preceding sections.

    Will the veiled sister between the slender
    Yew trees pray for those who offend her
    And are terrified and cannot surrender
    And affirm before the world and deny between the rocks
    In the last desert between the last blue rocks

> The desert in the garden the garden in the desert
> Of drouth, spitting from the mouth the withered apple-seed.

The syntactical routing in this passage is uncommonly obscure, even for *Ash Wednesday*. So much appears to be suspended in parenthetical apposition that it becomes difficult to separate the apposition from the transitive progression. The passage appears, however, to plot out something like this: the recusant, those who offend the veiled sister, cannot surrender in order to affirm and deny the world, or care and not care; they cannot reject "the withered apple-seed" of fallen nature and time. "Affirm" and "deny," like "care" and "not to care," have no stated direct objects; if the objects were, as it first seems, the desert and the garden, respectively, then "spitting from the mouth the withered apple-seed" would become contradictory, unless everything between that last phrase and "surrender" four lines before it were to be taken as an awkwardly long parenthetical elaboration. In any case the language at this point becomes indefinite and musical in a way suggesting that the language representing "the world" before has now begun to be transposed into the idiom of the prior, renewed experience of the "higher dream." As the poet's consciousness thus separates itself in its very form from "those who walk in darkness," there emerges perceptual illusion in which the poet seems to be expressing his own effort to achieve the spiritual state that the others of the world have rejected. Thus he is restored in a gauzy, dreamlike transformation of identity to the presence of the Lady who "made strong the fountains and made fresh the springs." Lines from *The Waste Land* seem apt:

> I sat upon the shore
> Fishing, with the arid plain behind me
> Shall I at least set my lands in order?

The ascent of the mystic stair in section III makes it clear that nature itself is fallen and yet may be made whole momentarily in this vision and restored in the vision to prelapsarian integrity. That the garden of the Earthly Paradise, short of transcendence itself, is metaphorically the goal in *Ash Wednesday* is evident in the transition from section III to section IV and in their proximity. The curiosity is that the first turning of this ascent is of the *second* stair. This could only mean that the first stair is already behind us in the poem and therefore must be identified as the condition of apathy and resignation described abstractly in section I and section II, where the strangely singing character of the language implies that the soul is already prepared to hazard devotional affirmation. In turn this would suggest that the surrealistic tableaus that are come upon at the different turnings of the stair are in fact symbolic of, or stand for, stages of the spiritual *descent* of the stair by which the poet had arrived in the first place in his state of apathy beyond even despair. In this phase he could not drink, for although trees flower and springs flow, the world is without God: that is, "there is nothing again"; and he must renounce the human face and the human voice for the veiled sister and silence of the revelation beyond speech.

The process by which the descent has taken place is more or less reviewed in the fragmentary scenes in memory in the struggle upward. The "devil" of the stairs "who wears / The deceitful face of hope and despair" is the tormenting ambivalence of *The Waste Land:* a different representation of April as the cruellest month. The aspect and cause of despair itself, alone, is imaged as the "old man's mouth drivelling, beyond repair, / Or the toothed gullet of the aged shark"—each of these being reductions in different ways of death and biological decay in unredeemed time. The hope, on the other hand, which had given way to despair, which had given way to conflict between the two and ultimately to apathetic inertia (since we are ascending, we are passing these stages of descent in reverse order of their taking place), is represented in images of sexuality in its innocent, procreative form—"slotted window bellied like the fig's fruit"; "hawthorn blossom"; "pasture scene"; and Priapus enchanting "the may time"—that is transforming by mythicizing the physical world—"with an antique flute."

> Blown hair is sweet, brown hair over the mouth blown,
> Lilac and brown hair;
> Distraction, music of the flute, stops and steps of the
>     mind over the third stair,
> Fading, fading; strength beyond hope and despair
> Climbing the stair.

Significantly, the purgatorial journey upward toward God appears to cease here and to be suspended on the achievement of an experiential plateau: not in the garden of the pagan god but one stage and *only* one stage past that garden in the garden of the Lady whom the pagan god now becomes in Christian apotheosis. Her ritualistic role, like the pagan god's, is regenerative and intercessory, to mediate between the believer and the world and to bring things to life—hence her making "strong the fountains and . . . fresh the springs," "cool the dry rock and . . . firm the sand." She redeems time, restores the original concordance between the self and nature ("restoring / With a new verse the ancient rhyme"). She is *behind* or *beyond* the garden god, but his flute is now "breathless" (his dispensation having been transcended), and she has but to gesture without speaking for creation to answer to her bidding. She is *between* the yew trees (which represent death and continuous life within the cycle of birth and death), and she walks between "the violet and the violet," presumably between morning and evening.*

The sequence from section III to section IV and their being structurally at the poem's center argue for their being *thematically* central to the meaning of Eliot's poem as well. In them it is implied that a pagan vitalist spirit has yielded to a Christian vitalist spirit. The space between them, then, is a kind of bridge or passageway between the two halves of the poem. It is implied that there is to be no further progression in this poem of the ascent to God. The emphasis—structurally and in the language— has fallen squarely on the cessation of progress, on suspension at an intermediate position, on intersection of the timeless with time. The simple preposition "between" has become a catalytic verbal agent. So, "And after this our exile" refuses to be read in only one way. In the *Salve Regina* prayer "our exile" is exile from God, and "this" is Time, beyond which we may be shown "into the fruit of thy womb Jesus." But if "this" and "our exile" are not in apposition, "this" can mean only the restored years, the temporarily redeemed time of the poem, and the "exile" is the eventual union with God, which will entail separation from the things of creation. "Here are the years that walk between," and it is this condition of betweenness that the speaker desires.

Although St. John of the Cross is concerned in the *Ascent of Mount Carmel* with "the obligation of Christian perfection," he discusses certain paradoxically "temporal advantages" that result from the detachment from temporal things:

> Although a man might not do this for the sake of God and of the
> obligations of Christian perfection, he should nevertheless do it
> because of the temporal advantages that result from it, to say
> nothing of the spiritual advantages, and he should free his heart
> completely from all rejoicing in the things mentioned above. And
> thus, not only will he free himself from the pestilent evils which we
> have described . . . but, besides this, he will withdraw his joy from
> temporal blessings and acquire the virtue of liberality, which is one
> of the principal attributes of God, and can in no wise coexist with

*In his commentary on the "Spiritual Canticle" St. John of the Cross interprets "morning knowledge" of God as essential knowledge of God, which is knowledge "in the Divine Word," and the "evening knowledge of God" as "the wisdom of God in His creatures and works and wondrous ordinances."

> covetousness. . . . He will find greater joy and recreation in the
> creatures through his detachment from them, for he cannot rejoice
> in them if he look upon them with attachment to them as to his
> own.

Since the sensual part of the soul cannot know God—"for it has no
capacity for attaining to such a point"—this limited revelation can be only
what Eliot calls a "token of the word unheard, unspoken"; nevertheless,
the "spiritual man" can, St. John of the Cross says, rejoice "in all things—
since his joy is dependent upon none of them—as if he had them all."
Perhaps the detachment he speaks of is signified in Eliot's poem in section
VI by the "wide window" through which the white sails flying seaward
are seen, the liberal frame of spiritual disengagement.

The logic, the structure, and the pattern of images in *Ash Wednesday*,
nevertheless, are and are not parallel with the commentaries of St. John of
the Cross in the same way that they are and are not parallel with *The Divine
Comedy*. The fact that both texts are alluded to directly and indirectly
means nothing in itself unless the odd insistence upon the divergencies as
well as the agreements is understood to be an aspect of the poem's
strategy and statement. The effect of the inexact correspondences to *The
Divine Comedy* is one of Dante's vision having been re-dreamed with its
components garbled and rearranged and reproduced in new but only
vaguely cognate images. The leopard, the lion, and the wolf of the
*Inferno*'s first canto associate suggestively, but only vaguely, with the
three white leopards of *Ash Wednesday*'s section II. The three levels of
Purgatory proper associate with the implied three stairs of the ascent in
*Ash Wednesday*. Dante's three dreams in Purgatory are suggested by "The
place of solitude where the three dreams cross" in *Ash Wednesday*, section
VI. The mortal death of Beatrice and then her subsequent supernatural
manifestation in the Earthly Paradise seem deliberately alluded to in *Ash
Wednesday*, section IV:

> Here are the years that walk between, bearing
> Away the fiddles and the flutes, restoring
> One who moves in time between sleeping and waking. . . .

In their first encounter in Earthly Paradise, Beatrice rebukes Dante for
having failed to learn from her death the folly of infatuation with the "brief
and passing" things of mortal life; the poet of *Ash Wednesday* says,

> I renounce the blessed face
> And renounce the voice
> Because I cannot hope to turn again.

Leah and Rachel in Dante's third dream, then Matilda, and then Beatrice
(the last two of whom are anything but silent) associate elusively with the
silent Lady (or Ladies) of *Ash Wednesday*. Beatrice's chariot drawn in the
Celestial Pageant by the Gryphen seems parodied as the "gilded hearse"
in *Ash Wednesday* drawn by "jewelled unicorns."

These examples can be multiplied, and they grow more complex. It is
therefore not simply an eccentricity worth remarking but a fact of thematic
significance that there is no true equivalent in *Ash Wednesday* of Beatrice in
her divine form and that the threshold of Paradise is not attained, although the equivalent of the zone of the Earthly Paradise appears to be.
Thus the garden of *Ash Wednesday* is not an image of the still point but an
image of *kairos*, of redeemed time. "The deracinated metropolitan," says
Nathan Scott, "wants again . . . to find himself living not amidst inert and
faceless mechanism but amidst a world which, in its every dimension, is
under the law of participation because all created things are indwelt by
grace and by holiness." That would seem to describe succinctly the theme
of both *The Waste Land* and *Ash Wednesday*. It points as well to the mutuality
of their concerns and to the transformations of those concerns shown by
the subtle kinship relation in their titles. What we see in Eliot, however, is
not the pantheism of Wordsworth and even less the naive sacramentalism
of Theodore Roethke. That among other things is what theistic structures
of Dante and St. John of the Cross are there in the background of *Ash
Wednesday* to keep us mindful of. As *Ash Wednesday* was latent in *The Waste
Land*, so the *Four Quartets* is latent in *Ash Wednesday*, an alternative when
the quest in *Ash Wednesday*, perhaps because the result is foreseen, fails.
*Four Quartets* restores the meaning in a different form. The time of pipe
and drum and dancing and commodious sacrament and concord and
rustic laughter and living seasons becomes

> The time of the coupling of man and woman
> And that of beasts. Feet rising and falling.
> Eating and drinking. Dung and death.

The ironic first gift reserved for age, for the one who in *Ash Wednesday*
pleads "not to be separated," is

> The cold friction of expiring sense
> Without enchantment, offering no promise
> But bitter tastelessness of shadow fruit
> As body and soul begin to fall asunder.

# Poetry of the Desert War:
# British Poets in Egypt 1940–45

*Bernard Bergonzi*

URING THE Second World War the cry "Where are the war poets?" was raised at intervals in Britain. There *were* war poets, of course, and the best place to have found them would have been in North Africa, on the battlefields of Egypt and Libya, or behind the lines in Cairo. The British army was continually in action between June 1940 and April 1943, fighting first the Italians and then the German troops of General Rommel's Afrika Korps. It was a war of rapid movement across empty spaces, fought in tanks and trucks.

Egypt was technically a neutral country but in fact a British-run protectorate. The life of Cairo, an ancient, cosmopolitan melting-pot of a city, was enriched by a large expatriate British population. Olivia Manning gives a vivid picture of the life and atmosphere of wartime Cairo in her *Levant Trilogy,* a brilliant sequence of autobiographical novels. In fact she provided readers back in Britain with one of the first accounts to reach them of the Cairo writers. In October 1944 she published an article called "Poets in Exile" in Cyril Connolly's monthly, *Horizon.* She described how the physical separation from Britain, and the slowness of the mails once the Mediterranean was closed, meant that the exiled writers had to generate their own literary life and outlets for publications. Hence, the several literary magazines that existed in Cairo, run by expatriates.

Manning herself was associated with *Personal Landscape,* a poetry magazine that had been founded as a semi-private platform for the work of a number of civilian literary exiles: Robin Fedden, a poet and travel writer; Lawrence Durrell, at that time known primarily as a poet; and the poets Bernard Spencer and Terence Tiller. Durrell worked at the British Information Office, while the other three were lecturers at the Fuad I University, where Robert Graves had briefly been professor of English in the 1920s. *Personal Landscape* soon opened its pages to other contributors. It had a strongly phil-Hellenic flavour—Durrell, Spencer, and Fedden had previously lived in Greece—and it published the work of George Seferis and Elie Papadimitriou. The magazine ran from 1942 to 1945, and its later issues included poems by a young officer, Keith Douglas, who had fought in the desert campaigns.

In her *Horizon* article Manning wrote, "Among the younger men whom the army has brought out here, Keith Douglas stands alone. He has been in contact with the enemy much of the time and he is the only poet who has written poems comparable with the works of the better poets of the last war and likely to be read as war poems when the war is over." Given the delays in publication and the postal service, this was probably written before Douglas's death in Normandy, just after the D-Day landings in June 1944. It was a perceptive judgment to have made at the time, and it has been vindicated by the subsequent growth of Douglas's reputation as the leading British poet of the Second World War. Manning also mentioned Hamish Henderson, who, like Douglas, had fought in the desert campaign, and two other poets in uniform, John Waller and G. S. Fraser, who were employed by the army on publicity and journalistic work.

*Personal Landscape* was not generally popular; it was regarded as a highbrow, mandarin production, with nothing to say to the ordinary fighting man in the desert, though it was appreciated by those with developed literary taste and judgment, and it published some distinguished work. *Personal Landscape*'s rival was *Salamander,* a magazine that went for undemandingly traditional poetry, francophilia, and a genteel romanticism. In 1943 an anthology of "war poetry" called *Oasis: The Middle East Anthology of Poetry from the Forces* was published in Cairo under the imprint of *Salamander.* (In 1980 it was reprinted in England as *Return to Oasis,* with much additional material.) Keith Douglas was unimpressed with the wartime flood of poetry publications: "No paper shortage stems the production of hundreds of slim volumes and earnestly compiled anthologies of wartime poetry, *Poems from the Forces,* &c."[1] He told Edmund Blunden with some satisfaction of his meetings with the *Personal Landscape* poets, Spencer, Tiller, and Durrell, and was scathingly dismissive of other Cairo magazines.[2] (Fraser heard from Durrell that the character of "Johnny Keats" in his *Alexandria Quartet* is partly based on Douglas.)[3]

With the passing of time, Olivia Manning came to take a cooler view of the Cairo literary scene. In *The Levant Trilogy,* "Castelbar," apparently a

1. Keith Douglas, *A Prose Miscellany* (Manchester, 1985), 119.
2. Ibid., 132.
3. G. S. Fraser, *Lawrence Durrell: A Study,* 2d ed. (London, 1973), 136.

composite of more than one Cairo poet, is an unattractive and rather absurd figure. Her 1944 article is historically important, but it restricts itself to the description of a milieu and its figures.

Soon after it appeared, G. S. Fraser published "Recent Verse: London and Cairo," a more sustained critical discussion, in *Poetry London X*, which attempted to sum up the work of the Cairo poets and establish a contrast between that and the poetry written and published in England. In this article Fraser distinguishes between the poetry published in London, which he sees as crisis-ridden, tormented by catastrophe and crying for redemption, and the poetry of Cairo, which is calm, conscious of the long perspectives of eastern Mediterranean culture and the need for restraint and good form, in both art and life. One pole is romantic, the other classical, and Fraser identifies himself with the latter in a sharp move away from the neo-romanticism he espoused when he contributed a long introduction to the New Apocalyptic anthology, *The White Horseman*, in 1941. The school of Cairo, writes Fraser, "has the poise and something of the sadness of maturity." As examples of "Cairo" poetry he quotes passages from the *Personal Landscape* poets, Durrell, Spencer, Tiller, and Fedden (though Fedden's lines are inexplicably attributed to another *Personal Landscape* contributor, the novelist Robert Liddell), and concludes with some lines of his own, translating Horace via D'Annunzio.

The contributors to *Personal Landscape* were serious about writing, and several of them were to become well known as poets and novelists. It is appropriate that Keith Douglas, who had an intensely professional approach to poetry and who let it be known that he intended to become a "major poet," should have appeared in it.[4] Robin Fedden, in his introduction to the 1945 anthology from the magazine, echoes Olivia Manning's praise: "We think, for instance, that Keith Douglas's war poems are near the top of the small body of presentable English poetry that the war has thrown off." However, Douglas was conspicuously absent from *Oasis* when it was published in 1943. Indeed, most of the contributors remain quite unknown, and the only two who went on to make any reputation as poets were Fraser and John Waller, though Erik de Mauny was to become a distinguished foreign correspondent for the BBC. Judged by the standards set by *Personal Landscape*, the poetic level of *Oasis* was decidedly low, and the anthology is pervaded by a note of populist amateurism. The windily verbose introduction by John Cromer seems to concede as much:

4. John Stubbs, "A Soldier's Story: Keith Douglas at El Ballah," *PN Review* 47 (1985): 26–29.

> From time to time in English literary circles the cry arises, 'where
> are our war poets?' That cry has been answered by the appearance
> of a number of anthologies and a continuous stream of books of
> poetry. It may not all be good poetry, but it is symbolic of the men
> of our time and the poetry of all time, that despite the crises and
> difficulties which surround them they continue to sing their songs
> and give out the benefit of their lyrical impulse and philosophic
> reflection.[5]

Keith Douglas would have greeted such sentiments with derision.
Nevertheless, he was opportunistically co-opted into the enlarged *Return
to Oasis*. This reprinted the 1943 *Oasis*, with a further section of "Previously Published Middle East Verse," which included several of Douglas's
poems. One of his drawings, an animated Cairo street scene, was reproduced on the back of the book. A third section was called "Previously
Unpublished Soldiers' Poems and Ballads," which for the most part
conveyed the same kind of dim amateurism as the original *Oasis*. But
Hamish Henderson's "So Long" was well worth printing; it is subtitled
"Recrossing the Sollum Frontier from Libya into Egypt, 22nd May, 1943,
in a lorry carrying captured enemy equipment":

> To the war in Africa that's over—goodnight.
>     To thousands of assorted vehicles, in every stage of
>         decomposition,
>     littering the desert from here to Tunis—goodnight.
> To thousands of guns and armoured fighting vehicles
>     brewed up, blackened and charred
>     from Alamein to here, from here to Tunis—goodnight.
> To thousands of crosses of every shape and pattern,
>     alone or in little huddles, under which the unlucky bastards
>         lie—goodnight. . . .

There is word-play within Henderson's sardonic declamation: "brewing
up" was the British soldiers' term for the tea-making they engaged in
whenever they could.

Another anthology, *Poems from the Desert: Verses by Members of the Eighth
Army*, with a foreword by Field Marshal Montgomery, appeared in England in 1944 and went into several editions. The poetic level is no higher
than in *Oasis*: the idioms are well worn, and some of the patriotic effusions
might have been written in August 1914. Nevertheless, the collection is of
some cultural and historical interest. The poems were written in response
to a competition organised by the Education Officer of the Eighth Army at
the end of 1942, after the El Alamein victory; only poems actually written

---

5. *Return to Oasis* (London, 1980), 10.

in the Western Desert could be submitted. The desert provided a subject and a theme. In battle it was a place of destruction and imminent death; at other times it represented vacancy and menacing emptiness. Yet it also had rich cultural implications for notionally Christian Englishmen. The idea of the "desert" carried many resonances from the Bible; so did "Egypt," with its suggestions of the Israelites in exile, and the typologically parallel exile of the Holy Family. There were, too, the ghosts of Caesar and Antony and Cleopatra. Terence Tiller called a collection of poems *Unarm, Eros,* and Douglas began his poem "Mersa":

> This blue halfcircle of sea
> moving transparently
> on sand as pale as salt
> was Cleopatra's hotel . . . .

One of the contributors to *Poems from the Desert,* M. St. J. Wilmoth, has a poem called "The Desert," whose idea is more interesting than its language:

> All these the desert is, and yet attracts
> The spirit with its rigours, as the cold
> And bitter pole attracts the compass-needle
> From the tropic's torrid zones, with the lure
> Of something strange and vast, in which the soul
> Can drown itself in its reflections,
> Unimpeded by the thousand cares of
> Daily life in cities and the haunts of men.

If the desert, which stood for death or emptiness, was one pole of the soldier's experience, the other was Cairo, which embodied density of experience and pullulating life. Two of the better poems in *Poems from the Desert*—"better" insofar as the writers try to focus on specific experiences, to which their language is more or less adequate—try to capture the alien feel of the city: J. Broome's "M. E. Medley" and N. A. Brown's "Western Oriental." Here is part of the opening of the latter:

> . . . Magnificent entrance, elevators by Otis,
> And a drooping donkey tethered to the door.
> Kite hawks hover high in sleepy circles,
> Malevolent outcasts, scavenging to live,
> Swoop to the gutter to pick at the scraps
> Of a syphilitic beggar drowsing there.[6]

Sleeping beggars, too, occur in Broome's poem.

6. *Poems from the Desert: Verses by Members of the Eighth Army* (London, 1944), 11–12, 35.

Cairo offered continual shocking contrasts between extremes of opulence and squalor, which were traumatically registered by the expatriate poets, whether civilian or military. Fraser eloquently recalled his impressions of Cairo in his posthumously published autobiography, *A Stranger and Afraid*:

> When I think of Cairo, now, I think of something sick and dying; an old beggar, propped up against a wall, too palsied to raise a hand or supplicate alms; but in a passive way he can still enjoy the sun. . . . The tenement which is crumbling away at one side, like a rotted tooth, the native restaurant, open to the night, from which there comes a soft clapping of palms on tables and a monotonous chanting; the maze of narrow streets that leads to a cul-de-sac, where a taxi has gone to die; . . . these things, and not things only, but people and incidents, are repeated; the baldish purple-looking ox that has collapsed in the gutter and is having its throat cut; the street accident with twenty shouting spectators in white galabyehs; the woman in black, sitting on the pavement, nursing her baby at a dusty breast; the legless beggar propelling himself forward, on a little wooden trolley, with frightful strength, with his hands.[7]

For the British expatriate writers, Cairo represented a quintessentially alien experience, where there were no clear bearings. The only part of its life to which they had access was the thin cosmopolitan milieu of the Egyptian upper classes, Hellenic or French in its inclinations, represented by bars and fashionable restaurants. Outside was a mass of poverty and deprivation, exemplified by the beggars in the streets. Whatever the superficial appeal of orientalist fantasies, the real Egypt was alien in all its aspects. Its Islamic culture was unintelligible to the outsider, and beyond that lay the Greeks and Romans, and the ancient past of the Pharaohs, symbolized by the Pyramids and other monumental relics. The more sensitive or observant had the sense of being in an environment that was quite indifferent to their passing presence (if the outcome of the El Alamein battle had been different, the British would have been shortly replaced by the Germans). In his 1944 article Fraser wrote:

> To visit Luxor and consider, in the brilliant air of Upper Egypt, the fallen basalt head of Rameses II, the serene, indifferent smile, or to watch an ox pulling a water wheel,
> eyes from the mud, and laughing
> filth and hunger steady as the sun. And sunk

7. G. S. Fraser, *A Stranger and Afraid* (Manchester, 1983), 120–21.

somewhere in all a patience of this ground,
   like the blind ox's round,
is to realise that there do indeed exist ancient and indifferent
civilizations in which all our excitements have somewhat of an air of
intrusion. The intruder, the barbarian invader, the danger from
outside, is nothing new in Greek or Egyptian history; and, indeed,
it is a danger which a great, corrupt, magnificent city like Cairo
feels perfectly capable of being able to absorb. The spiritual crisis in
Cairo is getting up in the morning and living through another day:
it is not anything so transitory as a war.[8]

(The quoted lines are from Bernard Spencer's "Egyptian Delta.")

The pervasive alienation offered a stimulus for poems, which could be
defensive or resigned or outraged; the same topics tend to occur. Thus,
Spencer has poems called "Egyptian Dancer at Shubra" and "Cairo Restaurant," while Tiller has "Egyptian Dancer" and "Egyptian Restaurant."
Tiller has a curiously cold poem called "Beggar," which has the effect of
fragmenting the subject into a cubist painting.[9] Keith Douglas's "Egypt"
reacts more vehemently to a female beggar:

A disguise of ordure can't hide
her beauty, succumbing in a cloud
of disease, disease, apathy. My God,
the king of this country must be proud.[10]

Fraser also wrote a poem called "Egypt"—by far the best poem, I think, in
the original *Oasis* anthology—which looks over the alien territory, taking
in the opposition between desert and city. Here are two of the concluding
stanzas:

The desert slays. But safe from Allah's justice
Where the broad river of His Mercy lies,
Where ground for labour, or where scope for lust is,
The crooked and tall and cunning cities rise.

. . . . . . . . . . . . . . . . . . . . . . . . . . . . . . . . . . .

In airless evenings, at the cafe table,
The soldier sips his thick sweet coffee up:

8. G. S. Fraser, "Recent Verse: London and Cairo," *Poetry London X* (1944), 215–19. (This,
the tenth number of the irregularly appearing magazine *Poetry (London)*, was published as a
substantial bound book.)

9. Bernard Spencer, *Collected Poems*, ed. Roger Bowen (Oxford, 1981), 30, 37; Terence
Tiller, *The Inward Animal* (London, 1943), 27, 31; *Unarm, Eros* (London, 1947), 24.

10. *The Complete Poems of Keith Douglas*, ed. Desmond Graham (Oxford, 1978), 89.

> The dry grounds, like the moral to my fable,
> Are bitter at the bottom of the cup.

Fraser's "The Streets of Cairo" brings in the inescapable beggars, and in a longish poem, "Monologue for a Cairo Evening," he looks back in a measured, reflective way at his experience of the city.[11]

More poems of merit were written about Cairo than about the desert, if for no other reason than that most of the poets, whether military or civilian, were not directly involved in the desert war. Spencer did write a short and uncharacteristic poem called "Libyan Front," and Tiller went into the desert to lecture to the troops and produced a rather embarrassed poem ("Lecturing to Troops") about doing so, which saw the soldiers as almost as alien as the denizens of the Cairo streets, "strange violent men, with dirty unfamiliar muscles / sweating down the brown breast, wanting girls and beer."[12] The point can be made differently by saying that most of the fighting men were not very good poets, as is apparent from *Oasis* or *Poems from the Desert*.

There were, however, some exceptions. Prominent among them was Keith Douglas, recognized at the time, and subsequently, as an outstanding poet. Another was Hamish Henderson, who has never had the recognition he deserves. Douglas, in one of his most powerful poems, "Cairo Jag," violently juxtaposes the city and the desert battlefield:

> Marcelle drops her Gallic airs and tragedy
> suddenly shrieks in Arabic about the fare
> with the cabman, links herself so
> with the somnambulists and legless beggars:
> it is all one, all as you have heard.
>
> But by a day's travelling you reach a new world
> the vegetation is of iron
> dead tanks, gun barrels split like celery
> the metal brambles have no flowers or berries
> and there are all sorts of manure, you can imagine
> the dead themselves, their boots, clothes and possessions
> clinging to the ground, a man with no head
> has a packet of chocolate and a souvenir of Tripoli.[13]

Schooled by recent critical thinking, we have learned to see the function of aporias and discontinuities, and "Cairo Jag" seems to me one of Douglas's

---

11. *Poems of G. S. Fraser*, ed. Ian Fletcher and John Lucas (Leicester, 1981), 71, 111, 118.
12. Spencer, *Collected Poems*, 26; Tiller, *Unarm, Eros*, 30.
13. *Complete Poems of Douglas*, 97.

best poems. Fraser preferred the poised and homogeneously satirical "Behaviour of Fish in an Egyptian Tea Garden," which is also admirable, though in a different way. It is perhaps the finest of all the expatriates' poems about Cairo.

Douglas left an interesting essay among his papers, "Poets in This War," written in about May 1943, after his experience of desert warfare. He refers with respect to the soldier-poets of the First World War, Owen, Sassoon, Sorley, and Rosenberg, and remarks that so far there had been no equivalents, notwithstanding the prevalence of anthologies and magazines of poetry. Douglas is contemptuous of the Middle East publications, which published effusions "from clerks and staff officers who have too little to do, and from the back end of the desert army." For Douglas, a war poet was essentially someone like Owen or Sassoon who had had direct experience of fighting. He attributes the absence of authentic war poetry to what later criticism would describe as the problem of "belatedness":

> There is nothing new, from a soldier's point of view, about this war except its mobile character. There are two reasons: hell cannot be let loose twice: it was let loose in the Great War and it is the same old hell now. The hardships, pain and boredom; the behaviour of the living and the appearance of the dead, were so accurately described by the poets of the Great War that every day on the battlefields of the western desert—and no doubt on the Russian battlefields as well—their poems are illustrated. Almost all that a modern poet on active service is inspired to write, would be tautological. And the mobility of modern warfare does not give the same opportunity for writing as the long routines of trench warfare.[14]

Douglas was right, up to a point. The experience of the trench poets of 1914–18 was unprecedented; they were the victims and witnesses of the rending of a civilization that had grown complacent after a long peace. The shadow of the earlier war hung over the later, and the participants knew what to expect. Yet the later war was not merely a continuation of the earlier. Douglas greatly underestimated the difference between the active, mobile warfare of the desert and the waterlogged stasis of the trenches, where men were likely to be passive victims of artillery bombardments or gas attacks. A tank commander in the hot empty spaces of the desert, as Douglas was, was physically and perhaps morally a freer being than the young infantry officers in the Great War. The mutual respect of the soldiers of the Eighth Army and the Afrika Korps, and of their comman-

14. Douglas, *Prose Miscellany*, 119–20.

ders, Montgomery and Rommel, looked back to an earlier, more chivalrous and individualistic mode of battle than the mass wars of the twentieth century.

In his essay, Douglas argued that if genuine war poetry was to be written, it would not be until the war had ended. In fact, he was already writing it. The poetry of the First World War has led to a general though inaccurate assumption that "war poetry" is necessarily pacifistic "protest poetry." Douglas was far from being a pacifist or even a reluctant civilian in uniform. He went straight from Oxford to the army, and he already had something of the temperament of a professional soldier. Indeed, while still at school he had seriously considered applying to enter Sandhurst rather than go to university; an "untitled autobiographical story" he wrote at the age of twelve begins, "As a child he was a militarist." When the Second World War broke out in September 1939, Douglas told a friend that he would join a good cavalry regiment and "bloody well make my mark in this war. For I will not come back." The conviction that he would not survive the war remained constant with Douglas, and was particularly strong during the last months of his life, on the eve of the Normandy invasion.

Yet if Douglas was a militarist, he was also an artist. In fact, he emerges from Desmond Graham's biography as a bewilderingly complex and even contradictory character. Graham sums up Douglas's career at his public school, Christ's Hospital, in these words: "A keen rugby player and swimmer, a dedicated horseman, a resolute opponent of authority and the injustices of boarding school life, a devoted member of the school's O.T.C. [Officers' Training Corps], a generally admired artist, it was as a writer that his reputation was most firmly based."[15] Douglas was, in embryo, a Renaissance man of many talents, though writing poetry was the activity to which he was increasingly dedicated.

In the cultural history of the twentieth century the combination of aestheticism and violent action that we find in Douglas had antecedents in futurism and was liable to take a proto-Fascist form. It had done so in Wyndham Lewis, and it is of Lewis, and notably of his accounts of his experience in the First World War, that I am reminded in parts of Douglas's masterly prose memoir of the desert war, *Alamein to Zem Zem*. Douglas shows a quasi-futurist delight in the clash of armoured masses, and his descriptions of death and dismemberment can be disconcertingly cold and detached. In the opening paragraph of *Alamein to Zem Zem* he writes:

15. Ibid., 17.

To say I thought of the battle of Alamein as an ordeal sounds pompous: but I did think of it as an important test, which I was interested in passing. I observed these battles partly as an exhibition—that is to say I went through them a little like a visitor from the country going to a great show, or like a child in a factory—a child sees the brightness and efficiency of steel machines and endless belts slapping round and round, without caring or knowing what it is all there for. When I could order my thoughts I looked for more significant things than appearances; I still looked—I cannot avoid it—for something decorative, poetic or dramatic.[16]

He had seen many deaths in the desert, which took horrible forms, as when men were burnt alive in tanks. He dealt with it all with extraordinary control, both psychological and literary, and his poems offer exact observation and a calm poise in facing extremity. But a darker side to Douglas emerged in the "Bête Noire" sequence he wrote early in 1944, after his return to England.

It was his thorough apprenticeship to modernism that distinguished Douglas from the amiable amateurs who contributed to *Oasis* and *Poems from the Desert*. In August 1943 he sent a letter to his friend J. C. Hall, who had preferred his earlier to his later, postbattle poems. In defending his recent practice Douglas, in effect, restates in a personal and existential way the modernist literary arguments of a generation earlier:

To write on the themes which have been concerning me lately in lyrical and abstract forms, would be immense bullshitting. In my early poems I wrote lyrically, as an innocent, because I was an innocent: I have (not surprisingly) fallen from that particular grace since then . . . . my object (and I don't give a damn about my duty as a poet) is to write true things, significant things in words each of which works for its place in a line. My rhythms, which you find enervated, are carefully chosen to enable the poems to be *read* as significant speech: I see no reason to be either musical or sonorous about things at present. When I do, I shall be so again, and glad to. I suppose I reflect the cynicism and the careful absence of expectation (it is not quite the same as apathy) with which I view the world. As many others to whom I have spoken, not only civilians and British soldiers, but Germans and Italians, are in the same state of mind, it is a true reflection. I never tried to write about war (that is battles and things, not London can Take it) . . .

16. Keith Douglas, *Alamein to Zem Zem* (London, 1966), 15.

until I had experienced it. Now I will write of it, and perhaps one
day cynic and lyric will meet and make me a balanced style.[17]

There is a bitter wisdom and assurance here. Douglas may have begun
with the earlier war poets—Owen, Sassoon, Rosenberg—as ideals, but he
went on to develop a new kind of war poetry, which had assimilated their
example, the knowledge of the war they had fought in, and of the literary
revolution that coincided with it. By now his achievement is generally
accepted; "Vergissmeinnicht" is a familiar anthology piece, a parallel to
Owen's "Futility" from the earlier war. The contrast between Owen's
anguish at the sight of a young dead English soldier and Douglas's
seeming coolness at a dead and decaying German points beyond differences of temperament to a difference in ways of apprehending war.
Direct emotion is repressed in Douglas, and emerges obliquely in the
language and descriptive detail. The poem has the directness of a poster,
and its directness needs to be balanced by the subtler attitudes of some of
Douglas's other war poems.

It is one thing to write a poem about a dead man, and it is another to
write a poem about killing a man, as Douglas does in "How to Kill," of
which these are the middle stanzas:

> Now in my dial of glass appears
> the soldier who is going to die.
> He smiles and moves about in ways
> His mother knows, habits of his.
> The wires touch his face: I cry
> NOW. Death, like a familiar, hears
>
> and look, has made a man of dust
> of a man of flesh. Being damned, I am amused
> to see the centre of love diffused
> and the waves of love travel into vacancy.
> How easy it is to make a ghost . . . . [18]

Douglas's poems offer a tension between feeling and apparent indifference, which can be harder for the reader to relate to immediately than
the anger of Sassoon or the pity of Owen, more innocent participants in a
different war. Tensions or contradictions were part of Douglas's life as of
his art; perhaps the greatest tension was between his wish to be a major
poet and his conviction that he would not survive the war:

17. Douglas, *Prose Miscellany*, 127.
18. *Complete Poems of Douglas*, 112.

I see my feet like stones
underwater. The logical little fish
converge and nip the flesh
imagining I am one of the dead.
("Mersa")

John Jarmain, a Cambridge mathematics graduate, served, like Douglas, through the North African campaign only to be killed in Normandy in June 1944 and, like Henderson, was in the 51st Highland Brigade. Jarmain was an older man, who was thirty-three when he was killed. He did not apparently contribute to the Middle East anthologies and magazines, though some of his poems were published posthumously in the *Middle East Anthology* edited by Waller and de Mauny, published in London in 1946. Jarmain's *Poems* appeared in 1945. His responses were simple and his mode of expression traditional; indeed, he is closer in feeling and language to Sassoon in his more reflective moods than to the far more sophisticated Douglas or Henderson. Most of Jarmain's war poems are very pedestrian. But "Tel-El-Eisa" written at El Alamein on November 26, 1942, while the battle was in progress, has an imagistic poignancy, though it could have as easily been written in the First World War as the Second:

Tel-El-Eisa is Jesus' hill,
Or so they say:
There the bitter guns were never still,
Throwing up yellow plumes of sand by day
And piercing the night across.
There the desert telephone's long lonely line expires,
Ends with a tangle of looping wires
And one last leaning cross.

"Sand" seems to me one of Jarmain's more successful poems. It explores the universal element of the desert war in its different aspects, making a Latinate pun in the final line:

We have seen sand frothing like the sea
About our wheels, and in our wake
Clouds rolling yellow and opaque,
Thick-smoking from the ground;
Wrapped in the dust from sun and sky
Without a mark to guide them by
Men drove alone unseeing in the cloud,
Peering to find a track, to find a way,
With eyes stung red, clown-faces coated grey.
Then with sore lips we cursed the sand,

Cursed this sullen gritty land
—Cursed and dragged on our blind and clogging way.
.................................................
Yet sand has been kind for us to lie at ease,
Its soft-dug walls have sheltered and made a shield
From fear and danger, and the chilly night.
And as we quit this bare unlovely land,
Strangely again see houses, hills, and trees,
We will remember older things than these,
Indigo skies pricked out with brilliant light,
The smooth unshadowed candour of the sand.

Buerat-el-Hsun. Jan, 1943[19]

Hamish Henderson survived the war; after taking part in the desert campaigns, he fought with the Italian partisans. In later years he became a distinguished authority on Scottish oral culture. I believe that he is of equal stature with Douglas as a war poet, though he is very much less well known, since his reputation rests on a single slim collection, *Elegies for the Dead in Cyrenaica*, published in 1948. A new edition appeared from a small Edinburgh publisher in 1977, and it is more than time for the book to be reprinted and made generally available again. Even anthologists have not served him well, compared with Douglas: he is not represented in Skelton's *Poetry of the Forties* or in Jon Stallworthy's *Oxford Book of War Poetry*. Because of the difficulty of locating his poems, I am, with the poet's permission, reprinting three of the *Elegies* as an appendix to this essay.

Like Douglas, Henderson was at the same time a fighting soldier and a very literary poet, who wrote out of a wide acquaintance with modernist poetry. Beyond this, the two poets are unalike. Douglas, though intensely individualistic, was in many respects a conventional Englishman of his class. His poetic points of reference were the trench poets of 1914–18, plus the major anglophone modernists. Henderson, although he had been educated at an English public school and at Cambridge, was a more exotic figure. He was a Highlander, who knew the Gaelic language and its poetry, and who was immersed in German literature and thought; he was both a Scottish Nationalist and a Marxist, in the mould of Hugh MacDiarmid. Fraser, a Lowland Scot of more empirical temperament, has left a lively account of his first meeting with Henderson in Cairo in 1941, and of their subsequent argumentative friendship:

> Hamish, a Marxist in the modern world, became when he
> considered Scottish history a Jacobite and a Tory. He was so eager

19. John Jarmain, *Poems* (London, 1945), 26, 27–28.

about the old feuds, which he felt stirring again beneath the surface of our time, that it was hard not to catch his enthusiasm. An age of battles! What a splendid prospect . . . if one had a temperament like his.[20]

Douglas responded to war with irony and toughness and a cool repression of feeling that can on occasion seem like an apotheosis of the ethic of the stiff upper lip. Henderson was not afraid to write rhetorically, to express emotion, even to rant, and to make abrupt shifts between poetic registers. In short, his poetry takes risks in a way that has evoked an embarrassed uncertainty in notionally admiring English critics such as A. T. Tolley and Vernon Scannell.[21] Henderson's *Elegies*, in their range of allusion, and their juxtaposition of literary and demotic speech, are reminiscent of Pound's *Cantos* or David Jones's masterpiece from the First World War, *In Parenthesis*.

Henderson has described Hölderlin as a major influence on the *Elegies*, and their form recalls Rilke's *Duino Elegies*. German and Gaelic poetry are invoked throughout Henderson's sequence: there are epigraphs from Goethe and Hölderlin, and from the Gaelic poet, Sorley Maclean, who also fought in the Western Desert and who contributed an introduction to the 1977 edition. Although Henderson began writing the *Elegies* in 1942, he did not complete them until 1947, and they broadly fulfil Douglas's belief that the best of the war poetry would not be written until after the war. Certainly, they take a broader perspective on the desert war than the other poets who fought in it. Henderson goes beyond the recording of simple personal experience, and in places he gives the genuine sense of a collective voice. At the same time, he is more single-minded than the other Middle East poets. There are no references to Cairo and its corrupt attractions, though in the Eighth Elegy Henderson, contemplating the ruins at Karnak, reflects on the transience of the successive civilizations that have existed in Egypt. But his main preoccupation is the desert, which, as other poets had seen, erased all distinctions. He wrote in his preface:

> It was the remark of a captured German officer which first suggested to me the theme of these poems. He had said: 'Africa changes everything. In reality we are allies, and the desert is our common enemy' . . . . The conflict seemed rather to be between 'the dead, the innocent'—that eternally wronged proletariat of

20. Fraser, *A Stranger and Afraid*, 136.
21. A. T. Tolley, *The Poetry of the Forties* (Manchester, 1985), 263–64; Vernon Scannell, *Not Without Glory: Poets of the Second World War* (London, 1976), 146–49.

levelling death in which all the fallen are comrades—and ourselves, the living, who cannot hope to expiate our survival but by 'spanning history's apollyon chasm' . . . . In the first part of the cycle, echoes of earlier warfare and half-forgotten acts of injustice are heard, confusing and troubling the 'sleepers'. It is true that such moments are intended to convey a universal predicament; yet I was thinking especially of the Highland soldiers, conscripts of a fast vanishing race, on whom the dreadful memory of the clearances rests, and for whom there is little left to sustain them in the high places of the field but the heroic tradition of *gaisge* (valour).[22]

No other British poets, as far as I know, saw the war in quite this way. As a Highlander, Henderson had an acute sense of history, which his Marxism reinforced and systematized. Marxism also provided a confident metaphysical vision and held out an ultimate remote hope for humanity. Henderson can write observantly and precisely of the desert landscape, as at the opening of the Second Elegy, which Sorley Maclean has praised: "The psycho-geographical impression of the Halfaya-Sollum area in the opening verse paragraph of the Second Elegy is as true to me as anything I have read in war poetry":[23]

> At dawn, under the concise razor-edge
> of the escarpment, the laager sleeps. No petrol fires yet
> blow flame for brew-up. Up on the pass a sentry
> inhales his Nazionale. Horse-shoe curve of the bay
> grows visible beneath him. He smokes and yawns.
> Ooo-augh,
>                    and the limitless
> shabby lion-pelt of the desert completes and rounds
> his limitless ennui.

Elsewhere, Henderson is defiantly rhetorical, as in the "Interlude" between the two parts of the book, which is called "Opening of an Offensive." It ends with lines about Highland troops advancing to the sound of the bagpipes, with an artillery bombardment in the background. Here Henderson sees the war as ideologically justified and necessary. With the recurring phrase "mak siccar," which means "make sure," Henderson looks back to one of the bloodier episodes in Scottish history, which he glosses in his notes: "After Bruce had stabbed the Red Comyn in Dumfries Kirk he was found outside the building by Lindsay and

22. Hamish Henderson, *Elegies for the Dead in Cyrenaica*, 2d ed. (Edinburgh, 1977), 59–60.
23. Ibid., 10.

Kirkpatrick. Lindsay asked if Comyn were dead. Bruce replied that he didn't know. 'Aweel,' said Kirkpatrick. 'I'll mak siccar.' "

> Now again! The shrill war-song: it flaunts
> aggression to the sullen desert. It mounts. Its scream
> tops the valkyrie, tops the colossal
> artillery.
>
> Meaning that many
> German Fascists will not be going home
> meaning that many
> will die, doomed in their false dream
> We'll mak siccar!
> Against the bashing cudgel
> against the contemptuous triumphs of the big battalions
> mak siccar against the monkish adepts
> of total war against the oppressed oppressors
> mak siccar against the leaching lies
> against the worked out systems of sick perversion
> mak siccar
> against the executioner
> against the tyrannous myth and the real terror
> *mak siccar*

This kind of writing makes English critics uncomfortable, and I am not claiming for it the poetic quality of other parts of the *Elegies*. But it is worth quoting as an example of a kind of declamatory political poetry that is rare in English, though common in other cultures.

Douglas and Henderson never met, though they shared acquaintances, such as Fraser and Waller. If they had, they may not have found much in common, given their differences in temperament and attitudes to reality, Douglas's cynicism confronting Henderson's Marxism. Nevertheless, they seem to me to be the two best "war poets" of the Second World War, using the term as we apply it to Owen and Sassoon and Rosenberg, to mean poets whose poetry expressed the reality of battle, the static warfare of the Western Front in the one case, the mobile action of the Western Desert in the other. What can be said of both Douglas and Henderson, for all their differences, is that they were poets who had learned the lessons of modernism. They knew that poetry is not only drawn from individual experience, however extreme and unique; it is also drawn from other poetry. They were very conscious in their art, which distinguished them from the many other would-be "war poets" who contributed to magazines and anthologies.

# *Appendix*

## Extracts from Hamish Henderson,
### *Elegies for the Dead in Cyrenaica*

### First Elegy
### END OF A CAMPAIGN

There are many dead in the brutish desert,
        who lie uneasy
among the scrub in this landscape of half-wit
stunted ill-will. For the dead land is insatiate
and necrophilous. The sand is blowing about still.
Many who for various reasons, or because
        of mere unanswerable compulsion, came here
and fought among the clutching gravestones,
        shivered and sweated,
cried out, suffered thirst, were stoically silent, cursed
the spittering machine-guns, were homesick for Europe
and fast embedded in quicksand of Africa
        agonized and died.
And sleep now. Sleep here the sleep of the dust.

There were our own, there were the others.
Their deaths were like their lives, human and animal.
There were no gods and precious few heroes.
What they regretted when they died had nothing to do with
        race and leader, realm indivisible,
laboured Augustan speeches or vague imperial heritage.
(They saw through that guff before the axe fell.)
        Their longing turned to
the lost world glimpsed in the memory of letters:
an evening at the pictures in the friendly dark,
two knowing conspirators smiling and whispering secrets;
        or else
a family gathering in the homely kitchen
with Mum so proud of her boys in uniform:
        their thoughts trembled
between moments of estrangement, and ecstatic moments
of reconciliation: and their desire
crucified itself against the unutterable shadow of someone
whose photo was in their wallets.
Then death made his incision.

There were our own, there were the others.
Therefore, minding the great word of Glencoe's

son, that we should not disfigure ourselves
with villainy of hatred; and seeing that all
have gone down like curs into anonymous silence,
I will bear witness for I knew the others.
Seeing that littoral and interior are alike indifferent
and the birds are drawn again to our welcoming north
why should I not sing *them*, the dead, the innocent?


*Seventh Elegy*
## SEVEN GOOD GERMANS

*The track running between Mekili and Tmimi was at one time a kind of no-man's land. British patrolling was energetic, and there were numerous brushes with German and Italian elements. El Eleba lies about half-way along this track.*

Of the swaddies
who came to the desert with Rommel
there were few who had heard (or would hear) of El Eleba.
They recce'd,
or acted as medical orderlies
or patched up their tanks in the camouflaged workshops
and never gave a thought to a place like El Eleba.

To get there, you drive into the blue, take a bearing
and head for damn-all. Then you're there. And where are you?

—Still, of some few who did cross our path at El Eleba
there are seven who bide under their standing crosses.

The first a Lieutenant.
When the medicos passed him
for service overseas, he had jotted in a note-book
*to the day and the hour    keep me steadfast    there is only the
decision and the will*
*the rest has no importance*

The second a Corporal.
He had been in the Legion
and had got one more chance to redeem his lost honour.
What he said was
*Listen here, I'm fed up with your griping—*
*If you want extra rations, go get 'em from Tommy!*
*You're green, that's your trouble. Dodge the column, pass the
buck*
*and scrounge all you can—that's our law in the Legion.*

*You know Tommy's got 'em . . . . He's got mineral waters,*
*and beer, and fresh fruit in that white crinkly paper*
*and God knows what all! Well, what's holding you back?*
*Are you windy or what?*
                          *Christ, you 'old Afrikaners'!*
*If you're wanting the eats, go and get 'em from Tommy!*

The third had been a farm-hand in the March of Silesia
and had come to the desert as fresh fodder for machine guns.
His dates are inscribed on the files, and on the cross-piece.

The fourth was a lance-jack.
                          He had trusted in Adolf
while working as a chemist in the suburb of Spandau.
His loves were his 'cello, and the woman who had borne him
two daughters and a son. He had faith in the Endsieg.
THAT THE NEW REICH MAY LIVE prayed the flyleaf of his Bible.

The fifth a mechanic.
                          All the honour and glory,
the siege of Tobruk and the conquest of Cairo
meant as much to that Boche as the Synod of Whitby.
Being wise to all this, he had one single headache,
which was, how to get back to his sweetheart (called Ilse).
—He had said
              *Can't the Tommy wake up and get weaving?*
*If he tried, he could put our whole Corps in the bag.*
*May God damn this Libya and both of its palm-trees!*

The sixth was a Pole
                          —or to you, a Volksdeutscher—
who had put off his nation to serve in the Wehrmacht.
He siegheiled, and talked of "the dirty Polacken",
and said what he'd do if let loose among Russkis.
His mates thought that, though "just a polnischer
     Schweinhund",
he was not a bad bloke.
                          On the morning concerned
he was driving a truck with mail, petrol and rations.
The M.P. on duty shouted five words of warning.
He nodded.
           laughed
                    revved
                          and drove straight for El Eleba
not having quite got the chap's Styrian lingo.

The seventh a young swaddy.
                              Riding cramped in a lorry
to death along the road which winds eastward to Halfaya
he had written three verses in appeal against his sentence
which soften for an hour the anger of Lenin.

> Seven poor bastards
> dead in African deadland
> (tawny tousled hair under the issue blanket)
> *wie einst Lili*
> dead in African deadland
>                              *einst Lili Marlene*


### Ninth Elegy
### FORT CAPUZZO

> *For there will come a day*
> *when the Lord will say*
> *—Close Order!*

One evening, breaking a jeep journey at Capuzzo
I noticed a soldier as he entered the cemetery
and stood looking at the grave of a fallen enemy.
Then I understood the meaning of the hard word 'pietas'
(a word unfamiliar to the newsreel commentator
as well as to the pimp, the informer and the traitor).

His thought was like this.—Here's another 'Good Jerry'!
Poor mucker. Just eighteen. Must be hard-up for man-power.
Or else he volunteered, silly bastard. That's the fatal
the—fatal—mistake. Never volunteer for nothing.
I wonder how he died? Just as well it was him, though,
and not one our chaps. . . . Yes, the only good Jerry,
as they say, is your sort, chum.
                              Cheerio, you poor bastard.
Don't be late on parade when the Lord calls 'Close Order'.
Keep waiting for the angels. Keep listening for Reveille.

# Three Hard Women:
# HD, Marianne Moore, Mina Loy

*Thom Gunn*

A COLLECTED POEMS is a monument, and it often gives you little sense of its author's early poetry, of the ways it seemed fresh, unprecedented, even outrageous, to its first readers. You would be hard put to guess what the *Lyrical Ballads* or the 1855 *Leaves of Grass* were like from Wordsworth's or Whitman's collected works, in which they have become scattered limbs. Redistribution and revision have made the originals hard to reconstruct.

I am concerned in this essay with some twentieth-century poets. Yeats, Marianne Moore, and Auden are merely the most famous of those who suppressed some of their early poetry and altered much of the rest out of all recognition. But the attempt to read a poet's early work for itself and not as part of a career meets more subtle obstacles among other modernists, in whose work such large changes of style took place, for here the obstacles may rather be in the reader's mind. Though *Prufrock* and *Harmonium* are printed as intact units at the start of the collected Eliot and the collected Stevens, you have to make an effort to see them as such, to separate the brilliant, self-willed cleverness of the younger men from the sobered meditations that came afterward. You tend to keep the latter in mind without meaning to, their weight anachronistically ballasting the early work. Nevertheless, whether the obstacles are outside or inside your mind, it is still worth trying to overcome them in order to read those first books for what they were at the time of publication.

For what they were. Asked in old age about her criteria in selecting material for the *Dial*, Marianne Moore said:

> I think that individuality was the great thing. We were not conforming to anything. We certainly didn't have a policy, except I remember hearing the word 'intensity' very often. A thing must have 'intensity.' That seemed to be the criterion.[1]

1. Interview with Donald Hall, *A Marianne Moore Reader* (New York, 1961), 266.

The words may sound moderate enough, but the individuality, nonconformity, and intensity she is speaking about are those of, among others, Gertrude Stein, e.e. cummings, Williams, and Stevens, all of whom she admired. However we may see it now, her generation saw itself as in revolt.

It is possible to speak of the essential conservatism of all poetry, which through its language, its metric, and so on, preserves and extends the values of tradition. Yes, but it does so through a paradox: for revolutionary activity is a firm part of that tradition. Catullus, for example, was conservative in that he adopted genres and meters from the past, but to his contemporaries he was revolutionary, for those genres and meters were un-Roman, many of them came from Sappho (the comic Lesbian of lost early Roman plays and hardly the most proper of models), and his subjects ranged from the religiously orthodox to the scandalously personal, with a marked emphasis on the latter.

I want, then, to insist on the obvious, because the obvious is in danger of being forgotten, that what we now call the modernists started by being revolutionary. I want to take a look at the first books of three members of the avant-garde in the years around 1920: HD's *Sea Garden* (1916), Marianne Moore's *Observations* (1924), and Mina Loy's *Lunar Baedecker*[2] (1923). I want especially to isolate these books from the respectability a "collected works" has granted even to Mina Loy by 1988, in an effort to read them as they were when they first appeared. It is, of course, no chance that the poets I have chosen are women: I am interested also in finding out how women responded in their poetry to being, for probably the first time in history, the comrades and equals of men in a generation of literary innovators.[3]

Many of the poems in *Sea Garden* may be called Imagist, but few are as subtle and none is as succinct as the two classic Imagist poems HD deliberately omitted, presumably because they did not fit thematically— "Oread" and "The Pool." The book opens with "Sea Rose," one of a series of sea-flower poems, and though it is unquestionably Imagist, it is very simply so. To compare it with Rossetti's "The Woodspurge," for instance, shows how straightforward it is. Rossetti's weed serves, for all the mathe-

---

2. This was the spelling of the book's title.
3. I refer to *woman poets* throughout. Three male poets I admire, Basil Bunting, Donald Davie, and August Kleinzahler, have tried to retain or revive the word *poetess*, but I find it impossible to use here, since it is not without its associations, and they are precisely those that Moore and Loy were trying to escape from.

matical brevity of presentation, as indeed "an intellectual and emotional complex [presented] in an instant of time." Because of a mere habit of observation retained during a period of grief, his plant becomes inextricably associated in his mind with that grief, loaded with an emotion that is irrelevant to the characteristics of the woodspurge itself. By contrast, HD's sea rose, described in an appropriately economical free verse line, short, qualifying, and nervous, is somewhat allegorical: clearly its enduring and unpretty hardness represents the kind of existence that the poet aspires to.

By sea rose I think she means not a marine plant, real or imagined, but an ordinary rose that has grown too close to the sea to achieve more than a minimal life, contrasted with the "spice rose" inland. She thus announces the sets of opposed images around which most of the book is organized. She is preoccupied with that edge between land and sea embodied in the paradox of the sea garden, where "sea-grass tangles with shore-grass," or where, as she says beautifully, addressing the sea,

> O privet-white, you will paint
> the lintel of wet sand with froth.

They tangle, they interpenetrate, and yet they are irreconcilable. The sea, being in constant movement, is like the bare demands of emotion or of impulse, and is by extension the place of adventure. The land is, of course, everything else: in "The Helmsman" she refers to "a slender path strung field to field"; land contains the connected, the habitual, even the rational, as opposed to the impulsive. Though at times she speaks with the exasperated folly of a Gothic heroine, in most of the poems she more calmly values the edge between land and sea, because it is the only place at which she apprehends life as not annihilated by too much violence on the one hand or paralysed by too much security on the other. The symbolism is familiar, but has a certain individuality from her passionate interest in the precarious existence of life-at-the-edge: her sea garden is composed of a number of flowers, real or mythical, whose very names are contradictions—sea rose, sea violet, sea poppy, monsters of endurance. The sea lily is as if carved out of stone by wind-blown sand:

> Sand cuts your petal,
> furrows it with hard edge.

It is an edge at the edge, quintessence of hardness. What she rejects, then, is ease, unstrenuous beauty—the spice rose, the soft grass of the uplands and lowlands, the garden pinks. She rejects honey but approves of the offerings to Priapus, which are, as in her Greek source, nuts, shrunken figs, broken pomegranates, crushed grapes, quinces.[4] Such things are also sweet, but theirs is a weathered, aged, abused, distilled, hardened, *enduring* sweetness, one that accords better with the saltiness of the sea.

The soft against the hard, ease against endurance, land against sea, the honeyed sweetness of fresh fruit against the subtler sweetness of nuts or dried fruit; but the book's dualism is not so rigid as I may make it sound. There are inconsistencies, one of them being in the presence, early in the collection, of the unsettling poem "Mid Day."

"Mid Day" is both an Imagist poem and a poem about the Imagist procedure, which may be said to consist of extracting images from their context and then treating them in isolation.[5] The speaker is distraught, "anguished—defeated," at the very beginning of the poem. The reader is not told what causes her feeling, and suspects that she does not know herself. She experiences a sense of dislocation: identifying first her "thoughts" and then herself with some black "hot shrivelled seeds" ejected from their pods to the paved path. Surely akin to the figs and the rocks, resistant and enduring, they are grouped in this poem with other images of dryness, but here of plants in the dryness of near-annihilation. She contrasts these seeds with a distant poplar, "bright on the hill," burgeoning triumphantly, which in *its* turn is performing a different function from the usual inland plants of *Sea Garden*, being strong and desirable in its fertility. The poem *is* anguished, obsessive, trapped within repetitive perceptions conveyed in repetitive language, and at the same time written with all the energy, tautness, and clarity of the best poems in the collection, the verse movement seeming like that of the speaker's desperate mind. When she gives up at the end, she is indeed defeated:

> O poplar, you are great
> among the hill-stones,
> while I perish on the path
> among the crevices of the rocks.

I have called the poem unsettling, and I do so not only because of its nightmare feeling of helplessness, but also because it implicitly denies all that I know of seeds. They are repositories of life, not the denial of it; the poplar started from a seed, after all; and I have often seen seeds sprouting

4. Joan Retallack, in "H.D., H.D.," *Parnassus*, vol. 12, no. 2 / vol. 13, no. 1 (1985), compares the passage in HD's poem with its Greek source. See pp. 70–71.

5. I echo Kenneth Fields in this sentence, Introduction, HD, *Tribute to Freud* (Boston, 1974), xxix.

from the crevices sunken between pavings, a possibility she does not envisage. The sense of the images is inconsistent with the scheme inaugurated by the first poem of the book, according to which you would expect such hard, dry, shrivelled things as seeds to possess a more enduring vitality than the soft inland life of the poplar. The anguish of the poem is all too convincing, then, because it seems involuntary.

"Mid Day" makes the overall plan of imagery in the book seem *willed*. The tone of most of *Sea Garden* is one, in fact, of a yearning toward the willed images. I want! I want! she cries. I want to be hard because I feel so soft. She admires the rigidity of stone and of statuary. The hero of "The Contest" is seen in terms of chiselled rock, of brass, cypress, white ash. The hero as statue is "Greek," and Greece is a highly symbolic place for HD—remote, hard, cool, "perfect." She has no wish to bring ancient Greece up to date, like Joyce; still less to make its terms those of an argument about living values, like Marianne Moore in "An Octopus." Fragments of plot in the less successful poems involve battle, imprisonment, religious ritual, all of a sort far from the experience of her London life. Her Greece (fifth century B.C. as seen by the Victorians) consisted of columns, white drapery, and colorless statuary.

Yet the tone of her yearning is more energetic than the state yearned after. She is typically caught in a state of dismayed wonder at her own helplessness, beseeching powers stronger than herself: "O wind, rend open the heat." She is only a step from whining. A sense of humor would have helped, but that apparently was not available. She keeps things dignified, however, by reverting time after time to the rhythms of incantation. The tone is far from flexible, but is nevertheless impressive, based in a discipline of taut emotion, which is in turn measured by an exquisite sense of pace.

What I hope to will into being is not yet here; in a way it is a dream. But in my hope I have already succeeded in distancing myself from the actual, so that it too has become a dream. The imagery of the poems in *Sea Garden* may be simultaneously exact and dreamlike—the black seeds of "Mid Day," the detached leaf sinking like "a green stone" in "Storm," or the fruit so strangely hindered in "Garden":

> Fruit cannot drop
> through this thick air—
> fruit cannot fall into heat
> that presses up and blunts
> the points of pears
> and rounds the grapes.

She attributes her own claustrophobia to the fruit: the heat is so "thick" that it actually distorts the fruit's original freedom to be what shape it chooses. There is a suggestion of fairy-tale or myth here: Kipling would have called it "How the Pear Got Its Point." And yet in our world pears *are* pointed, grapes *are* round.—But just a minute, I thought she wanted less malleability, not more? Or is she just unsure of what she wants, sure only that she wants something out of reach? The anxiety that is undercurrent to HD's constant beseeching indicates a terror of the world she lives in, where shape is already determined, however soft the thing taking shape, and where she has little chance of entering the shape and texture of marble in a putative Greece.

As late as 1953 the editors of a British anthology of new poetry considered "Naked Sensitives" a just description of some of its female contributors. That is the way people still expected woman poets to be. And though what was avant-garde in *Sea Garden* was the technical in quite a narrow sense, and though HD certainly disturbed no tradition of female *feeling*, yet to see her merely as a naked sensitive, woman as a passive yearner, does not do justice to the individuality of her book. For in an odd way the poetry yearning after what is hard and self-contained, after what does not need to yearn, realises something of its desire in the very style of its yearning, which is hard it seems with the hardness of desperation and unfulfilled desire.

Marianne Moore's first authorized collection, *Observations,* was not published until 1924, and by then she had for several years identified herself with the avant-garde. HD was one of the most avant of that garde, and of course she was among Moore's greatest admirers, yet it takes an effort even to consider the two poets in the same sentence. Where *Sea Garden* is anguished, *Observations* is self-possessed. Moore's strong desire for social decorum, for an unprivate speech, paradoxically makes her book far more adventurous than HD's eight years before; in tone, subject matter, metric, and structure of the individual poem, she experiments confidently and widely.

She was considered a difficult poet from the start, as HD could hardly have been, and her first unorthodoxy, in the metric, is visible from a mere glance at the pages of the book. The poets in that experimental generation had individually to make up a free verse of their own. There is no possibility of mistaking the measure of any one of my three woman poets for that of the others. Each has been distinctly evolved. Moore's free verse seems to be influenced by prose writers, her long sentences like those of Henry James receptive to a quantity of physical detail and abstract qualification. When you think of Moore's metric, though, you think primarily of syllabics, which both preceded and succeeded a few years of free verse. The two measures as used by her sound exactly alike (in fact some of her poems that first appeared in the one form were later rewritten in the other), though they looked different on the page, where her syllabics were remarkable for the most shockingly casual enjambements yet to be seen in poetry.

However, "a thing must have 'intensity.' " The sentences look loose and wandering, the rhythms look random, but they introduce a whole new type of conversational compactness into poetry. If they are influenced by James, it is by the *spoken* rhythms of the last novels, all of which, I remember, were dictated.

The attitude of the younger Marianne Moore was patrician, in a sense, in that it was half wilful and half genuinely eccentric. She waived the whole question of distinctions between verse and prose by treating it as simply irrelevant, and her doing so must have been deeply annoying to those who had always considered that poetry, in its rhythms, diction, and subject matter, should be in some way "elevated." She was obscure, sophisticated, learned, allusive; she wrote to please herself, her mother and brother, and her fellow experimenters; and she emphasized intelligence more than feeling (though there *is* feeling in the poetry, usually just below the surface, and as Helen Vendler has pointed out in her excellent essay, much of it is painful): you find in Moore, often quite nakedly and separably, what you can only call thought.

It *is* thought, too, in the old-fashioned sense, as opposed to the "thoughts" of "Mid Day," which were not properly anything but fleeting notions, panicked reactions to an unexplained anguish. Yet Moore's thought is often not easy to follow: abstract, subtle, heavily qualified as it is, she may not so much change the subject in the course of a poem as minutely shift the ground of emphasis—stepping very slightly to the side of the subject to address a similar but far from identical matter, as for example at the end of the cat's speech in "My Apish Cousins" (later renamed "The Monkeys").

This last poem brings up the matter of her experiments in poetic structure, which were extraordinarily bold; a few specimens of them may be found in the talking-animal poems in *Observations*, though these are merely specimens, and you might well say that in Moore's poetry there are almost as many structures as there are different poems. "My Apish Cousins" starts with descriptions of animals in a zoo, to pause finally on a cat of vivid presence, who then takes over the second half of the poem with an increasingly complicated speech about art. The style of the poem is one of extreme sophistication; the structure of extreme crudity. That is one of the jokes, of course. The further incongruity, of the speaker with his speech, is another joke, a very broad one. Yet there is no likelihood of its being taken simply as a nonsense poem: the cat is somewhere between the talking animals in Lewis Carroll and those in Dante for, at the same time as she is making her preposterous jokes, Moore seems completely serious in what she gives him to say, however ambiguous it becomes toward the close.

Two other poems in the collection consist of monologues by animals—"Dock Rats" and "Black Earth" (later "Melancthon")—and continue the same combination of joke with serious intent. The first expresses a passion for place through the urbane voice of a rat; the second is a lengthy meditation by an elephant who celebrates the joy of the body, questioning the relation between inner and outer values in a tone both agile and thoughtful. Both poems are exquisitely written, but neither has survived into the current "complete" collection of Moore's poems. A fourth poem, "An Octopus," containing a talking jay, has survived, but minus the jay, who acted as an essential though arbitrary link in the original version. There the jay shares a ledge of the mountain with the wild orchid Calypso; the orchid's name is Greek; but the jay "knows no Greek" and therefore cannot converse with her: in this way the reader is introduced to the matter of Greek ethics and style that are taken up in the second half of this long poem. The jay is an associationistic link (a comic one) in an associationistically organized poem. (In the later version there is no link at all but a gap. The reader is left with a juxtaposition of elements that may recall the juxtapositions in Pound's Cantos.) This unrevised version is one of the wildest experiments Moore was ever to make in the putting together of a poem: one detail leads to another by, it seems, mere whim, but you are eager to stay with the poem and worry out the meanings because of its sheer attractiveness, line after line.

From about 1917, Moore was thus one of the chief innovators—and possibly, as R. P. Blackmur suggests, taught Pound by her example even as she learned from him. Her most complicated experiment with poetic structure was in one of the latest poems in the book, "Marriage." This is the only place here, moreover, where you might expect Moore to be speaking as a woman. It is possible to imagine finding "female" characteristics elsewhere in her writing, but they are largely asexual, being also present in the writing of a male like Henry James. There are indeed some sharp satirical references to the ways in which men patronise women, notably in "Sojourn in the Whale," where the oppressed stepdaughter is both Ireland and the female sex. But her tone is pretty impersonal, and in that poem there is no use of the first person (though, typically, the second is used several times). When she does say "I" in her poetry, it is not like the "I" of HD or Mina Loy, being much closer to the representative first person of the nineteenth-century English essayist. In "Marriage," I have said, you expect Moore to speak as a woman. But she doesn't, exactly; she preserves an apparent distance. In her old age she went so far as to add a note of demurral in the *Complete Poems*, disclaiming personal relevance— this is, she says, simply an accumulation of "statements that took my fancy." Such a remark fools no one. Nobody writes one of her longest poems without some sort of emotional interest in the subject. Barbara Guest believes that it was composed on the occasion of the Bryher-MacAlmon wedding: it is amusing to imagine Moore thinking "if even these two people are marrying, maybe it is time to get my feelings straight on the subject."

Getting feelings straight, however, is not an apt description of the poem. In structure it is perhaps unique. Her title suggests an essay, her later demurral a commonplace book. It has been described as a debate; Vendler speaks of it as a vacillating. William Carlos Williams's piercing phrase for it is "an anthology of transit," since it is necessary, as he says, to move rapidly through the poem in reading it. It is not random in arrangement, though. To my mind, Moore preserves a certain balance between Adam and Eve, the husband and the wife, favoring—or disfavoring— them about equally. The technique is complicated by the shifting ironies of tone both in Moore's own voice and in the many voices she quotes as she goes along. Hers recurs again and again to a seeming or real impartiality that is impossible to fathom. Marriage, she says in the first sentence, is a thing

> requiring public promises
> of one's intention
> to fulfill a private obligation.

For all the balance of the epigram, it is merely one of those shallow truths that most of us discover in our teens. But it is one point of view, and she is already off on something else: she, and the reader, are already in transit. By the end of the poem, marriage has been seen from almost every point of view, and almost always ironically: as a social struggle, as a contest between egos, as a power game—she mentions

> the spiked hand
> that has an affection for one
> and proves it to the bone.

The one point of view not taken explicitly into account, as Blackmur noted fifty years ago, is the sexual, which is referred to only through the conventional emblems of the apple (as in Eden) and the fire (as in St. Paul). The poem ends with the image of a successful marriage, only possible as the result of the statesmanship of "an archaic Daniel Webster," under whose statue is written

> 'Liberty and union
> now and forever';

> the book on the writing-table;
> the hand in the breast-pocket.

One must be of positively archaic simplicity to be able to accept it, she suggests. The flexible and subtle emulator of James is hardly interested in a union as fixed as a crude statue, its terms as permanent and frozen as the stone Bible before it and the immovable half-concealed hand of the male whose mind is made up—values absolute, unchangeable, taken for granted.

I am not trying to suggest that Moore was a moral relativist—she was anything but—yet she makes it clear in another poem how much she valued "accessibility to experience." To resist marriage, to remain flexible, she had to be even harder than the statue of Daniel Webster, hard as the armored animals that flocked into her poetry as she got older, protecting herself from the surrounding pressures: she would not marry; she would not give up her options. Neither would she, when she could help it, write as a woman any more than as a man; and so one of her forms of courage in *Observations* is to write virtually without gender. There is nothing wrong with that; after all, it is what many men do all the time. She is merely claiming as her own one of the privileges of the male.

In "O Hell" Mina Loy rejects the "excrements" of the past with a stylish defiance. The careful condensation of her language qualifies what might appear to us a childish iconoclasm. To us, perhaps, but hardly to the reader of the 1920s, for even the steadiest among that generation seem to have felt unbearably hampered by the sheer weight of the Victorian inheritance and showed an almost hysterical impatience to throw it out into the street.

Yet it is not as "modern" a poem as it looks. I would suggest, first, that the title is not a flapper's expletive, but a memory of (or reference to) the Blakean hell that is the home of energy as opposed to the establishment church of heaven. After all, in another poem the poet sees herself as "ostracized . . . with God."[6] And there are other echoes from *The Marriage of Heaven and Hell:* in line 6, "Our person is a covered entrance to infinity," and in the last sentence the lineaments of desire become divine when she evokes "Goddesses and Young Gods" (provocatively placing the female before the male!).

No writer passively inherits "the" tradition; you make your own choices, your own incongruous combinations of literary parents. If in this poem Loy takes Blake as iconoclastic sponsor for her iconoclasm, she elsewhere claims relationship to more recent poets like Laforgue. It is the present she emphasizes, aligning herself deliberately and almost programmatically with the avant-garde by including in *Lunar Baedecker* a group of poems praising Joyce, Brancusi, and Wyndham Lewis.

Her contemporaries often compared her with Marianne Moore—naturally enough, since they were both clever women who had started publishing at about the same time. Each had developed her own inimitable kind of free verse; neither went "in fear of abstractions"; both tended toward the epigrammatic. Yet, for all the resemblances, what a difference!

The poem "Lunar Baedeker," a witty guide to the moon as literary symbol, consists of a series of details that are simultaneously image and epigram. It is an effect special to Loy, to be perfected in her poem of World War II, "Omen of Victory." The rather jerky emphases of the short verses suit the overall tone of self-conscious cleverness. Frequency of adjectives, alliteration, internal rhyme and half-rhyme, a dandyish fondness for the obscure epithet—all contribute to a tone of deliberate artificiality. The clotted phrases do not seek to look unstudied, and could never occur in the midst of Moore's equally elaborate discourse with *its* air of conversational improvisation.

The greatest difference is to be found in her attitude toward the human body. For HD, it was sublimated into emblems like the sea rose; for Moore, it did not exist; for Loy, it was a necessary part of her subject matter. Not that she thought of sexuality as just a matter of mutual fondlings in the sunshine; she and "Johannes" in "Love Songs" are far from the divine adolescents of "O Hell."

The full thirty-four-part sequence of "Love Songs" that had been printed in the magazine *Others* in 1917 was greatly abridged in the book versions published during Loy's life, but I agree with Virginia M. Kouidis (in *Mina Loy, American Modernist Poet*) that the long version is preferable,

6. I perhaps wrongly interpret "with" as "by." Mina Loy's use of prepositions is unusual elsewhere as well.

and moreover should be read as a single poem, repetitive disillusionment
its rhythm and subject. All forms of it, in any case, open with the lines:

> Spawn of Fantasies
> Sifting the appraisable
> Pig Cupid
> His rosy snout
> Rooting erotic garbage

The reader's initial disorientation resulting from Loy's lack of punctuation
is an essential part of the meaning. It is appropriate to the shifting and
indecisive nature of romantic love. Does "Sifting" belong to Cupid, purposeful with his phallic snout, or to the "Fantasies," daydreams review-
ing themselves like pornographic tapes? Both are possibilities, and in
keeping them open, Loy looks forward, as she does in other ways, to later
developments of experimental poetry. The work shifts constantly between possibilities, specifically between those of fantasy and reality, and
Ms. Kouidis suggests that it thus shows considerable resemblance to
"Prufrock" (though dates preclude the likelihood of influence one way or
the other). There is this difference, however: Prufrock's are merely speculative fantasies, but the speaker of "Love Songs" has a real love affair.
The longer version of the poem ends with the line "Love—the pre-
eminent littérateur": whether as "Pig" or literary hack, Cupid will always
be making busy work for himself. Thus, while Prufrock will return to his
speculative fantasy, the speaker of "Love Songs" will return to her attempts to substantiate her fantasy. They are both idealists, but she deals
with actual events, and is moreover energetic in speech to the very end.

Loy writes as a woman, and as a woman standing up for herself. She
does not do so as dutiful follower of a political program, but as expression
of a quite unforced indignation at the comedy of male complacency, and
not incidentally as exploration of new poetic material, of which the potential excites her as a writer. The battle of the sexes in "Love Songs" is
between "shuttle-cock and battle-door," a phrase compact with contemporary daring and undated wit. In "Parturition," which would count
among her best work if it were cut by half, she writes what I take to be the
first poem ever about experiencing labor pains and childbirth. And in
"Sketch of a Man on a Platform" she satirizes with admirable vigor the
man who is busy, *too* busy, at being a man.

For all her aggressive modernism and feminism, she identifies with a
traditional genre more easily than most of her great contemporaries—that
of satire. Her satire is never so absolute as in "Der Blinde Junge," which I

readily follow Yvor Winters and Kenneth Fields in considering her most moving achievement.

It may be conveniently set against another poem in the collection, "Ignoramus," an attractive combination of languages recalling nursery rhyme, philosophy, polite small talk, and Rimbaud-like dream excursion. Its subject, an idealised tramp, the Clown of Fortune, owes something perhaps to the Shakespearean fool, his idiom the cunning wisdom of the innocent. "Breakfasting on rain," he is a cheerful vagabond who has created a satisfactory alternate world of his own. There is no hint of idealisation, however, in "Der Blinde Junge," which is about another of the vagrants that fascinated Loy all her life, a blind beggar on a Vienna sidewalk after World War I. The poem is written with a relentless bitterness. The Futurist conception of war as a global hygiene, with which Loy had possibly flirted some years before, is dismissed at the start of the poem, thirteen words punctuated with a blunt rhythm that is almost no rhythm and merely emphasizing, it seems, the uncompromising nature of the statement made:

> The dam Bellona
> littered
> her eyeless offspring
> Kriegsopfer
> upon the pavements of Vienna

War is no goddess working toward either hygiene or glory, but a slovenly animal that "litters" the street with her "litter," human puppies born blind and staying blind, whom it immediately abandons, offerings like this youth,

> this slow blind face
> pushing its virginal nonentity
> against the light

The dim questing movement is scarcely human. The phrase "virginal nonentity" combines powerfully with the specifics to sharpen the accuracy of the observation: he is merely a virgin to the complex life allowed the entities passing by. In the lines,

> Pure purposeless eremite
> of centripetal sentience,

it might seem for a moment, even, that her contempt has turned against the pathetic youth himself, but it has not, being still directed against the forces that made him pathetic. She uses arcane vocabulary to deadly effect. "Eremite" suggests the Keats of "Bright Star," but she uses it with a difference: for the self-containment of the hermit, like that of the virgin, has been brought about not by a choice but by a maiming. Implicitly she attacks the values of a culture through such words, embedded as they are in the classics of our poetry. The lines that follow look at first glance even more impersonal—perhaps affectedly so—but reading them aloud, you realise that the greater sweep of their rhythm suggests the growing scope of her indignation: in them she describes, by showing its termination, the delicate mechanism of the sighted human being. "Horologe" and "index" indicate that it *is* a mechanism, but "carnose" and "tendon" that it is an organic one, too sensitive for repair:

> Upon the carnose horologe of the ego
> the vibrant tendon index moves not
>
> since the black lightning desecrated
> the retinal altar

If you are used to the immediate effects of an Ann Sexton, then of course such writing cannot stay you. But if you take the poem as slowly as one by HD or Moore, you see that such language cannot be improved on for the kind of compression that is the peculiar property of poetry. The sensitive mechanism has its holiness, she goes on to say—and the connection of holiness with the *wholeness* of the adolescent body is already familiar from "O Hell." This adolescent, however, is no young god, but a dreadful abandoned puppy.

> A downy youth's snout
> nozzling the sun
> drowned in dumfounded instinct

She ends the poem with what starts as a conventional didactic address, but its iambic eloquence is interrupted by the deliberate lameness of the last line, recalling her from the temple of rhetoric to the mere fact on the sidewalk:

> Listen!
> illuminati of the colored earth
> how this expressionless 'thing'
> blows out damnation and concussive dark
>
> Upon a mouth organ

There is a brilliant etymological pun on "illuminati"; and another pun on "blows out," for the youth tries to *extinguish* the great terrors by *blowing out* through the apertures of his mouth organ (or harmonica), producing the least eloquent of music, something like the whine of the baby animal. Which brings you back to the beginning again.

Pity may be evoked by the poem, and it inevitably is, but it isn't *in* it. Loy is a tough writer, and sentiment in the usual sense is seldom present in her work. Her overt feeling in this poem is of contempt, turned upon the rest of us, the illuminati reading her poem, complacently assuming that we are heirs to all culture. She has come far from simple iconoclasm, and equally far from the Laforguian self-cancellations of "Love Songs": she is hard, pure, unrelenting. The controlled anger and indignation of the poem make it the equal, to my mind, of the best of Pope or Swift.[7]

Hardness was a quality sought after by the avant-garde poet during the period marked approximately by the years 1910 to 1925. It was considered a corrective to what appeared the softness of the poetry in the years preceding. It took the form of an emphasis on clarity, explicitness, and sharpness of language and image, accompanied by an equal emphasis on objectivity or the appearance of it: at that time Pound, Williams, and Eliot were much taken with analogies between science and poetry.

That is a summary of what everybody knows already. My impression, however, is that women, aware of certain stereotypes about female passivity, felt understandably even more compromised than the men by the real and imagined softness of writing before 1910. It is perhaps relevant to recall here that in the anthology Pound assembled late in life, *Confucius to Cummings,* his one woman poet from the nineteenth century was Mrs.

---

7. There is one collection of Mina Loy's poetry in print, *The Last Lunar Baedeker,* published by the Jargon Society in 1982 and by Carcanet Press in 1985, edited by Roger Conover. For its existence I cannot be too grateful, all the more because Mr. Conover has made substantial additions of poems never before available in book form; but it can hardly be said to contain a critical text, and there are too many typographical errors in it (which are reproduced verbatim in the British edition). These errors are more serious than those we may find in current editions of HD or of Marianne Moore, in that the reader of Loy has little opportunity to compare this text with any other. Therefore, I append a list of the most serious below, supplying emendations either from other printed versions or from my own guesses: Conover edition, p. 3, 1.10: *to* should read *of* (as in Kouidis);
p. 8, 1.8: *is* should be *in;*
p. 21, 1.1: *satinize* should be *satirize;*
p. 57, 1.1: *Peninsular* should be *Peninsula* (?);
p. 63, 1.18: *magneta* should be *magenta;*
p. 91, 1.2: *sitting* should be *sifting* (but Kouidis has *silting*);
p. 180, 1.18: *interstate* should be *intestate* (?);
p. 182, 1.7: *efflugence* should be *effulgence.*
(I have not listed misprints in the introduction and notes.)

Browning rather than Emily Dickinson or even Christina Rossetti. No wonder his female contemporaries needed to show that they could write hard poetry, too.

"We were not conforming to anything," Marianne Moore recalled; and so in reaction—who is to say how far conscious?—these three women published their astonishing early poetry: HD's representing the hardness of passivity; Marianne Moore's the hardness of resistance; and Mina Loy's the hardness of aggression. Later, in different ways, their poetry softened somewhat, and none of them, in my view, often approached again the concentrated brilliance of their first work.

Nevertheless in that work they established, I hope for good, that hardness is not the prerogative of male poetry. As various writers have pointed out, hardness, softness, and derivative terms used in literary criticism look back to an obviously sexual origin. But there is no reason that good woman poets should be limited by the symbols of gender. If Jane Austen hadn't been in the novel, then they needn't be in poetry, another state in what is, after all, a free country.

# Ezra Pound in Paris

## Robert von Hallberg

MORE THAN any other American writer, Ezra Pound has been identified with the international movement in the arts known as modernism. His poetry above all, but also his efforts as literary, music, and art critic, as editor and publicist, have made it seem inevitable that he should be known as the premier American avant-gardist. T. S. Eliot, Wallace Stevens, Ernest Hemingway, William Faulkner, and Gertrude Stein were, of course, all experimenters in verse or prose, but no other career has seemed to literary historians so properly captured by the term *avant-garde*. Pound's coming to live in Paris in 1921, then, ought to have been a signal event in literary history, because the international avant-garde was already well established there, as he well knew. One might imagine no more direct contact between Anglo-American poetry and the styles of international movements such as futurism, Dada, and surrealism. Yet, as Pound critics have long known, the contact did not set off sparks. After three years, Pound backed off from the Paris scene and settled in Rapallo. What I want to suggest here is that Pound, unencumbered by any single notion or theory of the avant-garde, made his affiliations to various avant-garde groups according to their momentary utility as instruments of literary criticism. The reasons for Pound's hesitation to affiliate himself with groups in Paris cast some light on the tension between national literary traditions and the internationalism of the avant-garde, and this tension persists in the writing of contemporary American poets.

Pound lived in Paris from January 1921 until autumn 1924. He often traveled to Italy during that time, but mostly he stayed in Montparnasse at 70 bis rue Notre Dame des Champs, just a few blocks from the famous carrefour Vavin. There are photos of the courtyard there, of the furniture he made for the apartment, and amusing stories about him boxing with Hemingway or practicing on the tuba (that was the instrument he managed to get at a bargain). The goings-on of this particular neighborhood during the 1920s are abundantly documented in dozens of memoirs and even a couple of histories, yet there is much about Pound's activities during these years that remains unknown. Having resolved to leave London, how did he decide so quickly at the end of 1920 to give up on hopes of returning to America? Was it really the appearance of a collection of prose sketches of small-town American life that persuaded him the American scene was hopeless? That is what he told John Quinn. It sounds unlikely, yet it may have been impressive to see that Alfred Knopf in 1920 was willing to present to the American literary world Edgar Watson Howe, author of *The Story of a Country Town* (1911), *Success Easier Than Failure* (1917), *The Blessing of Business* (1918)—and organizer of the Don't Worry Club. Pound had already been burned by such people: Ed Howe came from Wabash County, Indiana, about fifty miles upriver from Wabash College, the site of Pound's failed effort in 1908 at academic respectability. One wonders, though, whether Pound's marriage did not bear on the decision to go to Paris, because in the fall of 1921, after seven years of marriage to Dorothy Shakespear, daughter of Yeats's one-time lover and lifelong friend, Olivia Shakespear, he became involved with a serious Englishwoman, Bride Scratton, who was married to the sort of unforgiving British military man Ford Madox Ford wrote about.

And why, less than four years later, did he leave Paris? He had always loved the city, and like virtually everyone else, he thought of it as the world's most civilized capital. In 1917 he wrote an essay entitled "Provincialism the Enemy." One counterweight to the provincialism responsible for the war, he thought, might be the tunnel (now due for completion in 1993) between England and France.

> There is something sinister in the way *the* tunnel disappears from
> discussion every now and again. . . . A definite start on the
> Channel Tunnel would be worth many German defeats. It belongs
> to a world and an order of things in which local princes with the
> right of life and death over their subjects do not exist, and wherein
> many other mediaeval malpractices pass into desuetude.

One imagines that the poet who wrote a disgusted farewell to London in *Hugh Selwyn Mauberley* (1920) would live gladly in Paris. Hugh Kenner says that if Paris had only been more interesting, Pound would have stayed. But when he looked back over his life in 1938 for the moments of greatest social conversation, he said, "If one is to measure merely by brilliance, the maximum I have known was at Picabia's of a Sunday about 1921 or '22." Those aren't the words of a man bored by Paris.

Many memoirists do report, though, that the Montparnasse scene peaked in 1924, and that soon thereafter a great many people, mostly

Americans, who cared little for poetry, fiction, painting, or music took over the bars and cafe terrasses. Roger Shattuck dates the last banquet ending the French scene in the summer of 1925 at the Closerie des Lilas—that was an evening designed to honor the poet Saint-Pol-Roux. In the later 1920s the international *Chicago Tribune* routinely focused on talk of the decadence of the expatriates. John Glassco's *Memoirs of Montparnasse* suggests that this was not merely the sensation-mongering of journalists. And yet one wonders about Pound's timing. For after apparently pondering the idea of parenthood for a year, Olga Rudge and Ezra seem to have decided quite deliberately in late 1924 to change their lives. Ezra left Paris in the week of October 9, 1924, and his daughter Mary was born nine months later on July 9, 1925. Possibly this was a little easier for Dorothy to bear once they had removed themselves from the social circles of Paris.

Until very recently it did not seem especially important to question the patronizing remarks of those who said that Ezra left because he could not make the splash in Paris that he had made twelve years earlier in London. The history of American poetry seemed little affected by the matter. Now the climate of literary opinion is different. Marjorie Perloff recently argued, in *Poetics of Indeterminancy* (1981), that Rimbaud has been much more important to American poetry than anyone, including a number of American modernist poets, had been willing to admit. In 1985 she published another book, *The Dance of the Intellect*, claiming that this influence has come into subsequent American poetry chiefly through Pound. And in her forceful new book, *The Futurist Moment* (1986), she argues strenuously that modern American poetry really does belong to an international movement in the arts; she suggests that the European isms—futurism, cubism, and Dadaism—are as important to the history of American poetry as the Anglo-Americanisms—Imagism, vorticism, and objectivism. The first of these three books built on Andrew Clearfield's 1978 essay in *Paideuma* showing Pound's indebtedness to the Dadaists; and Richard Sieburth looked still more closely at this phase of Pound's career in an important essay in the *South Atlantic Quarterly* (Winter 1984). It seems clear now that there is indeed an "other tradition" to which American poets have been more attentive than literary historians; clear, too, that American poets like Pound have been rather quiet about part of their debt to the French and Italian writers of 1885–1920. That T. S. Eliot learned some of his art from Jules Laforgue is very well known; the French symbolists of Laforgue's generation enjoyed a vogue around Harvard University when Stevens and Eliot were studying there. But when Eliot appeared socially in 1922 wearing green face powder, he was repeating for the Bloomsbury set something Alfred Jarry had done in Paris: Baudelaire had dyed his hair green, but Jarry did his face and hands in green as well. The French avant-gardists of the years just before World War I had a sense of the literary life as theatre that fascinated British and American poets. (Incidentally, Virginia Woolf, Clive Bell, and the Sitwells missed the point of the face powder: Osbert Sitwell guessed that Eliot was trying to get sympathy for his suffering in a difficult marriage.)

Beyond the writings of the scholars I've named, though, one might have taken the same lesson from very recent poets. In one of the *Dial* Paris Letters, Pound said that "the real criticism of an author is found not in the incompetents who talk about him, but in the creating writers who follow him." The writings of Charles Olson, John Ashbery, John Cage, and David Antin suggest that aleatory techniques, reliance on instinct and association, and spoofs on the pretensions of high art may have been part of what post-World II poets inherited from their modernist predecessors. Apollinaire summed up his era by saying, "We learned to laugh." We know that Olson in the 1950s believed he could learn from Rimbaud as well as from Pound; and that Ashbery felt he had to go to Paris to find a nurturing literary milieu. In order that these recent poets not be seen as mere sports of literary history, one wants to establish that they are speaking to the central issues of their art. When Ashbery admits that he tries to balance meaning and meaninglessness in his poems, one wonders, though, about how far the literary traditions of Wordsworth, Matthew Arnold, and Emerson, say, can be made to stretch. If only William Carlos Williams among the great American modernist poets was working in a line of poetry deriving from Rimbaud and leading to the surrealists, one must question whether American poetry has been genuinely cosmopolitan; whether the English and American literary traditions have not effectively prevented certain lines of artistic development from thriving until very recently; whether the utopian aspirations of Anglo-American modernism did not perish in World War I; and finally whether Robert Lowell and Philip Larkin will not in the end seem the postwar poets writing in English with the most accurate awareness of what their literary tradition permits. That is to say, if Perloff largely overestimates (as I think she does) the importance of French poetry to American writers, if the American modernists were charmed only by the rhetoric and theatrics of the French and the Italians, not by the avant-gardist program, there is that much more reason to think that Cage, Ashbery, Olson, Duncan, Antin, and others may come to look like curious figures who tried to do in English what was possible only in French. One thinks of Renaissance efforts to bring quantitative meters into English.

In May 1928 Samuel Putnam and his collaborators on the *New Review* gave a dinner in the rue de l'Odéon in honor of Pound. When the evening was well under way, a surrealist pulled out a dagger and made as if to stick it in the back of the guest of honor. Robert McAlmon grabbed the surrealist arm, and a seltzer bottle on the head restored the peace. But what if Ezra, say, had been wounded? This *scandale* would have raised long ago some of the issues that interest Perloff, Clearfield, and Sieburth. It is not altogether unheard of for surrealists to attack each other, or even others. But why attack Pound? He was no surrealist, yet he was perhaps the only American poet of the time whose stature was recognized by the French avant-gardists. The American writers in Paris in the 1920s did not generally mix in French literary circles (few of them spoke French well); Pound was an exception. In 1919 Pound's old schoolmate from the University of Pennsylvania, William Carlos Williams, published a clairvoyant "Prologue" to a book of improvisations in *The Little Review*:

> Imagine an international congress of poets at Paris or Versailles, Remy de Gourmont (now dead) presiding, poets all speaking five languages fluently. Ezra stands up to represent U.S. verse and de Gourmont sits down smiling. Ezra begins by reading [Eliot's] "La Figlia Che Piange." It would be a pretty pastime to gather into a mental basket the fruits of that reading from the minds of the ten Frenchmen present: their impressions of the sort of U.S. that very fine flower was picked from.

Williams (like Matthew Josephson and Kenneth Rexroth) thought that Pound's literary taste was outmoded, that French writers could not take his sense of the art seriously. But they certainly did take Pound himself seriously. The question I want to raise by telling a story is: how far was Pound willing to go to keep up with the French avant-garde?

In the winter of 1921, when Pound arrived in Paris, surrealism was still *ab ovo* among the Dadaists. In the following summer, André Breton and several collaborators set plans for a Congrès de Paris, and the events that followed mark the end of Dada. On January 3, 1922, *Comoedia* ran an article entitled "Défense de l'Esprit Moderne" signed by Robert Delaunay, Pound's friend Fernand Léger, Amadée Ozenfant, Jean Paulhan, and Roger Vitrac.

> Au mois de mars prochaine s'ouvre à Paris un *Congrès international pour la détermination des directives et la défense de l'esprit moderne*. Tous ceux qui tentent aujourd'hui, dans le domaine de l'art, de la science ou de la vie, un effort neuf et désintéressé, sont convié à y prendre part. Il s'agit avant tout d'opposer à une certaine formule de

dévotion au passé—il est question constamment de la necessité
d'une prétendu retour à la tradition.

(This March in Paris there will be an international congress to
establish the guidelines and the defense of the Modern Spirit. All
those who today in art, science or life pursue this new and
disinterested effort are invited to take part. It is above all a question
of opposition to a particular form of devotion to the past—it is
constantly a question of the necessity of a supposed return to
tradition.)

What must Pound have thought of all this? Maybe Williams's imaginings
of two years earlier would be tested after all. Pound was eager then to
make contact with the lively literary people of Paris. As Clearfield and
Sieburth have shown, he was friendly with the Dadaists, ready to publish
in their journals, and enthusiastic about bringing them into *The Little
Review*. French writers and many others—Belgian, Dutch, German, Spanish, Italian, Russian, and English writers responded enthusiastically to
the call—were asking questions that Pound could not bother with: "Has
the Modern Spirit always existed? Among so-called modern objects, is a
top hat more or less modern than a locomotive?" Pound's friend Picabia
did have some sense of humor about the questions being proposed for the
agenda. Once he finally signed on for the Congrès, he suggested inquiry
into the difference between the sun and the moon. Perhaps Marinetti and
the Italian futurists were alone in their enthusiasm for "the great Futurist
Railroad," as he unembarrassedly put it; Whitman was the last American
poet who could speak in pious tones of a locomotive. The American
modernists knew better than to speak of a literary revolution in terms of
subject matter.
    One month after the first announcement of the Congrès, Tristan Tzara
told the organizing committee that he could not participate. Breton became angry, insulted Tzara, and offended nearly all by the way he
chauvinistically publicized the rift. A protest against Breton's manage-
ment of the Congrès was called for February 17 at the Closerie des Lilas,
and a motion censuring him was proposed by Erik Satie and signed by
over forty of the artists present. This restaurant is well known in American letters because of Hemingway's mention of it in *The Sun Also Rises*,
but its history in French literature goes back to Verlaine and the symbolists who gathered there in the nineteenth century. Breton was being
summoned to a particularly auspicious courtroom. Pound knew the restaurant well because he used to meet Hemingway there, and it was
probably there, too, that he heard the story told in Canto XVIII about

Zaharoff the international munitions dealer, for it was Zaharoff's as well as Hemingway's cafe. The now pricey Closerie is a five-minute walk from Pound's studio. About fifty writers and artists gathered there in mid-February. Pound's friends Cocteau and Brancusi were there. Louis Aragon, Philippe Soupault, Paul Eluard, Picasso, and Matisse went to it as well. And there were Americans, too: the New Jersey-born painter and photographer Man Ray, the poet Matthew Josephson, and probably Slater Brown. Pound apparently stayed away. One of the broadsides published to promote the Congrès said "Bonjour Pound" on it, but he seems not to have returned the greeting—not even in his Paris Letter of March 1922. The forthcoming new biographies of Pound may tell us just where he was on February 17, but for now I take his absence as a sign that he was apprehensive of the differences he must have felt between himself and the French writers he knew. In January 1922, at just the time the Congrès was being discussed in the press, he visited Cocteau and read some of his Villon opera. Cocteau giggled at Pound's expense, because he found anything medieval funny. Pound could not have enjoyed the joke much.

He and other English and American poets knew that the French (and earlier the Italian) call to abandon literary traditions was unattractive if taken seriously. Two and a half years before Cocteau laughed at the Villon, Pound had met Eliot for a walking tour of southern France. Eliot went alone to the caves at Dordogne and returned to London, as Hugh Kenner has noted, to write "Tradition and the Individual Talent." When Eliot reviewed the Dadaists in 1921, he said that a special effort was needed to treat them intelligently. Because the French literary tradition is so much a part of the cultural life of France, he claimed, there is no parallel between the polemics concerning tradition in the two nations. Dadaism he treated as a sign of cultural malaise. Pound, too, was reluctant to take at face value the Dadaist rejection of literary tradition. In 1917 he wrote that "the phrase 'break with tradition' is currently used to mean 'desert the more obvious imbecilities of one's immediate elders' "—and this is the way he continued to think of the Dadaists for over twenty years. "The young frenchmen of 1920 had NO elders whom they cd. in any way respect." Neither Pound nor Eliot allowed the Dadaists to challenge his sense of the fruitfulness of literary tradition. And Pound's closest French collaborator, Cocteau, knew that the French literary tradition was not something that could be eliminated anyway: "TRADITION APPEARS AT EVERY EPOCH UNDER A DIFFERENT DISGUISE, BUT THE PUBLIC DOES NOT RECOGNIZE IT EASILY AND NEVER DISCOVERS IT UNDERNEATH ITS MASKS."

Pound regarded the Dadaists as a tonic, medicinal force, and merely that. "That anyone shd. have tried," he wrote in 1938, "to use Picabia's acid for building stone, shows only the ineradicable desire of second-rate minds to exploit things they have not comprehended." Picabia and the Dadaists were "carrying on the satiric heritage of Laforgue." Sieburth said in his book on Pound and de Gourmont that Pound read *L'Education Sentimentale* "less as a masterpiece of fiction than as a work of historical and sociological analysis." This was the prose tradition, as Pound saw it. And in his words, "Prose is perhaps only half an art." Pound believed that poetry "asserts positive emotional values and works toward emotional synthesis. Prose arises from an instinct of negation, proceeds by intellectual analysis, and presents something one wants to eliminate." He did not expect great poetry to come from the Dadaist effort, only a momentary clarity. And Cocteau must have seen the matter similarly: "Scepticism is a bad conductor of poetry. That is why poetry has no great hold in France, a country which is much too knowing." When the diagnostic impulse behind Dada began to lead to a positive literary program, as it did in Breton's hands, Pound could certainly not go along. For the prose tradition, Breton expressed contempt: "clarity . . . a dog's life" is the way he put it in the 1924 manifesto.

The Congrès de Paris was to meet in March of 1922, but the whole project collapsed after the trial of Breton at the Closerie des Lilas. It was toward the end of March, as Lawrence Rainey has established, that Pound went south to research in Italian libraries the life of Sigismundo Malatesta, who neither wore a top hat nor drove a locomotive. And furthermore, Rainey shows, Pound's Malatesta was very much a product of nineteenth-century romantic historiography. When he had finished with these Cantos, Pound wanted yet another historical subject matter; Thomas Jefferson was next, he wrote to his father in 1924.

If Pound's interaction with the French avant-gardists is to count heavily for literary history, one must find the evidence in the poetry itself. Clearfield and Sieburth cite Pound's pastiche, "Kongo Roux," which, written in French, appeared in the Dada journal *Le Pilhaou Thibaou*. This is an amusing parody in Dada manner of Saint-Pol-Roux (1861–1940), the French poet whom Roger Shattuck spoke of as the Rabelais of the symbolist period, and whom Breton thought of as a precursor of surrealism. But "Kongo Roux" is only a joke, a hoax, and if that were all Pound's involvement with the Dadaists amounted to, nothing much could be claimed for these years. Pound did, however, undertake poems in his Paris years that he regarded as by far his most important work to date, the Malatesta Cantos. These four Cantos (VIII–XI) were originally planned to be just one; however, the project grew enormously as Pound wrote. They now take up twenty-five pages in the New Directions edition of the *Cantos*, and the manuscript drafts number over a thousand pages in the Yale archive. Pound plainly labored to get these Cantos just right. So they are the poems, written in 1922–23, where one should be able to measure the effects of Pound's Paris years.

Marjorie Perloff sees those effects in the way that Pound tends, as she puts it, "to create a flat surface, as in a Cubist or early Dada collage, upon which verbal elements, fragmented images, and truncated bits of narrative, drawn from the most disparate contexts, are brought into collision." The result, she says, is a poem that transforms history into a "play of language." Anyone who has read these poems through without the aid of a historical companion volume is likely to want to agree: names, dates, documents, and editorial commentary do seem to swirl around all more or less on a plane. Pound juxtaposes sections of a narrative of Sigismundo's activities with passages from letters taken from his postbag. Although the art of juxtaposition was plain in Pound's poetry before he came to Paris, this is the technique of the Dadaists and later of the surrealists. Here Pound seems more heavily invested than ever in this technique, because formerly he had not juxtaposed large hunks of historical material. Before I challenge Perloff's notion of verbal play in these Cantos, I want to concede to her viewpoint certain other characteristics these poems share with their French counterparts.

Roger Shattuck notes that Apollinaire's 1913 collection of poems, *Alcools*, was criticized by reviewers for its mixture of different styles. Avant-garde poems do not observe unity of subject or style; serious lines often sit next to playful or even nonsense lines. Two principles are at stake here: (1) the coherence—that is, internal consistency—of the poem as artifact; and (2) what Arnold spoke of as the high seriousness of great art. Avant-garde poets reject both principles. Poems have been invaded by newspaper clippings to show that internal consistency counts not at all for these poets. And in place of Arnoldian seriousness they have repeatedly insisted on absurdity as the province of art. As for the greatness of any art, that too is in question. In the 1918 Dada manifesto Tzara said that art "hasn't the importance that we, old hands at the spiritual, have been lavishing on it for centuries."

On the opening two pages of Canto VIII, the first of the Malatesta Cantos, one can hear several different styles. The first four lines are colloquial of course—"'Slut!' 'Bitch!'"—but also urbanely ironic about this low style—"sous les lauriers." A few lines down the page Pound as editor interprets in a businesslike fashion: "Equivalent to: . . . ." As Perloff has remarked, Pound makes Sigismundo sound more like a Wall Street broker than a fifteenth-century condottiere, but a broker with some witty self-consciousness: "At any rate nothing wd. give me more pleasure / or be more acceptable to me." Pound admires urbanity and credits Sigismundo with the ability to move freely from this straightforward prose to the ludicrous pomposity of formal political communiqués—"the aforesaid most illustrious / Duke of Milan" and so on. I want to stress the tone of urbanity here, because more than verbal play is involved. Pound's juxtaposition of various styles is designed to lead one to conclusions about the nature of the characters who are responsible for producing such language.

Sigismundo is admirable in Pound's poem for his straight-dealing and largesse with artists, and for his irony about his own political activities. For many avant-gardists, political intrigues but also the pretensions of artists like Alberti, the designer of the Tempio, were on the face of it absurd. At the very end of the Malatesta Cantos, Pound tells this story of Sigismundo and his steward:

> And one day he said: Henry, you can have it,
> On condition, you can have it: for four months
> You'll stand any reasonable joke that I play on you,
> And you can joke back
>     provided you don't get too ornry.
> And they put it all down in writing:
> for a green cloak with silver brocade
> *Actum in Castro Sigismundo, presente Roberto de Valturbus . . .*
> *sponte et ex certa scienta . . . to Enricho de Aquabello.*

That is the note on which these Cantos conclude: a good-natured joke about art. Sigismundo, after twenty-two years of intrigues, is ready to give the Tempio to his steward for a small playful wager. (The manuscript drafts show that what Sigismundo is wagering is his cloak, not the Tempio, but Pound's ultimate text seems designed to suggest that the Tempio itself is the prize.) Pound's intention, I believe, is not to display the Tempio as a hoax, nor to suggest that the political actions of Sigismundo, Francesco Sforza, and Pope Pius II were absurd. Through it all Sigismundo was clear and consistent in trying to recover his hereditary right to Pesaro; Sforza was consistently out only for himself; and Pius was determined to see Sigismundo hanged. The objectives of the political agents in the story are portrayed as firm and understandable. Just as firm was Sigismundo's commitment to securing the labors of the best artists of his day, most notably Piero della Francesca and Alberti. When at the poem's end Sigismundo is ready to give it all away, Pound makes two points about Sigismundo's humanity: he did not believe that he could really possess the work of the artists he patronized; and at the end of a long series of political defeats, nothing was more important to him than the sort of good fellowship that puts the labors of ambition and the pride of possession in reasonable perspective.

My point about the various styles of these Cantos and the jokes too being intended as evidence of personal character bears directly on the development of recent avant-garde writing. In a 1912 futurist manifesto, Marinetti said: "Destroy the *I* in literature: that is, all psychology." Seven years later Tzara published a letter in Breton's *Littérature* claiming that "if there is a common characteristic to be found in people who are creating today's literature, it will be that of anti-psychology." Recent American poets, from Ashbery to the Language poets, have employed chance techniques of composition in order to eliminate psychology, the presence of human character, from poems they would rather regard as, in Perloff's words, "verbal play." But Pound's Malatesta Cantos do not, I think, suggest that he was particularly enthusiastic about the antipsychological efforts of Marinetti and Tzara. On the first page of the second Malatesta Canto these lines appear:

> And he fought in Fano, in a street fight,
> and that was nearly the end of him;
> And the Emperor came down and knighted us . . . .

Throughout most of the poems, Pound employs the third-person form common among modern historians, but periodically these first-person plural statements undermine the illusion of distance between Pound and Sigismundo, as though Pound were being swept into Sigismundo's service quite literally. Technically speaking, Pound is sticking to his source documents, one of which was the chronicle constructed by Sigismundo's comrade-in-arms, Gaspare Broglio. But rhetorically, Pound is permitting himself to take his characters seriously as individuals and to move toward and away from them at particular points in the narrative, as though Sigismundo were an individual who commands more or less sympathy at one moment or another, the way one's friends do. Moreover, the importance of this narrative method becomes obvious in the last Malatesta Canto, when Pound says: "And we sit here. I have sat here / For forty four thousand years." Some months before writing these lines Pound read in manuscript Eliot's effort at the omniscience of Tiresias, and must have been reminded not of the antipsychological voices of French writers but of the all-inclusive voice of Whitman behind both Eliot and Pound, and of his own first, failed effort at that perspective in the 1917 Cantos published in *Poetry.*

There is a photograph of Pound with Tzara, Cocteau, Man Ray, and several others posing in front of the Jockey Club in 1923. Pound is at the very center of the group. That's the way we think of him, as one who wanted to be always at the center of artistic activity. "The intellectual capital of America," he wrote in the Picabia number of *The Little Review,* "is still Paris." In the photo he is wearing a very large beret and a velvet jacket, leaning on his cane, and that should remind us of how in Paris, as in London, he was deliberately more than a little out of date. "There was a touch of Whistler about him," Sylvia Beach said. In fact Whistler lived for the last decade of the nineteenth century in the rue Notre Dame des Champs. Pound knew where his real bearings were. In December 1922 he wrote in the *Dial* that "the latest real news of the French is still Flaubert, Corbière, Laforgue, and Rimbaud. The rest is what I believe skilled city editors dismiss as 'unimportant if true.' " There his cards are on the table. No wonder that he was so enthusiastic about Julien Benda's critical book *Belphégor* (1919), which argued against those poets of the years *before* the Great War who overstressed feeling and instinct at the expense of intelligence. Pound saw to it that this commonsensical, reactionary book was serialized in the *Dial* in 1920; in Paris it must have seemed dated.

At times Pound was unsure of the distinctions between futurism, vorticism, cubism, and so on, but the Dadaist phase that Sieburth and Clearfield have analyzed had distinct limits. Dada was for him not a movement capable of producing serious art. When the Dadaists began to become surrealists, Pound got on with his library research. This means, I think, that recent American poets attempting to develop the poetics of Breton and his French contemporaries must do so without the encouragement of Ezra Pound's example. They are going out on a limb that would not bear their Anglo-American predecessors. Pound's relation to his French contemporaries leaves one thinking that American modernism was a good deal more conservative than the continental variety. Why this should be so is difficult to say with any exactness. The causes must be an interweave of national intellectual traditions, the bent of various individual temperaments, and of course accident. But as late as 1920 Pound referred to the Pre-Raphaelites in *Mauberley* as an English movement of opposition that foreshadowed E. P.'s career. Even Pound may not have been able to spring quickly and wholeheartedly from the earnest objectives of that group to the ironic jests of the Paris Dadaists.

The literary critical tradition of England—Pound, like Eliot, surely knew his Johnson, Wordsworth, Coleridge, and Arnold—holds to the notion that the function of literature is to illuminate the *meaning* of experience, not its absurdity. And the American literary and popular belief in improving and explanatory literature was obviously held by Pound, whom Stein called a "village explainer." Pound was never a writer to leave much to chance; the aleatory techniques of continental modernism could not have suited him deeply. In 1921 he was becoming insistent about causation, prediction, and prevention, specifically about the causes of the First World War and about how another war might be predicted or prevented. Even his effort at Dada, "Kongo Roux," is focused, as other Paris Dada texts were not, on just these political and economic issues. (Pound seems not to have known much about the more political Berlin Dadaists.) From his reading of documents concerning fifteenth-century condottieri emerged poems indicting Sforza and Pius for the narrow provinciality and meanness that destroys artistic efforts and produces war. A tunnel might help to leash local princes . . . . Although Pound may in fact have left Paris for personal reasons having to do mostly with Dorothy and Olga, the reasons why he must be seen by literary historians and younger poets as standing at some distance from his continental contemporaries are not hard to see plainly, especially in his major poetry.

# "Necessary Murder":
# The Auden Circle and the
# Spanish Civil War

## George Mills Harper

WHEN THE Spanish Civil War broke out on July 5, 1936, Auden and his Circle were ideologically committed to the Republican cause. Having convinced himself that the writer should "Make action urgent and its nature clear,"[1] Auden decided in September to join the International Brigade. "I shall probably be a bloody bad soldier," he said, "but how can I speak to/for them without becoming one."[2] But he did not fight in Spain. Arriving in January to broadcast propaganda for the government, he was "profoundly shocked and disturbed"[3] to discover churches closed, and he was embarrassed by the demands made of him. His one published article is little more than its title suggests: "Impressions of Valencia."[4]

Equally unconvincing as propaganda was his only other public comment on the war, the ambitious and provocative poem entitled "Spain." Although Auden came to consider it "trash," which he was "ashamed to have written,"[5] his friend Spender called it "the best poetic statement in English of the Republican case."[6] Written upon his return to England in

---

1. "To a Writer on His Birthday," in *Poetry of the Thirties*, ed. Robin Skelton (London, 1964), 169; hereafter cited as *PT*. The writer was Christopher Isherwood.
2. *The English Auden: Poems, Essays and Dramatic Writings 1927–1939* (London, 1977), xviii; hereafter cited as *EA*. Auden was writing to his friend E. R. Dodds.
3. Ibid.
4. Published in *The New Statesman*, January 30, 1937. For the text of this brief article, see *EA*, 360–61.
5. When Auden granted Skelton permission to use early texts of five poems, he asked Skelton "to make it absolutely clear that 'Mr W. H. Auden considers these five poems to be trash which he is ashamed to have written' ": "Sir, No Man's Enemy," "A Communist to Others," "To a Writer on His Birthday," "Spain," and "September 1, 1939" (*PT*, 41).
6. *World within World: The Autobiography of Stephen Spender* (London, 1977), 247; hereafter cited as *WW*.

March 1937 and published in May, "Spain" was in effect Auden's last word about the Civil War.[7] Why he never spoke of his visit again remains a minor mystery despite his explanation, more than twenty-five years later, that "I did not wish to talk about Spain when I returned because I was upset by many things I saw or heard about."[8]

It is not clear why or how soon Auden became "ashamed" of his famous poem. But we can determine which sections were especially displeasing. When he revised the poem, he omitted stanzas 18, 19, and 22 and made an important revision of another. Although he changed only two words in stanza 24, they were the source of significant controversy and embarrassment. Shifting from predictions about the future to observations about the present, he wrote:

> To-day the deliberate increase in the chances of death,
> The conscious acceptance of guilt in the necessary murder;
> To-day the expending of powers
> On the flat ephemeral pamphlet and the boring meeting.[9]

Both friends and enemies probably objected to Auden's implication that the Republicans had deliberately increased the chances of death and condoned the necessity of murder. The most bitter reaction came months later from George Orwell, who had observed the methods of the Communists in Spain at first hand. He referred to Auden and his Circle as members of "the soft-boiled emancipated middle class" to whom "such things as purges, secret police, summary executions, imprisonment without trial, etc. etc. are too remote to be terrifying. They can swallow totalitarianism *because* they have no experience of anything except liberalism." Quoting eight lines from Auden's "Spain," he focused on the phrase "necessary murder" to illustrate the failure of "nearly all the dominant writers of the 'thirties' " (that is, Auden and friends). I must quote at length:

> The second stanza is intended as a sort of thumb-nail sketch of
> a day in the life of a "good party man." In the morning a couple of
> political murders, a ten-minutes' interlude to stifle "bourgeois"
> remorse, and then a hurried luncheon and a busy afternoon and
> evening chalking walls and distributing leaflets. All very edifying.
> But notice the phrase "necessary murder." It could only be written

7. The royalties from "Spain" went to Medical Aid for Spain (*EA*, xviii).

8. Hugh D. Ford, *A Poet's War: British Poets and the Spanish Civil War* (Philadelphia, 1965), 288, n. 8. Auden was disturbed by what he had "learned about the treatment of priests."

9. I quote from p. 11 of the rare first edition published by Faber and Faber in May 1937.

by a person to whom murder is at most a *word*. Personally I would not speak so lightly of murder. It so happens that I have seen the bodies of numbers of murdered men—I don't mean killed in battle, I mean murdered. Therefore I have some conception of what murder means—the terror, the hatred, the howling relatives, the post-mortems, the blood, the smells. To me, murder is something to be avoided. So it is to any ordinary person. The Hitlers and Stalins find murder necessary, but they don't advertise their callousness, and they don't speak of it as murder; it is "liquidation," "elimination," or some other soothing phrase. Mr. Auden's brand of amoralism is only possible if you are the kind of person who is always somewhere else when the trigger is pulled. So much of left-wing thought is a kind of playing with fire by people who don't even know that fire is hot. The warmongering to which the English intelligentsia gave themselves up in the period 1935–39 was largely based on a sense of personal immunity.[10]

Not satisfied with that diatribe, Orwell reiterated his denunciation on the following page:

It is the same pattern all the time; public school, university, a few trips abroad, then London. Hunger, hardship, solitude, exile, war, prison, persecution, manual labour—hardly even words. No wonder that the huge tribe known as "the right left people" found it so easy to condone the purge-and-Ogpu side of the Russian regime and the horrors of the first Five-Year Plan. They were so gloriously incapable of understanding what it all meant.[11]

Orwell was not, of course, entirely unbiased. As a Trotskyite, he had observed the persecution, imprisonment, and even execution of his comrades in the P.O.U.M., which was defeated in the feuding among factions of the Republicans.[12]

But Auden did not need Orwell's destructive criticism to make him realize the superficial cleverness of his lines: he had already changed "deliberate increase" to "inevitable increase in the chances of death" and "necessary murder" to "fact of murder."[13] And unlike Day Lewis, Rex Warner, and other friends, Auden had never expended his power "On the

10. *Such, Such Were the Joys* (New York, 1953), 184–85.
11. Ibid., 186.
12. Orwell's *Homage to Catalonia* may be the best book written about the Spanish Civil War as Auden suggested to Hugh D. Ford: "some" of "the many things I saw or heard about . . . were described better than I could ever have done by George Orwell, in *Homage to Catalonia*" (288, n, 8).
13. See *EA*, 210–12, for the revised version dated April 1937.

flat ephemeral pamphlet and the boring meeting." By the time "Spain" was published (May 29, 1937), he had, I think, concluded that he had been deceived by Communist propaganda. Sometime that summer, when he visited Spender and his wife in Kent, Auden "stated emphatically that political exigence was never a justification for lies."[14] Two years later, in an essay entitled "I Believe," he wrote: "It is always wrong in an absolute sense to kill, but all killing is not equally bad; it does matter who is killed." As an epigraph for that essay he chose a maxim from Blake: "Everything that lives is Holy."[15] He cited Blake, also, in an unfinished essay about "the Artist and the Politician" to deny emphatically that the end justifies the means:

> Perhaps it is necessary that thousands should be martyred for the sake of that General Good which Blake called the plea of the hypocrite and the scoundrel. But neither I nor anyone I care for shall be among the martyrs if I can help it, and I find your complaisance disgusting.[16]

He is apparently addressing left-wing extremists who have accused him of "unrealistic bourgeois idealism."

Auden was obviously embarrassed that he had been deceived in the naive assumption that the issue in Spain was simply good versus evil, Communism versus Fascism. He had, of course, stated in a striking phrase a rationalization of the "necessity for violence,"[17] which had been accepted by most of his contemporaries among writers. Many of them justified their stance by the worn but still useful theory of "the greatest good for the greatest number." Any murder or atrocity could be justified by Day Lewis's rhetorical question: "Will the use of violence in this particular, concrete situation benefit the majority of persons concerned?"[18] Auden himself, in an essay on "The Good Life," had insisted—in 1935 note—that "Unless the Christian denies the value of any Government whatsoever, he must admit, as Schweitzer did when destroying trypanosomes, the necessity for violence, and judge the means by its end."[19] Spender entitled Part 3 of *Forward from Liberalism* "The Means and the Ends." In order to make "the transition [from Liberalism to Communism] as short as possible," "deliberate violence" must often be

14. WW, 247.
15. EA, 379, 372.
16. Ibid., 402.
17. Ibid., 353.
18. Quoted in Symons, *The Thirties: A Dream Revolved* (London, 1960), 142.
19. EA, 353.

used: ". . . if there is another world war," Spender argued, ". . . humanity will have to choose between protracted chaotic conditions and some
kind of government by machine gun and terror. Of these the best would
be the ruthless force from which a new and juster order might emerge."[20]
That is, if not "necessary murder" at least "desirable murder."

Upon being urged to join the Communist Party and go to Spain,
Spender agreed, but not as a member of the International Brigade because, in his words, "I could not see what qualifications I had as a
soldier."[21] By July 1937 he had made three trips to Spain—first as a
reporter for the *Daily Worker*, next as a broadcaster for the Socialist Party in
Valencia, and finally as a delegate to a Writers' Congress in Madrid. As a
result of his experiences at the Congress, he became thoroughly disillusioned over the Communist cause in Spain. Called ostensibly "to discuss
the attitude of the Intellectuals of the World to the Spanish war," the
Congress also had a "hidden theme": "the Stalinists versus André Gide,"
whose recent book about his impressions of Russia had infuriated the
Communists. Once considered "the greatest living French writer," Gide
"became overnight a 'Fascist monster', 'a self-confessed decadent bourgeois', and worse"; and the Russian delegates denounced Trotsky and
Gide in the same breath. Spender concluded that "the Congress . . . had
something about it of a Spoiled Children's Party": "Speeches, cham-
pagne, food, receptions, hotel rooms, were a thick hedge dividing us
from reality."[22]

Spender and Auden were signatories of a famous questionnaire (dated
June 1936) addressed "To the Writers and Poets of England, Scotland,
Ireland and Wales." Insisting that "The equivocal attitude, the Ivory
Tower, the paradoxical, the ironic detachment, will no longer do," the
twelve signers posed the following question: "Are you for, or against, the
legal Government and the People of Republican Spain? Are you for, or
against, Franco and Fascism?"[23] It must have taken courage to fail to
respond or to oppose writers who "have seen murder and destruction by
Fascism in Italy, in Germany." "To-day," they said, quoting Auden, "the
struggle is in Spain," then warned: "To-morrow it may be in other countries—our own." When the editors of the *Left Review* published selected

---

20. *Forward from Liberalism* (London, 1937), 281.
21. *WW*, 211.
22. *WW*, 243. For further details of Spender's impressions, see 238-47, and cf. Symons,
who suggests that "the Spender of 1951 was a different person from the Spender of 1937 and
so wrote of the Congress differently" (128).
23. For the entire text of "The Question," see Hynes, 414.

replies in the fall of 1937, their count was 127 for, 5 against, 16 neutral, and 1 unclassified.

The stance, the thought, and even the rhetoric of most of the published replies are expected. All the Auden Circle and most other writers were "for." But Eliot and Pound were listed as "neutral" and Shaw as "unclassified." Although "as a Communist [I] am generally on the Left," he said, "in Spain both the Right and Left so thoroughly disgraced themselves in the turns they took in trying to govern their country before the Right revolted, that it is impossible to say which of them is the more incompetent."[24]

The most distinguished writers not listed were W. B. Yeats, E. M. Forster, and Virginia Woolf. Like Shaw, Yeats had sympathized with the Fascists in the early thirties and, like Shaw, had withdrawn by the time of the Civil War. Like Shaw also, Yeats refused "to hold one form of government more responsible than any other": "Communist, Fascist, nationalist, clerical, anti-clerical, are all responsible according to the number of their victims." He suggested to Ethel Mannin that she should read "The Second Coming," which had "foretold what is happening."[25]

It should be said perhaps that Yeats had been concerned about the concept of "necessary murder" long before the Spanish War. In April 1919 he upbraided his friend George Russell (AE), who was sympathetic to the Russians: Iseult Gonne "likes Russian Communism no more than I do," Yeats wrote, then quoted her:

> 'But Mr. Russell tells me that he has information from a source which can be relied on—or some such phrase—that they have only executed 400 people,' that is why I sent you certain comments on the figure, as well as on the figure of 13,000 which was published some time ago as coming from the Russian government itself.[26]

After quoting a Labourite in the House of Commons to the effect that " 'the present Russian government is worse than that of the Autocracy,' " Yeats concluded: "I consider the Marxian criterion of values as in this age the spear-head of materialism and leading to *inevitable murder*"[27] (italics mine). The concept is stated more philosophically in *A Vision*, upon which he worked from October 1917 to April 1925. In his explication of Phase 25 of the Great Wheel, Yeats made an acute character analysis of the over-

24. This response was given a place of prominence on the inside of the front cover.
25. *The Letters of W. B. Yeats*, ed. Allan Wade (London and New York, 1955), 850-51; hereafter cited as *L*. See another letter to Mannin, dated March 1, 1937 (885).
26. *L*, 655.
27. Ibid., 656.

zealous reformer. I quote from a manuscript in which the language is stronger than that of the book.

> At 25 this insensitiveness can be very terrible—that of the judge, who orders a man to the torture, that of the statesman, who accepts massacre as a historical necessity. I think of Luther's apparent indifference to atrocities committed now by [,] now against [,] the peasants according to the way his own incitements veered.[28]

Men of this Phase are "born as it seems to the arrogance of belief"; Newman and Calvin, in particular, were on Yeats's mind. He also cited George Herbert and George Russell as "Poets of this phase [who] are always stirred to an imaginary intensity by some form of propaganda."[29]

The Woolfs and E. M. Forster remained more aloof from politics than the Auden Circle. Forster, who had become (in the words of Samuel Hynes) "the generation's father figure,"[30] was urged repeatedly to take a stand on the left. He was invited in 1935 to attend the Paris meeting of the International Association of Writers for the Defence of Culture, and before that largely Communist assembly, he testified simply to his liberal beliefs. A more "famous statement of Bloomsbury liberalism" appeared in September 1938 in the *London Mercury*. Entitled "Credo," it is a courageous statement of Forster's personal faith. One sentence is often quoted: "I hate the idea of causes, and if I had to choose between betraying my country and betraying my friend, I hope I should have the guts to betray my country."[31] Because he maintained this unswerving stance in a time of great crisis, Forster was, of course, accused of "escapism," of retreat to an Ivory Tower. A short time later he defended his "English" faith against that of Russia and Germany. "Their conclusions are the same," he said; they "are working out a faith which is in the interests of the herd and against those of the individual . . . neither of them has any use for the Ivory Tower." "We are here on earth," Forster concluded, "not to save ourselves and not to save the community, but to try to save both."[32]

In the same month (December 1938) he made a much stronger statement of his personal faith in a review of Christopher Caudwell's *Studies in a Dying Culture*. Caudwell argues, in a chapter on "Pacifism and Violence," that "the only way to secure peace is by a revolutionary change in

---

28. Cf. *A Critical Edition of Yeats's 'A Vision'* (1925), ed. George Mills Harper and Walter Kelly Hood (London, 1978), 108.
29. Ibid., 109.
30. *The Auden Generation: Literature and Politics in England in the 1930s* (London, 1976), 338.
31. Quoted in Hynes, 302.
32. *London Mercury* 39, no. 230 (December 1938): 124, 130.

the social system, and that ruling classes resist revolution violently and must therefore be overthrown by force."[33] Ostensibly addressed to Communists, Forster's strong disagreement was, I suspect, directed also at his own left-wing acquaintances:

> As for their argument for revolution—the argument that we must do evil now so that good may come in the long run—it seems to me to have nothing in it. Not because I am too nice to do evil but because I don't believe the Communists know what leads to what.[34]

"Democracy is not Beloved Republic really, and never will be," Forster concluded. "But it is less hateful than other contemporary forms of government."[35]

The Woolfs published two left-wing collections (New Signatures and New Country), but Virginia at least disapproved of the politics and poetry of left-wing intellectuals—Auden, Day Lewis, Spender, and MacNeice, in particular. Asked to address the Worker's Educational Association at Brighton, she chose, as symbol of her criticism, the tower: not Forster's Ivory Tower or Yeats's ruined tower "half dead at the top" but rather the leaning tower of Auden's "Spain," stanza 7:

> As the poet whispers, startled among the pines,
> Or where the loose waterfall sings compact, or upright
> On the crag by the leaning tower:
> 'O my vision. O send me the luck of the sailor.'

"Conscious of their middle-class birth; of their expensive educations," the writers of the leaning tower are not, Woolf observes, "altogether upside down, but slanting, sidelong . . .; they do not look any class straight in the face: they look either up, or down, or sidelong. There is no class so settled that they can explore it unconsciously." Lacking the power "that creates characters that live, poems that we all remember," these "great egotists," the leaning tower writers, "wrote about themselves honestly, therefore creatively": "They told the unpleasant truths, not only the flattering truths. That is why their autobiography is so much better than their fiction or their poetry."[36] Although Woolf is speaking of the autobiographical content of their art, it should be said that all the Circle except

---

33. *Studies in a Dying Culture* (London, 1957), 96.
34. Forster's review entitled "The Long Run" appeared in the *New Statesman* 16 (December 10, 1938), 971-72. See Hynes, 338-39.
35. Quoted from Forster's "What I Believe" (1939), in Symons, 160.
36. "The Leaning Tower," in *Folios of New Writing* (London, 1940), 28.

Auden wrote autobiographies. Spender's *World within World* is especially important to any study of the thirties.

From January to July 1938 Auden and Isherwood were in China gathering material for a book about the Sino-Japanese War. Since they did not know Chinese and saw no battles, the book they produced, *Journey to a War*, is farcical as reportage.[37] However, the experience led Auden to write a remarkable but difficult series of sonnets and "Commentary" under the subtitle of "In Time of War"—not *the* war or *a* war note but all war, especially the European war that Auden and his friends expected. Like "Spain," the twenty-seven sonnets represent a three-part philosophical commentary on past, present, and future. But there is an important difference: the sonnets deal with man individually rather than collectively—man "upon his little earth" contemplating "The universe of which he is both judge and victim"[38]—and they make appeal not to action but to compassion.

Sonnet XXVII, the last in the book but fourth from the last in the revision for *Collected Poems*, is representative. The different first lines in the two versions are arresting: "Wandering lost upon the mountains of our choice,"[39] which became "Chilled by the present, its gloom and its noise."[40] "We dream of a part / In the glorious balls of the future," Auden concluded,

> But we are articled to error; we
> Were never nude and calm like a great door,
>
> And never will be perfect like the fountains;
> We live in freedom by necessity,
> A mountain people dwelling among mountains.[41]

He was, I think, particularly pleased with the paradoxical phrase "freedom by necessity." He expanded it in a line of the "Commentary," "Some took Necessity, and knew her, and she brought forth Freedom"[42] and finally explained it in "I Believe": " 'Freedom', as a famous definition has it, 'is consciousness of necessity'."[43] Many of his friends were no

---

37. See Hynes, 341-49.
38. *EA*, 262-63.
39. Ibid., 262.
40. W. H. Auden: *Collected Poems*, ed. Edward Mendelson (London, 1976), 156; hereafter cited as *CP*.
41. *EA*, 262.
42. Ibid., 268.
43. Ibid., 373.

doubt aware that Friedrich Engels was the source of the "famous definition."[44]

Auden and Isherwood returned from China via Japan and the United States in July 1938. At that time, apparently, they decided to move to New York, arriving on January 26, 1939, the very day Barcelona fell and with it the hopes of the Spanish Loyalists. Two days later, on January 28, the archetypal poet of the century died. Auden began immediately to write one of his most moving poems, "In Memory of W. B. Yeats." The symbolic landscape of the first section makes clear that Auden is writing not only about Yeats but also about his own generation and by extension Western civilization:

> O all the instruments agree
> The day of his death was a dark cold day.[45]

In the second section Auden lightened his vision of the nightmare and chaos of politics with a suggestion that the "healing fountain" of art could "Teach the free man how to praise."[46] Almost at once, possibly before the poem appeared on March 8 in the *New Republic*, Auden composed a third section for the middle. Thinking perhaps that the prophetic claim of his first version was too optimistic, he admitted that "poetry makes nothing happen," though "it survives. . . / A way of happening, a mouth."[47]

During this time or soon thereafter Auden was writing the fragments that were to become "The Prolific and the Devourer: The Artist and the Politician." One brief paragraph suggests that he was recalling his recent poem:

> Artists and politicians would get along better in a time of crisis like the present, if the latter would only realise that the political history of the world would have been the same if not a poem had been written, not a picture painted nor a bar of music composed.[48]

In August 1935, in that "hour of crisis and dismay," Auden had asked Isherwood rhetorically, "What better than your strict and adult pen" could "Make action urgent and its nature clear?"[49] In four tumultuous years the wheel had come full circle: "If the criterion of art were its power

---

44. See Herbert Greenberg, *Quest for the Necessary* (Cambridge, 1968), 73.
45. *EA*, 241. In *CP* "All the instruments agree" reads "What instruments we have agree" (197).
46. *CP*, 198.
47. Ibid., 197.
48. *EA*, 406.
49. *PT*, 169.

to incite to action," Auden observed, "Goebbels would be one of the greatest artists of all time," then added as the last note for his unpublished essay on "The Artist and the Politician": "Tolstoi, who, knowing that art makes nothing happen, scrapped it, is more to be respected than the Marxist critic who finds ingenious reasons for admitting the great artists of the past to the State Pantheon"[50]

By this time, clearly, Auden and his Circle were thoroughly disillusioned with Marxism and Russian Communism. If any lingering scrap of faith remained, it was destroyed by the nonaggression pact signed by Germany and the Soviet Union in August 1939. In the following month Auden was agitated by the death of another of his culture heroes, Sigmund Freud, who

> . . . showed us what evil is, not, as we thought,
> deeds that must be punished, but our lack of faith,
>     our dishonest mood of denial,
> the concupiscence of the oppressor.[51]

Earlier in the same month Auden had been devastated by Hitler's invasion of Poland. His shocked reaction was reflected immediately in "September 1, 1939," another of the "trashy" poems he professed to be ashamed of. One reason for leaving England, he said later, "was precisely to *stop* me writing poems like 'September 1, 1939.' " He described it as "a hangover from the U.K.," then added, "It takes time to cure oneself."[52] Since it is one of the most famous poems of the thirties, I must ask what Auden hoped to cure himself of. The first stanza sets both tone and theme:

> I sit in one of the dives
> On Fifty-Second Street
> Uncertain and afraid
> As the clever hopes expire
> Of a low dishonest decade:
> Waves of anger and fear
> Circulate over the bright
> And darkened lands of the earth,
> Obsessing our private lives;
> The unmentionable odour of death
> Offends the September night.

50. *EA*, 406.
51. *CP*, 216.
52. *EA*, xx.

After parenthetical historical allusions to Luther, Hitler, and Thucydides to explain that

> Those to whom evil is done
> Do evil in return,

Auden observes himself in "this neutral air" of New York,

> Where blind skyscrapers use
> Their full height to proclaim
> The strength of Collective Man.

Three stanzas then develop the theme that "Faces along the bar [this fort] / Cling to their average day"

> Lest we should see where we are,
> Lost in a haunted wood,
> Children afraid of the night
> Who have never been happy or good.

Having surveyed, with marvelous compression, "the whole offence . . . / That has driven a culture mad," Auden shifted to the first person:

> All I have is a voice
> To undo the folded lie,
> The romantic lie in the brain
> Of the sensual man-in-the-street
> And the lie of Authority
> Whose buildings grope the sky:
> There is no such thing as the State
> And no one exists alone;
> Hunger allows no choice
> To the citizen or the police;
> We must love one another or die.[53]

Auden rejected this stanza in revision before rejecting the entire poem. The last line, apparently, was particularly "dishonest": we must die anyway, he commented ironically.[54]

The "folded lie" is, I take it, a reference to the "*clever* hopes" (italics mine) of the "low dishonest decade." Auden is talking to himself. The change of landscape may not have been wholly responsible for "a change of heart," but in 1939 he thought the move to America was necessary. "No, God willing," he wrote to a friend, "I never wish to see England

---

53. *EA*, 245-46, *PT*, 280-83.
54. See Hynes, 384.

again. All I want is when this [war] is over, for all of you to come here."[55] It may be said, therefore, that Auden's aspersion of cleverness and dishonesty is not only about himself and his friends but also about England and Western civilization.

By the end of the "low dishonest decade" most of Auden's Circle had even less faith than he that the "affirming flame" of their art could affect what Yeats had called "this foul world in its decline and fall."[56] Yet the "negation & despair" of Auden's Circle produced a virtual flood of poetry, fiction, and criticism. Unlike Yeats, they did not yet "think it better that in times like these / A poet's mouth be silent," but many were ready to admit that "in truth / We have no gift to set a statesman right."[57] Auden's "New Year Letter (January 1, 1940)" reflects the disillusionment of his own "lost generation." Sitting in a church, perhaps, rather than "one of the dives / On Fifty-Second Street," he accuses the Devil of "selling us down the river," and now

Repenting of our last infraction
We seek atonement in reaction
And cry, nostalgic like a whore,
'I was a virgin still at four.'[58]

Musing bitterly, he surveyed in twelve sardonic lines the landscape of despair:

Who, thinking of the last ten years,
Does not hear howling in his ears
The Asiatic cry of pain,
The shots of executing Spain,
See stumbling through his outraged mind
The Abyssinian, blistered, blind,
The dazed uncomprehending stare
Of the Danubian despair,
The Jew wrecked in the German cell,
Flat Poland frozen into hell,
The silent dumps of unemployed
Whose *areté* has been destroyed . . . ?[59]

---

55. *EA*, xx.
56. "A Bronze Head," in *Last Poems and Two Plays* (Dublin, 1939). For the text of the poem, see W. B. Yeats, *The Poems: A New Edition* (New York, 1983), 340; hereafter cited as *P*.
57. *P*, 155.
58. *CP*, 176.
59. Ibid., 166.

No longer thinking "That the worst rogues and rascals had died out"[60] nor that "The State would wither clean away" in "the Millennium / That theory promised,"[61] Auden and his followers could only write and wait, even though they were aware that

> No words men write can stop the war
> Or measure up to the relief
> Of its immeasurable grief.[62]

60. *P,* 207.
61. *CP,* 175.
62. Ibid., 166.

# "Or, Solitude":
# A Reading

*Seamus Heaney*

A N UNEXPECTED sensation of furtherance: that is what I remember of my first reading of Donald Davie's poem "Or, Solitude" in an issue of *New Statesman* late in 1965. What exactly the poem meant I could not have said, nor could I have formulated my response in the terms I now propose, yet the actual experience of the lines did constitute a poetic "happening." In them, the consensus that usually allows the English imagination to order reality on a domestic scale had been for the moment refused, and English poetry was receiving one of its rare visitations of strangeness. The roof had come off, and the sensibility was being exposed to something both unlimited and adjacent. One might have called the poem visionary, except that it concluded with a rhetorical curtailment which seemed to climb down from that high mode. Or one could have called it evocative, except that it intended something far more declarative than that word would suggest. Even the poet himself had difficulty determining where the poem had got to and what he was to make of it. For example, the first line of the fourth stanza—the point where the turn occurs, where what is being apprehended begins to declare itself—was revised between its first book appearance in *Essex Poems* (1969) and its publication in *Collected Poems 1950–1970*. I will discuss the change later, but I adduce it here as a symptom of the new combination of improvisational process and fastidious wording that made Davie's *Essex Poems* not only the essential volume in his own career, but an important event in the history of British poetry over the last quarter of a century.

"Or, Solitude" is, as the poet noted in the 1970 *Collected Poems*, the subtitle of Wordsworth's "Lucy Gray": "Oft had I heard of Lucy Gray: / And, when I crossed the wild, / I chanced to see at break of day / The solitary child." It is not surprising, therefore, that Davie's melody retains a certain intoned pathos, and that his *mise-en-scène* involves a presence who is part genius of place, part a phantom of sentiment:

A farm boy lost in snow
Rides his good horse, Madrone,
Through Iowan snows for ever
And is called "alone".

Because gone from the land
Are the boys who knew it best
Or best expressed it, gone
To Boston or Out West,

And the breed of the horse Madrone,
With its bronco strain, is strange
To the broken sod of Iowa
That used to be its range,

The transcendental nature
Of poetry, how I need it!
And yet it was for years
What I refused to credit.

In some obvious ways, this is an "American" poem. It is set in Iowa; it has a source in nineteenth-century frontier literature, uses terms like "range" and "farm boy" (not "farmer's boy" or "labourer"), and works with elements that are typical and even expected: snows, prairie, bronco. It is also American in the way it shifts memories of several Frostian winter-pieces from New England to the Midwest, and is susceptible to the idiom of Hart Crane. The "broken sod" has surely been wakened from the dream with which Crane invested the prairie in the closing lines of "Proem: Brooklyn Bridge." But this is at the same time an "Essex poem" in the way that the transition from the third to the fourth stanza involves both disjunction and projection, for such transitions are a feature of many of the lyrics in the volume and mark Davie's admission into his poetic practice of Black Mountain influences. Finally, "Or, Solitude" is an "English" poem in the way it confines the spaciousness to which it is genuinely open within a form and cadence deliberately related to *Lyrical Ballads*.

The concerns—Englishness, Americanness, the inner and outer weather of countries and countrysides—constitute a poetic ground from which the individual lyrics in *Essex Poems* do not aspire to detach themselves. On the contrary, as Davie wrote about the poems of Charles Olson and Ed Dorn in relation to their wayward learning, "they emerge from it only to burrow back into it." Similarly, the thematic concerns of these lyrics refuse to melt away and leave the poem orphaned within its linguistic limits. This is partly for biographical reasons, Donald Davie having been on the verge of making his move from England to the United States at the time of their composition. As a result of this impending departure, he was pondering with acute personal urgency not only the physical differences between a North Sea climate and a Pacific one, but also the cultural and psychological consequences of living a committed life in these extremely contrasting milieux. For somebody as bonded to England as Davie was, not just by nurture, speech, and service in war-time, but by an affection consciously deepened and sharpened by literary study and poetic vocation, the prospect of practising his art in a land-scape unhallowed by communal association, unsalted by known dialects and pungent place-names, was necessarily fraught with intense self-questioning.

Testing and disturbing as these uncertainties must have been at a private level, there was a further level of questioning to which they were attendant but not subsidiary. This involved the ongoing dialogue and tension in Anglo-American literary culture, the doubt about native English parochialism that had been planted by Ezra Pound fifty years earlier and remained inescapable by anyone alive to the shifts and reverberations of poetic energy in the 1950s and 1960s. That was the era of A. Alvarez's anthology, *The New Poetry*, with its notorious assault on "the gentility principle" in English letters, the debilitating conviction that "life is always more or less orderly, people always more or less polite, their emotions and habits more or less decent and more or less controllable." It was also the era of translation, when the first flush of the new postwar poetry from Eastern Europe was entering the insular consciousness. Davie was alive to it all, translating from Pasternak's Russian "The Poems of Doctor Zhivago" and swerving beyond the usual gentility-bound preference for Anglophile Eliot into the less travelled (in England) realms of Pound. He was still alive to it when he wrote "An Afterword for the American Reader" in *Thomas Hardy and British Poetry* (1972); there he glosses "gentil-ity" as "civic sense" or "political responsibility" and inclines to value these qualities above the liberties and assumptions of American poets who are "rapt and exalted bards together, in a sublime democracy." Three years after *Essex Poems*, six thousand miles away from Essex, Davie was still productively in two minds, except that his corrective example was now drawn from British tradition and it was American practice that was perceived to be in need of correction.

*Essex Poems* is the volume where Davie's poetry jumped ahead of what might have been expected of him. That is to say, the reasonableness, the scrupulous discursive impulses, the acrid relish of landscapes, all of which attained a certain fullness of expression in *Events and Wisdoms*

(1964), might have continued to issue in surely based poems of a still traditionally English sort, poems where the voice issued from a well-defined persona, which functioned as statements by that persona, bulletins relayed from a composed intelligence that had claims upon us because of its consistency and intentness. What happened instead was a breakaway by the voice from its recognizably social espousals, its tones of irony, discretion, or severity. The language was now more the vehicle of its own heuristic assays, the poem typically an action rather than an address. Although not all the poems in the volume belong to this "new" mode, whatever unifies the book and gives it an excited feeling of access is the result of some such change in the poetic process itself. One has a great sense of risks being taken, of a poet who is inclined to keep the colt tightly reined-in getting ready to let go and be carried in an unexpected direction. This does not involve abandonment of control, because, at every living moment of the unexpectedness, concentration, alertness, and balance are vitally important. Rather, it involves an abandonment of the self to art, a new stage in what Davie called in 1959 "the long struggle back to English poetry considered by the poet as a way of spiritual knowledge."

That may sound high-flown, but it is typical of the earnestness that enters Davie's writing almost every time he addresses the work of Ezra Pound or ponders its implications for the practice of subsequent poets. It is also consistent with his adducing of Pound as the sponsor of poetry as an art to be thought of in terms of other arts (a making no less than a saying) and his radical pursuit of this conception to the point where he considered we might "sell the pass on poetry from the start by refusing to consider any metaphysical or ontological grounds for the poetic activity." At a more practical and commonsensical level, this "new aesthetic" issued in statements like the one he made in the course of an exchange with Alvarez, printed in the first issue of the review (1962): "A man who is emotionally immature can, by dint of the passion he has for literature, transcend his emotional immaturity for the sake of the poem he is writing."

All in all, therefore, by the time he came to write "Or, Solitude," the pressure of the concerns underlying its final stanza was deep and constant:

> The transcendental nature
> Of poetry, how I need it!
> And yet it was for years
> What I refused to credit.

Those boys who best expressed the land have gone from it, and the farm boy lost in snow is thereby already symbolic and late-comerly. He is a manifestation of Lucy Gray, a revenant from the desert places in Robert Frost's poem of that name, which includes another snowbound consciousness intuitively responsive to the links between desolations *in here* and *out there*. But he is also directly sprung from a book to which Davie directs attention in his note in *Collected Poems 1950–1970*. Hamlin Garland's *Boy Life on the Prairie* contains a poem called "Lost in a Norther" where the farm boy rides in a blizzard, for days on end, numbed and solitary:

> Lost on the prairie! All day alone
> With my faithful horse, my swift Ladrone.
> And the shapes on the shadow my scared soul cast.
> Which way is north? Which way is west?
> I ask Ladrone, for he knows best,
> And he turns his head to the blast.

That the horse in Davie's poem is called not Ladrone but Madrone is a lovely waver since it may encompass an oblique *hommage* to the ratiocinative talents of Yvor Winters at the very moment when a Wintersian type of aesthetic is being left behind. Writing of this "great doctor of abstractions" in *These the Companions*, Davie noted with pleasure the unexpected earthiness of the man's conversation, a "halting monologue about the behaviour of Canadian waxwings . . . or the multiple nice distinctions within the botanical family that includes the great madrone." But whatever the reason for the switch of the horse's name, the musical effect remains the same, and as the Madrone/"alone" rhyme tolls, it opens a path into a pristine aural domain, a prairie spaciousness conjured by the after-echo of words like "Iowan snows," "gone from the land," and "range." Yet the terrain is also obstinately physical, thanks to another cluster of harder, more abrupt effects; for example, the rhyming of "need it" and "credit," while it occurs in a sentence that addresses a theme ultimately to be named "metaphysicality," keeps faith at the same time with the bluntness and cloddishness of ploughing. There is a little shudder to it, a sense of coming-up-against, an intimation of the out-thereness of what is being talked about.

In fact, this push toward a reality independent of categories that are primarily psychological and social has been an abiding concern of Davie's poetics, and there is in "Or, Solitude" a vindicating energy, a given-from-beyond quality that distinguishes other Essex poems and sets them in special poetic relation both to "the real world" and to the writer's intentions. The writing "goes itself"; it conducts and transmits that ontological neediness to which Davie was alluding in his crucial essay, "Two Analogies for poetry." So it is no surprise that "the transcendental nature / Of poetry" should have been revised later to "The metaphysicality / Of poetry." He needs "metaphysicality" more because, presumably, it represents a more extreme embrace of risk, a more exposed commitment to poetry as a genre that must justify itself not simply "as a way of getting or keeping in touch or practising group therapy."

The phrase "the transcendental nature of poetry" allows for an interpretation of the poem that would go something like this: because of the fetch and persuasiveness of these Iowan absences, I am inclined to credit my knowledge of reality as previous, extensive, and irrational, and I am also inclined to think of poetry as massaging and assisting that not uncomplacent feeling of being a Wordsworthian "inmate of this active universe." But "the metaphysicality of poetry" is much more "sculptured." It insists that there is a divide between the poetriness of poetry and the rest of our experience, that to conceive of poetry as having a conciliatory relation with our nature or an obligation to flatter our humanity is to conceive of it too laxly. The very sounds of "the metaphysicality of poetry" are more faceted and resistant, their hardness stands off, whereas there is something alluring, tenebrous, and perhaps inflationary about "the transcendental nature of poetry."

This reading of "Or, Solitude" has permitted itself to be affected by Donald Davie's writings on what he desires for and from poetry because I believe that in this case we are dealing with one of those poems in which poetic action and theoretical effort manage to coalesce. It happens to bridge the gap (perceptible in the sixties to himself and to his readers) between the poems he was given to write and the poems he would have liked to have written; it accrues as the bonus of long meditation on the consequences for English poetry of the achievements of the international modernists. It salutes the immoderacy and exorbitance of the expectations they had from art ("how I need it!"), yet by the constricted means it employs—short lines, a curtailed musicality that finally settles for speech over singing tones—it opts for a poetry that is ultimately more Hardyesque. So, in spite of what I said at the beginning about this being an American poem, and in spite of its obvious reach beyond the native limits, the final critical emphasis must be placed on its domestic force. Years before the publication of Davie's book on the desirable moderating effect that Hardy's "scientific humanism" might exercise on postmodernist poetry, "Or, Solitude" arises involuntarily out of the questions which provoked that book and by its curtailed music enacts the conclusion which the book would proffer:

> Are not Hardy and his successors right in severely curtailing for themselves the liberties that other poets continue to take? Does not the example of the Hardyesque poets make some of those other poets look childishly irresponsible?

# A Shared Humanity:
# "In the Stopping Train" and
# "The Whitsun Weddings"

## Mark Jarman

These are my customs and establishments.
It would be much more serious to refuse.
—Philip Larkin
"The Importance of Elsewhere"

A man who ought to know me
wrote in a review
my emotional life was meagre.
—Donald Davie
"July, 1964"

I N HIS recent collection of lectures, *Czeslaw Milosz and the Insufficiency of Lyric*, Donald Davie argues that, because of twentieth-century history, the lyric poet has lost the privilege of being responsible only to himself and his emotions. Therefore, he must find a way to speak for more than himself. The late twentieth-century search for a more representative self is not peculiar to our era. Keats sought it in his attempts at empathy, in the very negative capability now associated with the self-involved lyric and against which Davie reacts. Davie himself has sought in his poems a larger expression, while at the same time acknowledging the limits of the lyric that make such an expression impossible. "In the Stopping Train," one of Davie's finest poems, is an attempt to understand the insufficiency of lyric by subjecting the poet himself to nearly merciless critical examination.

It is helpful to compare Davie's poem, from his 1977 volume of the same name, with the title poem of Philip Larkin's 1964 collection of poems. "In the Stopping Train" seems, in part, a response to "The Whitsun Weddings" and not merely because both record journeys on stopping or local trains, but because the former presents a totally different role for the poet from that of the latter. The irony is that Larkin, in his poem, is not nearly as wrapped up in himself as Davie is in his. Yet Larkin's detachment from his subject has been cause for serious criticism, and quite rightly.

First of all, justifying his own ways to those of his fellowmen has never been the problem for Larkin that it is for Davie, except as Larkin has been too much like other people, letting "the toad work squat" on his life for example, or not enough like them, as in "Annus Mirabilis" where he admits to being a very late bloomer. Larkin is at his best when posing as the curious observer or when absent altogether. His self-effacement has been called smugness, though it might be seen as modesty. Davie's self-examination is not its opposite exactly, but more a search for humility, for atonement. But Davie is a Christian poet, and Larkin is not.

Existential anxiety is not present in "The Whitsun Weddings." Once Larkin boards his train on a hot Saturday afternoon at Whitsuntide, he feels "all sense / Of being in a hurry gone." The windows are down, the cushions are hot, but he pretty much has the car to himself, and after observing the urban landscape giving way to countryside as the train makes its way from Lincolnshire to London, he begins to read. The landscape is important to Larkin, especially as it retains its rural features and as they are lost or marred. Despite the poem's fame, stanza 2 is worth quoting entirely.

> All afternoon, through the tall heat that slept
>     For miles inland,
> A slow and stopping curve southwards we kept.
> Wide farms went by, short-shadowed cattle, and
> Canals with floatings of industrial froth;
> A hothouse flashed uniquely: hedges dipped
> And rose: and now and then a smell of grass
> Displaced the reek of buttoned carriage-cloth
> Until the next town, new and nondescript,
> Approached with acres of dismantled cars.

All of Larkin's strengths are present here, including his love of and doubts about pastoral England: his eye for the telling image—those cattle, that hothouse, those canals—his extraordinary gift for the simple yet perfect imagistic phrase, "the tall heat," and even his way of pointing to a poem's central intelligence, the annoyed reference to "the reek of buttoned carriage-cloth." Yet it is the little drama of the poem, beginning in the third stanza and continuing through the next six until the end, that requires an assessment of Larkin's particular, even peculiar temperament as a lyric poet. It requires one because, in this poem at least, none is offered by the poet himself.

Both American and British critics have noted Larkin's superior air in this poem. Blake Morrison in his book *The Movement* says that Larkin "seems to patronize as well as to pity" the working-class wedding parties he observes at each train depot. Merle Brown in an essay on Larkin's audience published in the *Iowa Review* in 1977 is downright censorious, but he puts his finger on the problem of how much the lyric poet can represent himself and others. Brown writes,

> In "The Whitsun Weddings" . . . Larkin takes on the sovereign privileges of . . . invisible, unnameable observing even though he also presents himself as a visible, existent, individual entity. He should have recognized that such a hybrid is inadmissible in poetry the likes of his. By bringing the act of attending into the scene, he has unknowingly committed an obscenity, in the sense that he has brought on stage what by its nature must occur offstage.

Strong stuff. But what Larkin has done in this poem is no more than what Tolstoy does in *War and Peace*, except that it violates our expectations of the first-person point of view, especially in a poem where we implicitly take that point of view to be the poet's himself.

What Larkin does is to presume to understand what is going on in the minds and hearts of the people he sees. Once he realizes the noise at each stop is not merely workers on the platforms but truly an event—the last weddings of the Whitsun week, portions of festivals that have marked the week for centuries—he is interested.

> Struck, I leant
> More promptly out next time, more curiously,
> And saw it all again in different terms.

Granted, the catalog of Larkinesque caricatures that follows is smugly satirical. On the platforms waving good-bye to the newlyweds are fathers with "seamy foreheads," "Mothers loud and fat," "An uncle shouting smut," and girls in their "parodies of fashion," including "jewellery-substitutes." Yet Larkin's eye is typically English, picking out as it does the limited expectations, the cheapness at the end of empire; what it sees has been a theme of British literature since World War II. But Larkin penetrates the phenomenon more deeply here, understanding it even as he seems to push it away, and to do this he assumes an omniscience based on shared experience. He observes that this event is witnessed in different ways, by children as "dull," by fathers as "Success . . . huge and wholly farcical," by the women as a "secret like a happy funeral," and by the girls themselves as "a religious wounding."

Free at last,
And loaded with the sum of all they saw,
We hurried towards London. . . .

Critics of this poem point out that Larkin either fails or refuses to see his place among the dozen marriages that have "got underway" on the train with him, and that he presumes even further to speak for them, when he notes,

                            none
Thought of the others they would never meet
Or how their lives would all contain this hour.

Only he sees this coming together, "this frail / Travelling coincidence," where in fact he is the odd man out. Although we might express irritation with him, to censor him is to deny the emotional accuracy of the poem. His removal from the others, his difference from them, may have resulted in complacent self-regard, but it is not alienation. It does allow him to see the event whole, and his personal affection for it is related to his love for England itself. When he recognizes what is going on, his response is "Yes." This response is an affirmation, too. Larkin affirms the persistence of Whitsun festivities. He also affirms the weddings themselves with the blessing that ends the poem, when he imagines that, after the train stops, what it holds will continue on "like an arrow-shower / Sent out of sight, somewhere becoming rain." Finally, however we may object to the condescending tone of this, it is not an emotion that any of the other passengers—the newlyweds—would have had; rather, it is one felt for them.

"In the Stopping Train" may be the poem Larkin's critics are looking for in "The Whitsun Weddings." Davie's train passenger would enjoy Larkin's serene outward look, too, if he believed it would do any good. But Davie's rage is inward and is aimed precisely at what divides him from others, including himself. The rhythm of "The Whitsun Weddings" is unhurried. Its eight ten-line stanzas rhyme *ababcdecde*; five of the eight dovetail with the stanza following them; all but the second line of each stanza is in iambic pentameter; only that second line, in iambic dimeter, registers the jolt of the train's stopping and starting, if it is meant to imitate anything. Davie's poem, in ten unnumbered parts, with stanzas appearing as couplets, tercets, quatrains, does not flow smoothly from strophe to strophe over bright knots of rhyme like Larkin's. Instead, it reflects in its lurching, enjambed, trimeter lines not only the speaker's anguish but the train's frustrating stop and start. Davie's train trip is neither as comfortable nor as magisterial as Larkin's. It lacks, too, Larkin's sweeping way with a metaphor in which he can speak of well-wishers left behind on boarding platforms

> As if out on the end of an event
> Waving goodbye
> To something that survived it.

But Davie's cramped, self-analytical ride does give us a narrative structure that exists as more than a route to an end. It is the mode by which the commonplace event—taking a train somewhere—is invested with the urgency to have understood oneself before the end of the journey. Davie's poem, then, has the greater symbolic and emotional resonance.

Part 1 of "In the Stopping Train" gets right to the matter, yet at the same time it begins probing for the heart of the poet's unhappiness.

> I have got into the slow train
> again. I made the mistake
> knowing what I was doing,
> knowing who had to be punished.
>
> I know who has to be punished:
> the man going mad inside me;
> whether I am fleeing
> from him or towards him.

The tone of puritanical self-loathing is quite clear, but is boarding this train "again" a recurrent error or, as he implies, a deliberate punishment? The self divided from the self has to be punished, in part, for his lack of charity.

> He abhors his fellows,
> especially children; let there
> not for pity's sake
> be a crying child in the carriage.
>
> So much for pity's sake.

This is the first of the bitterly humorous remarks made at the speaker's own expense throughout the poem. Is there a crying child on the carriage to which the "So much for pity's sake" has been directed? Or does the wish defeat any notion of pity, even that suggested by the expression "for pity's sake"? The fascination of this poem is the total lack of objectivity. No flowers will be observed, no architecture or landscapes will be noted simply for pleasure as in the Larkin poem. Instead, language about them will be analyzed.

> Jonquil is a sweet word.
> Is it a flowering bush?
> Let him helplessly wonder
> for hours if perhaps he's seen it.

Davie zeroes in on the culprit—it is the artist, the man going mad inside him with a self-involved passion, who "never needed to see, / not with his art to help him." It is this figure, too, who has hatreds and loves, though false. He is the passionate figure who, for reasons not yet clear aside from his selfishness, must be punished.

Meanwhile, he displays for us his various artistic and intellectual strengths as he tries to understand his situation. The play of language, of tones of voice, and of rhythm predominate in Davie's poem, whereas in Larkin's imagery and metaphor are foremost. Part 2 of "In the Stopping Train" contains the most moving of Davie's wordplay; it is affecting because it touches on the larger symbolism of this ride.

> A stopping train, I thought,
> was a train that was going to stop.
> Why board it then, in the first place?
>
> Oh no, they explained, it is stopping
> and starting, stopping and starting.

Here, "they" are adults; the exchange recalls their voices. In this section there *is* a child in the carriage after all. Having understood the adult assurances, Davie says, "I saw the logic of that; / grown-ups were good at explaining." But the starting and the stopping of the train do not keep it from getting to the end of the line. As broad as the hint becomes here— "even expresses have to do that"—still, there is a power in this internal dialogue, this analysis of memory. The child Davie is not sure the adults understand his anxiety about riding such a train, and the adults show this by ending the conversation.

> Well, they said, you'll learn
> all about that when you're older.
>
> Of course they learned it first.
> Oh naturally, yes.

Is it mortality, then, that has been the source of the inner man's, the artist's madness? The resentful tone of the last lines is mitigated by one of resignation. This is one of the poem's quietest moments.

Davie shows a distinct temperament in part 3; that is, it is distinct from Larkin's ironic detachment. Regarding the reckless traffic on the highway that runs beside the train, the "passing and re-passing" of cars with "a recklessness like breeding," "he is shrieking silently: 'Rabbits!' " To follow this with the refrain "He abhors his fellows" may be seen as an understatement. Yet the British use of the rabbit, despite its cutesified transformation in *Watership Down*, is instructive. Larkin's "Myxomatosis," ostensibly about the disease spread to control the rabbit population in Britain after World War II, ends with lines that could be meant to indict an aspect of the British character,

> You may have thought things would come right again
> If you could only keep quite still and wait.

And there is in *The Wind in the Willows*, of all places, Kenneth Grahame's characterization of the rabbits who never wish to be involved, whose response is *"Do* something? Us rabbits?" Davie's epithet here may carry these connotations, along with the angry one of the sterile condemning the mindlessly procreative. Yet, this dissonance is resolved.

> Yet even the meagre arts
> of television can
> restore them to him sometimes,
>
> when the man in uniform faces
> the unrelenting camera
> with a bewildered fierceness
> beside the burnt-out Simca.

Confronted by the record of urban, probably terrorist violence, in which "his fellows," individuals like those he has been cursing, have been victimized and the representative of order, "the man in uniform," must make sense for the masses watching, Davie is capable of what he claims to lack—pity, perhaps even charity.

Lest we be seduced by this harmonic moment, however, the splenetic voice returns in part 4, growling, "What's all this about flowers?" He observes that "Some people claim to love them." Here the poet is faced with the full power of a word's meaning and the need to justify it to his own intelligence.

> Love *them*? Love flowers? Love,
> love . . . the word is hopeless:
> gratitude, maybe, pity. . . .
>
> Pitiful, the flowers.

Again, as with the rueful "So much for pity's sake," the notion of pity being misaligned with its object has wit. But "love" is the most important word in the poem, the word the poem resolves on, its last word, in fact. These flowers are pitiful because they are merely words, or merely a word, and the poet "can name them all, / identify hardly any." The madness, the passion, and the spleen here are vented because of an inability or a refusal to apply to reality the names the poet has for it, including "love." Nominalists make for anxious Christians.

Part 5 is interesting for a number of reasons. First, though not the most important, is that in Davie's recent *Selected Poems* (published by Carcanet), it has been deleted from the poem. Second, and more important, it helps to characterize the speaker, to identify him more closely with Davie (perhaps considered irrelevant in the Carcanet edition). It is subtitled *"Judith Wright, Australian."* Why would this particular character be thinking about the Australian poet Judith Wright? It would be simple enough to say that, well, Donald Davie is the speaker and he thinks of quite a lot of things to do with English literature, especially contemporary sorts. Has Davie carefully created a fictional self or selves for this poem? We already know the character has a literary bent; here he is giving an opinion that appears first to be gratuitous but, on a closer look, is not. Our speaker is occupying his time with more than internal agony and outward grousing. He is writing or thinking about somebody else.

> Judith Wright, Australian,
> 'has become,' I said,
>
> 'the voice of her unhappy,
> still-to-be-guilty nation.'
>
> Wistfully I said it,
> there in the stopping train.

A literary man can be believed to be writing or thinking about a review, for example, as he takes even the most miserable of rides; after all, he has time, and there is the leisure to work on a train. The greater import here, however, is that Davie has recognized that a poet can be the voice of an entire nation. Though guilt is that nation's inheritance, he assigns Wright's voice to it wistfully, with a melancholy wish. Australia's history has been, though it is no longer, bound up in England's. England has had its voices, but the singular spokesman has faded along with empire. For whom today does the contemporary English poet speak? Here he speaks only for himself and his own guilt.

In part 6 the poem turns and the speaker faces himself.

> The things he has been spared. . . .
> "Gross egotist!" Why don't

his wife, his daughter, shrill
that in his face?

Love and pity seem
the likeliest explanations;
another occurs to him—
despair too would be quiet.

These lines look back to the rumination of part 5 and ahead to those to come. What he has been spared is any concern for or obligation to anything besides his profession. Here "Love and pity" are introduced, although this time not as part of a witty self-satire, but as solemn recognitions of his family's indulgence. They are joined by another motive, in a play on Thoreau's famous observation, here personalized and all the more poignant. Our speaker himself is living a life not of quiet desperation but, if his inner turmoil is an indication, of noisy desperation. His self-disgust is partly with the ridiculous figure cut by the ranting inner man. Love, pity, and despair, in the form of those closest to him, regard his anguish sadly and quietly.

Part 7 is the most rhythmically compelling of the poem. At this point, rather than apologize, Davie rears up and justifies his professional activities in martial terms.

Time and again he gave battle,
furious, mostly effective;
nobody counts the wear
and tear of rebuttal.

He has not shrunk from controversy. He has even been proud of the stands he has taken, although there is some question about their lasting importance. Finally, playing on his favorite metaphor of poetry as sculpture, an art worked in a durable medium, he admits that his intellect and emotions have been "hardened" by his engagements. One can make a list of the many stands Davie has taken in his career, the areas of intellectual and artistic endeavor he has pronounced for—and against—and recognize this as an honest assessment of the man by the man himself. The phrase "Time and again" that begins each of the section's five quatrains and the rhymes in each stanza, rare in this poem, give the section its power. Yet the single most powerful stanza in the poem derives its strength from an apparent disruption.

Time and again, oh time and
that stopping train!
Who knows when it comes to a stand,
and will not start again.

Once more, the emblematic nature of this train is emphasized; the subject and the form could not be more closely welded.

Part 8 brings a change of tone, one that approaches the second stanza of "The Whitsun Weddings." As I have argued, there is a calmness, even a serenity, to Larkin's point of view that allows him to see the big picture, or what he imagines to be the big picture, without coming himself to any sort of intense self-realization. That is not his point, to be sure. Davie, on the other hand, shows us active and painful self-division. As he recognizes this state for what it is, he detaches himself from it so to speak, and in this section speaks more in Larkin's disinterested tone. Part 8 is also subtitled, in parenthesis, "Son et Lumière." It is as if the window of the stuffy car were opened for a moment.

> I have travelled with him many times
> now. Already we nod,
> we are almost on speaking terms.
>
> Once I thought that he sketched
> an apologetic gesture
> at what we turned away from.

He describes how his traveling companion's glasses caught the light as he turned away, and comes to the following passage of deft, impressionistic landscape painting.

> I knew they had been ranging,
> paired eyes like mine,
> igniting and occluding
>
> coppice and crisp chateau,
> thatched corner, spray of leaf,
> curved street, a swell of furrows,
>
> where still the irrelevant vales
> were flowering, and the still
> silver rivers slid west.

This is called having your cake and eating it, too. Though the spectacles blind the viewer and though the vales are called "irrelevant," the self-laceration is missing here in words like "crisp," "thatched," "spray," "curved," "swell," "flowering," and "silver." The sounds are gorgeous and forgiving.

Perhaps they hint at a reconciliation not to occur in this poem. An intenser rhythm returns in part 9, albeit with a sprightliness that includes a recognition of the landscape's redemptive properties. Here, too, the play of voices is most apparent and effective. If for this character "words alone are certain good," then admitting this leads to a sort of acclamation of what our fellow can do—play with words.

> The dance of words
> is a circling prison, thought
> the passenger staring through
> the hot unmoving pane
> of boredom. It is not
> thank God a dancing pain,
> he thought, though it starts to jig
> now. (The train is moving.) "This,"
> he thought in rising panic
> (Sit down! Sit down!)
> "this much I can command,
> exclude. Dulled words, keep still!
> Be the inadequate, cloddish
> despair of me!" No good:
> they danced, as the smiling land
> fled past the pane, the pun's
> galvanized *tarantelle*.

This may be the most emotionally complicated section of the poem, since the dull words tie him to the earth ("cloddish"), tend to embarrass him as he grows excitable about their possibilities ("Sit down! Sit down!"), and bring on a "rising panic" with its connotations of terror and the power of Pan. The "dancing pain" becomes a "jig," and the words, despite Davie's demurral, do dance. The landscape smiles, and the hot boredom of the poet's self-examination gives way, as was hinted in the previous section, to a momentary forgiveness in which we can hear not only the immediate wordplay on pane/pain, but reverberations between those words and the words "pun," "panic," and the important initiating circumstance, "punishment." The punishing slow pace of this self-criticism has yielded, despite impending panic, to the play of words, yet still within the prison of language.

Davie is too much the puritan to let himself off on a gaudy note of consolation or to let his poem become a pastoral. The final part, its tenth, is at once the most varied tonally, the most self-revealing, and the most moving. The play becomes self-punishment again as Davie "pummels his temples."

> 'A shared humanity . . .'
> . . . 'Surely,
> surely that means something?'

> He knew too few in love,
> too few in love.
>
> That sort of foolish beard
> masks an uncertain mouth.
> And so it proved: he took
> some weird girl off to a weird
> commune, clutching at youth.
>
> Dear reader, this is not
> our chap, but another.
> Catch our clean-shaven hero
> tied up in such a knot?
> A cause of so much bother?
>
> He knew too few in love.

By the end of Larkin's poem, he knows many in love, e.g., all the newlyweds. But Davie knows, he claims, "too few." Yet detachment like Larkin's could hardly be ascribed to what Davie does know and has observed. In one of the most risky satiric caricatures I can imagine, Davie first skewers what appears to be a contemporary, perhaps the victim of a midlife crisis, "clutching at youth." Then he turns on himself and plays on the doubleness he has presented throughout the poem to emphasize that in no way are we to mistake "our chap" for "another."

> Catch our clean-shaven hero
> tied up in such a knot?
> A cause of so much bother?

What adds to the chill of this portrait is its echo of one in a similarly structured and similarly emotional poem, from Davie's *Events and Wisdoms*, "After an Accident."

> Death is about my age,
> Smiling and dark, clean-shaven.

The "shared humanity" that must mean something has been glossed in numerous ways throughout the poem, as Davie responds to his possible carriage mates, to the remembered wisdom of grown-ups, to the traffic outside the train, to his wife and daughter, to the enviable position of Judith Wright who speaks for her nation, and to himself. Davie may not know what he means, but he does know how it feels to share the humanity of others, to be human. Larkin, on the other hand, does know what a shared humanity means, for others if not exactly for himself.

The most compelling and most ambiguous line in this section is the refrain, "He knew too few in love." Michael Schmidt has read it simply as

"He loved too few people." That is the reading that makes the most sense. Yet there are subtler overtones that are compelling, too. In his knowledge of others there was not enough love. Of those he knew, too few were in love—even in love like the foolish bearded man with his weird girl. A commune might, indeed, be the sort of community Davie claims to know nothing of, a weird one as far as he can tell. The reproach implicit in this line is a Christian one. The Christian admonition, to love one's neighbor as oneself, compels Davie in many of his poems. No less does it here.

My distinction that Davie is a Christian poet and Larkin is not might seem strange only because the occasion of Larkin's poem is a Christian holiday. Yet Larkin's interest is in what characterizes the object of his affection; this has little to do with Christianity. In his most famous poem, "Church Going," he affirms the perpetuation of custom much as he does in "Show Saturday"—"Let it always be there." This is his theme in "The Whitsun Weddings" as well. Davie's concerns as a Christian are the salvation of his soul and the fellowship of his fellowmen. It makes sense that as a Christian poet he would be distressed by the self's interference with these aims, especially as it uses language to obstruct them. Furthermore, it follows that he would find the lyric insufficient to express the obligations of a modern poet. "In the Stopping Train" tests the limits of the form, whereas "The Whitsun Weddings" goes beyond the form inadvertently and, perhaps, dubiously. What is tantalizing is to imagine a form in which the achievements of both poems—the intensity of self-revelation and the understanding of the experience of others—are shared.

# Eating Your Words:
# Dante as Modernist

## Gabriel Josipovici

THERE ARE two and only two kinds of modern artist: the one who feels that certain things can no longer be done, and the one who has never known such feelings. The trouble with the attitude of the former is that such knowledge erodes confidence and eventually leads to silence; the trouble with the attitude of the latter is that whatever he produces soon comes to seem irrelevant and outdated, no matter how good a craftsman he is. The greatest artists of the century have been those who have accepted that they have eaten of the apple and yet somehow found means of avoiding or evading the stark conclusion to which that ought to lead. This is what unites Eliot and Stevens, Valéry and Yeats, despite all their differences. Recent attempts to treat Stevens as a latter-day Keats or to replace Eliot by Hardy in the pantheon of modern poetry have not been convincing, though one can see why they have occurred: poets and critics have been desperate to find a tradition that would absolve them from having to make the impossible choices of modernism; but as with theological attempts to bypass the insights of Kierkegaard and Nietzsche, they have demonstrated only that there is no escape.

But one could also argue that the recognition of the dilemma can lead to a renewal of art rather than its extinction. Proust was able to write A`la recherche only when he accepted that he could not write like the Goncourts, and it is surely not by accident that Wallace Stevens placed the same poem at the head of both his Collected Poems and his Selected Poems, and that the poem "Earthy Anecdote" deals with precisely the issue we are considering: every time the bucks go clattering over Oklahoma the firecat bristles in the way, forcing them to go either to the right or to the left; yet when eventually the firecat closes his bright eyes and sleeps, leaving the direct way open, the poem comes to an end.

One way modern artists have had of coming to terms with the dilemma is to search for allies in other ages, other traditions. Proust turned to the Arabian Nights, Eliot to Dante and Donne, Kafka to the Bible, Brecht to Chinese stories and poems. Just as it is often a relief when a friend confesses to having experienced feelings one might have been tempted to think were peculiar to oneself, so an artist can take heart from realising that others, in distant times and places, encountered and overcame the problems that seem to him so paralysing. Think of Dante. Did he too not, like the bucks of Wallace Stevens, try first to run straight up the mountain toward his goal and find himself forced back by those medieval firecats, the lion, the leopard, and the wolf? He learned the hard way that in order to go up you must first go down, and that there is no straight road but that he who would truth reach "about must and about must go." Where language is concerned he learned that we cannot confer automatic authority on our work by use of an authoritative language, but that the use of the vernacular does not by itself confer authenticity, any more than Latin confers authority. The equivalent of the spiral downward and upward in linguistic terms is the forging of a vernacular that *through use* becomes both authentic and authoritative.

Dante, as Eliot sensed, has much to teach us about the temptations of false and superficial solutions to questions of morals, metaphysics, and aesthetics; so, rather than rehearsing once again the old yet still crucial debates of modernism, I propose to look in some detail at the closing cantos of the *Inferno*. For it is only by submerging ourselves in an artist's world that we can understand the choices with which he presents us and which we can use to illuminate our own lives and work.

As you approach the centre of an inverted cone—which is, after all, what Hell is—you naturally find yourself going faster and faster as the circumference grows smaller and the incline steeper. At the end of the *Inferno* Dante—and the reader with him—is going to zoom through the centre and, turning as he climbs down the hairy flanks of Satan, King of the Underworld, climb up to find himself in sight of the stars for the first time and at the foot of the mountain of Purgatory. From the point of view of God he has not been going down in his long journey through Hell, but up, so that the journey from the rim of Hell to the tip of Purgatory is one long ascent. It is only in our inverted world, as denizens of Satan's kingdom, that it has seemed as though we were going down.[1]

Dante is careful to make connections between the beginning and the end of the *Inferno* and between the beginning of the *Inferno* and the beginning of the *Purgatorio*. In *Inferno* XXXIII Ugolino dreams of a wolf,

---

1. See John Freccero, "The Pilgrim in the Gyre," in *Dante: The Poetics of Conversion* (Harvard, 1986).

which reminds us of the third of the beasts of Canto I, and in talking of the relation of bodies to souls on earth in Canto XXXIII Dante uses the unusual word *ruina* ("ella ruina in si fatta cisterna"; "she falls headlong into this cistern," 133) which takes us back to the striking image of the pilgrim Dante falling back at the start: "Mentre ch'i ruvinava in basso loco" ("while I was ruining down into the depths," I.61). Both echoes help us to see how foolish it was of the pilgrim to try to run straight up the mountain. At the same time the echoes of *Inferno* I in *Purgatorio* I, so well brought out by Singleton,[2] help to confirm us in our sense that at the start of the second canticle Dante is once again in the position he was in at the start of the first, at the foot of a mountain surrounded by desert and water, but that this time it will be possible for him to climb to the very top.

As always in Dante the theological and the artistic cannot be separated. Artistically, the poet wants to bind his great structure together, and to give us a sense of a huge physical and mental distance to be traversed and of how that distance can be compressed in the imagination. Theologically, Dante wants to remind us that the poem is about himself, about *his* escape from the dark wood of his life, *his* conversion and purgation to the point where he can answer to his own name (at the top of the mountain of Purgatory), and finally be ready to see God as well as to write the poem we are reading (at the end of *Paradiso*). For this to become possible he has to arrive at a new understanding of his relation to the world—to other people, that is, and to language.

In a sense the whole poem is about the relations between speech and love. It is about the right and wrong uses of both, for we can understand the right only when we have grasped its opposite, and the wrong uses of love are inseparable from the wrong uses of language. As the poem accelerates in the lower reaches of the cone of Hell, the cantos cease to be distinct, and we need to read XXXI–XXXIV as a single unit. We are in the lowest of the nine pits, the place where the treacherous are stuck for all eternity. Though even here Dante is concerned to make us grasp nuances, distinctions (between treachery to kindred, to country, to guests, to lords and benefactors), the four kinds merge imperceptibly into each other as earlier distinctions did not.

Yet what this merging should alert us to is that in reality *all* the circles merge into each other, that it is ultimately one state being explored from beginning to end of the *Inferno*. In *Paradiso* Beatrice tells Dante that all the

2. "In Exitu Israel de Aegypto," in *Dante: A Collection of Critical Essays*, ed. John Freccero (Englewood Cliffs, 1965).

souls are really gathered together in the great rose, and it is only to accommodate Dante's earthly understanding that they are reflected in the different planetary spheres. This is because theologically Heaven does not recognise the distinctions between better and best. But even in Hell the divisions are only an accommodation; ultimately, there is no difference between Francesca, clinging to the man she loves, and Ugolino, gnawing at the head of the man he hates.

St. Augustine had argued that there are basically only two attitudes we can adopt: *amor sui* and *amor dei* (love of self and love of God). Once we put love of ourselves at the centre of our affective life we are already headed down the cone of Hell toward Satan's gaping mouth—unless we are supple enough in spirit to repent, to reorient our will, which, in this life, is always a possibility. This is why there is a symmetrical relation between Hell and Purgatory as well as between Hell and Paradise.

Dante makes this clear, as I have suggested, by placing at the beginning and end of the *Inferno* two episodes that could not at first sight be more different, but are in fact profoundly similar. For Dante the pilgrim and perhaps for us the first time we read the poem, they do indeed seem very different, but one of the functions of the journey is, after all, to teach both Dante and ourselves how to read aright. We are able to do this because Dante the poet, who is the product of the journey, gives us the clues to both ways of reading, though it is only when we, too, have got to the end that we can read the beginning as it ought to be read.

In both Canto V and Cantos XXXII–XXXIII we come across two figures, only one of whom speaks. Yet the two are bound together through eternity, Paulo and Francesca by a desperate love, Ugolino and Ruggieri by hatred; the first two embrace and remember how they kissed, the second two eat each other and remember other acts of cannibalism. Both Francesca and Ugolino make long speeches—among the longest in the entire poem—which evoke the horror and pity of the listener and lead to a dramatic response from the pilgrim Dante. Yet the poet Dante takes care to give us, the readers, the chance to experience the speeches quite differently from either the way the speaker wishes them to be taken or the way the pilgrim understands them. And in both cases we who come seven centuries after Dante have the advantage of seeing in the reactions of speakers over the intervening centuries how easy it is to misread, to take, in Dante's terms, the letter for the spirit. That does not mean, however, that we can afford to feel superior, for there is no certainty that we, too, are not misreading in our turn.

"Una medesma lingua pria mi morse" is how Canto XXXI begins; "One and the same tongue first stung me, so that it tinged both my cheeks, and then it supplied the medicine to me."[3] It is typical of Dante that in this simple and straightforward account of the effect of Virgil's words on him he should also give us the key to the whole canto, for its theme is language and the division of tongues. Soon Dante and Virgil come upon the giant Nimrod, said to be the chief builder of the Tower of Babel, which led to the fragmentation of peoples and languages. The giant cannot speak any language we or the pilgrim can understand. "Raphel may amech zabi almi," he howls, and Virgil says to him: "Stupid soul, keep to thy horn and vent thyself with that when rage or other passion takes thee" (70–72). Then, turning to Dante, he explains, "He is his own accuser. This is Nimrod, through whose wicked device the world is not of one whole speech" (76–78). Nimrod, who had wanted to bypass speech and build a tower that would allow him to assault God and wrest his power from him, finds himself robbed of speech. Dante makes the point that to speak at all we have to make an initial sacrifice. The baby cries when it wants food; learning to talk gives it a new mastery of the world, but only at the cost of some repression of immediate desire. To speak means to learn the language of others, and to abide by its laws. Responsibility to speech is thus bound up with the acceptance of the fact that we are not alone in the world with our desires. But if speech can help us to interact with others, such an initial repression results in gain as well as loss. It is another example of the need to go to the right and to the left if one is to move forward. The pattern of the acquisition of speech, moreover, parallels the central lesson of the poem, that love of God rather than love of self is what allows man to fulfil his true potential: "In his will is our peace" (*Par.* III.85). And we go on reading the poem seven centuries after it was written precisely because Dante does not simply assert this but demonstrates it in action.

At the end of Canto XXXI we come to the frozen lake of Cocytus, which will be the setting for the next two cantos. Here the sinners are frozen into the ice, locked together in a parody of communal life and demonstrably incapable of the movement that alone can lead to salvation: Dante's physical movement through Hell and up the mountain of Purgatory, and the spiritual movement of those who repented in this life and are now in Purgatory.

When Dante enters this area of supreme cold, he calls on the Muses for help:

3. I use Singleton's lucid prose translation throughout: *The Divine Comedy, Translated, with a Commentary by Charles S. Singleton,* 6 vols. (Princeton, 1971–73).

It is not without fear I bring myself to speak, for to describe the
bottom of all the universe is no enterprise to undertake in sport or
for a tongue that cries *mamma* and *babbo*. But may those ladies aid
my verse who aided Amphion to wall in Thebes, so that the telling
may not be diverse from the fact.

(XXXII.5–12)

The "tongue that cries *mamma* and *babbo*" is the baby's, but it is also the
vernacular, which Dante chose for his poem, refusing the authority of
Latin. These opening remarks of Canto XXXII thus make the point that
with the help of the Muses, trusting himself to the guardians of tradition,
his child's language can develop and extend so as to take in even what is
farthest below speech, as later he will have to deal with what is farthest
above it. As we would expect of Dante, he does in the end indeed return
to the image of the child: "Now will my speech fall more short, even in
respect to that which I remember," he says of his final vision, "than that of
an infant who still bathes his tongue at the breast" (*Par*. XXXIII.106–8).

So Dante walks over the icy lake and sees the first group of sinners,
those who, like Cain, have been treacherous to kindred; and then he
comes to those who, like Antenor, the Trojan who betrayed Troy to the
Greeks, have betrayed a country or a cause. We are at line 124 and need to
start reading closely: "Io vidi due ghiacciatti in una buca" ("I saw two
frozen in one hole," 125). Two in one, but what kind of union do they
form? At the end of the whole poem Dante will contemplate the mystery
of the Trinity, and in Canto XXXIV of the *Inferno* he will see a parody of it in
Satan's three heads. But here already we are set to explore the nature of
unity and community.

The theme of the episode that follows is now adumbrated in typical
Dantean style, not by assertion but by an apparently precise description
of what the pilgrim sees: "And as bread is devoured for hunger, so the
upper one set his teeth upon the other where the brain joins the nape"
(127–29). Put very simply, the theme is this: what is the food that man
most needs? What is the bread that will truly satisfy his hunger? We are
fortunate to have a translation of the whole Ugolino episode by one of our
finest poets, Seamus Heaney, and it is no insult to him to say that his
translation just doesn't work. It is an early piece (it can be found in *Field
Work*, 1979), and I suspect that today he would probably agree that he was
just trying too hard:[4]

4. Heaney's most recent volume, *The Haw Lantern* (London, 1987), contains a beautiful
translation of *Beowulf*, ll.26–52, which shows a much more personal and relaxed attitude to
the translation of ancient poems than does his Ugolino translation, and is consequently
much more successful, it seems to me.

I walked the ice
And saw two soldered in a frozen hole
On top of other, one's skull capping the other's,
Gnawing at him where the neck and head
Are grafted to the sweet fruit of the brain,
Like a famine victim at a loaf of bread.
So the berserk Tydeus gnashed and fed
Upon the severed head of Menalippus
As if it were some spattered carnal melon.

This is Heaney at his most Lowellian, and the passage is certainly power-ful. But the power is that of the grotesque. Dante, for example, has no "spattered carnal melon," and "Like a famine victim at a loaf of bread" loses the wonderful way in which Dante, like Aeschylus, gives us images of wholesomeness even in the depths of Hell. For the line says nothing about famine victims, only about the way bread relieves hunger; in doing so, of course, it points us to the bread of the sacrament, but only by way of that most ordinary and natural activity, the eating of good bread to satisfy us after honest toil.

And yet, of course, Dante is too great an artist simply to set good against bad, correct against incorrect behaviour, the natural against its perversion. He makes the journey down precisely in order to understand the reasons for the perversion of the good, the nature of evil. The episode of Ugolino is the greatest exploration in literature (along perhaps with Kafka's late story, "The Fasting Showman") of the implications of the fact that the mouth is used both to masticate food and to utter speech and that it cannot do both at the same time. What Dante is going to suggest, and demonstrate, is that ultimately, if it comes to a question of choice, speech is a better food than food. But there is a long way to go before we can understand this.

To describe Ugolino gnawing at his enemy's neck and head, Dante chooses an image from the siege of Thebes: "non altrimenti Tideo si rose / le tempie a Menalippo per disdegno." Heaney misses that "for rage" by simply talking about "the berserk Tydeus." In his version it could have been hunger that drove Tydeus mad, but Dante is careful to tell us that he fed on the other not out of hunger but out of rage—"per disdegno." The image makes us realise that we are not dealing with three separate themes in these cantos, the themes of childhood, language, and love (and their perversion), but one theme that unites them all. For we are here in a world of utter regression, where adults have gone back to babyhood, wanting, wanting, wanting, and back even further, to bestiality—the ultimate regression that lies in wait as a possibility for each one of us.

Having described the scene, the poet follows a familiar strategy by having the pilgrim enquire of the damned about their condition: "O you who by so bestial sign show hatred against him whom you devour, tell me the wherefore" (133–35). John Freccero, in a fine essay to which I am greatly indebted,[5] has made the point that signs exist only within society and that a bestial sign is a contradiction in terms, the sign of the giving up of signs. Dante is here dealing with what lies beyond words, and as usual he is punctilious in his poetic response. On the one hand, we must not assimilate bestiality to our system of signs and thereby falsify its import; but on the other, without designating it by our signs we would remain in its power. Dante's solution here is not unlike Chaucer's in the General Prologue: the pilgrim wanders through Hell in an oddly innocent way. He talks as though everything around him were perfectly normal and as though there was no problem in conveying what he is experiencing: "Tell me the wherefore," he says to the sinner in the ice, "on this condition, that if you with reason complain of him, I . . . may yet requite you in the world above, if that with which I speak does not dry up" (135–39). Heaney, subscribing to a romantic aesthetic, which says that art must be what it tells, has no room for irony or the deferral of meaning: the task is his to squeeze as much horror as he can out of the scene. But since in the end he has only words, he always falls back in failure. Dante, on the other hand, is prepared to be patient. The calmness of the narration and the narrator's lack of horror are the truly terrifying aspects of the episode.

Without a break we move into the next canto. Again the horror of the scene is conveyed by the pilgrim's down-to-earth narration. But as the scene unfolds, we start to go back in our own minds to an earlier scene and to hold the two in balance.

> Tu vuo ch'io rinovelli
>   disperato dolor ch'l cor mi preme
>   gia pur pensando, pria ch'io ne favelli.
>
> (XXXIII.4–6)
>
> (You will have me renew desperate grief, which even to think of
> wrings my heart before I speak of it.)

Thus the figure in the ice. And we recall Francesca:

> Nessun maggior dolore
>   che ricordarsi del tempo felice
>   nella miseria.
>
> (V.121–23)

5. "Bestial Sign and Bread of Angels," in *Dante: The Poetics of Conversion*.

(There is no greater sorrow than to recall, in wretchedness, the happy time.)

The tone is the same, though the two passages naturally differ about the earlier time. Ugolino's remark is actually closer to what lies behind both passages, Aeneas's first words of the story of his adventures before he reached Carthage: "Infandum, regina, iubes renovare dolorem" ("A sorrow too deep to speak do you order me, O queen, to tell once more," *Aeneid* II.3–6). But where Aeneas calls the sorrow "infandum," beyond speech (from which our word *infant* comes), Ugolino, like Francesca, is actually only too glad to speak, though doing so is painful.

But they are glad for different reasons. Francesca wishes to tell the world about her great love; Ugolino, on the other hand, speaks so that "my words are to be seed that may bear fruit of infamy to the traitor I gnaw" (6–8). In other words his story will merely act out in verbal form his revenge on the one he is condemned to bite forever in hatred. It is worth noting, too, the inversion here of the idea of seed and fruit: for Dante there can be growth from the baby's babbling, from *mamma* and *babbo* to the entire *Commedia*; for Ugolino the act of speech is only another form of cannibalism and vengeance.

And yet the tale he tells seems to be full of pathos and has often been taken as such. The Monk in *The Canterbury Tales* retells it as an example of tragedy, and tragedy for him is in essence pathetic. In so doing he fills it out and makes it even more of a tear-jerker than it is in Dante. But he is in effect only "reading" the story as Ugolino himself would have us read it, not as Dante wants us to. For Ugolino is silent on two crucial issues, one I think through deliberate choice, and the other through a kind of psychological compulsion. I will come to the second aspect in a moment. As for the first, it is important to note that throughout his speech Ugolino says nothing at all about *his own guilt*. Yet, as the footnotes tell us, and as we can guess from the fact that he is where he is, Ugolino is himself a traitor; he betrayed his city, Pisa, to its enemies, before being betrayed in turn by his erstwhile ally, Archbishop Ruggieri.

Francesca had said to the pilgrim: "If thou hast so great desire to know our love's first root, I shall tell as one that weeps in telling" (V.124–26). Ugolino says: "If my words are to be seed that may bear fruit of infamy to the traitor I gnaw, thou shalt see me speak and weep together" (9). Yet the really striking fact is that Ugolino does not weep. (We will see later why weeping is a physical impossibility in this part of Hell.) And though he speaks, and at length, it is clear that his motive is not to recount what has happened in the past but to take present revenge on his enemy.

To that end he begins by explaining to Dante who he and his victim are: I am Count Ugolino, he says, and this is Archbishop Ruggieri. "Now I will tell you why I am such a neighbour ['tal vicino'] to him. How, by effect of his ill devising, I, trusting in him, was taken and thereafter put to death . . ." (15–18). Both "neighbour" and "trust" are being misused here, for Ruggieri and Ugolino form a parody of neighbourliness, and their mutual trust was in the service of betrayal of their city. Ugolino leaves it to Dante, as a Florentine, to draw his own conclusions about the neighbourliness and trustworthiness of Pisans, and this the poet duly does at the end of Ugolino's speech (79–90). In this outburst against the Pisans Dante makes two points that help us retrospectively read Ugolino's own story correctly, and it is therefore worthwhile jumping forward to it for a moment. First he compares Pisa to Thebes, and then he castigates the city for putting his [i.e., Ugolino's] children "to such torture." Dante has already referred to Thebes twice, and as Freccero reminds us, the city was a byword in antiquity and the Middle Ages not just for treachery and brutality, but for the mutual destruction of its ruling family. Oedipus killed his father, and then his two sons killed each other as they fought for possession of the city. Thebes is thus an apt symbol for the City of Man, which St. Augustine contrasted with the City of God. It is the place where each man is for himself, and where a neighbour is only a person who occupies space you might have yourself, who eats food you might yourself wish to eat, and who is likely to betray you if you do not betray him first.

But what, then, of the City of God? In paraphrasing Dante's remarks about what the city did to Ugolino's children I did not do justice to Dante's precise words: "non dovei tu i figliuoi porre a tal croce" ("You should not have put his children to such a cross," 87). The words cannot help but alert us to a quite different father-son relationship from that in Oedipus's family, one in which a cross figures not as an instrument of torture but as an instrument of redemption. Just as the image of the bread evoked echoes of a world far from the immediate one before the pilgrim Dante's eyes, so here his own words remind us of another world, unknown to the denizens of Hell, but known to us. In the City of God fathers and children will trust each other, and each will work for the good of the community. By the time Dante wrote the *Commedia* his hopes of the realisation of such a city on earth had all but vanished, but that did not stop him understanding that it was nevertheless the only alternative to Thebes. In this poem the psychological, the metaphysical, the aesthetic, and the political can never be separated.

Let us return now to Ugolino's account of his experiences. He powerfully conjures up the tower in which he and his four little children were shut up, and then tells of his terrifying dream of a wolf being ripped to pieces by pursuing hounds. He goes on: "When I awoke before the dawn I heard my children, who were with me, crying in their sleep and asking for bread. You are cruel indeed if you do not grieve already, to think what my heart was foreboding; and if you weep not, at what do you ever weep?" (37–42). Though he had said that he would "speak and weep together," now he tries to draw tears of sympathy from his listener. To this end he describes how he heard the tower door being nailed up ("e io senti'chiavar l'scio di sotto / a l'orribile torre," 46–47), those lines Eliot used so well as an image of solipsism in *The Waste Land*. (In fact Eliot must have sensed how much of this canto was about the ultimate solipsism that is the regression into bestiality, and must have felt its power more acutely than we can, since he had just recovered from a breakdown.) Ugolino goes on to say how he looked into his children's faces, "without a word": "Io non piangea, si dentro impetrai" ("I did not weep, I so turned to stone within," 48). Everything comes together in this simple line, the theme of tears again, the impossibility of tears then, and how, instead of the bread for which the children had asked (39), Ugolino can only give them stone— the stone he has now become.

The image of the self as stone, unfeeling and indifferent, is one that had long haunted Dante. He had written some wonderful sestinas about a *donna pietra*, a stony woman or belle dame sans merci, who tormented him by her indifference, and he knew well what it was like to reach the point where we can no longer feel. Here, instead of the traditional criticism by the sensitive lover of the indifferent beloved, we have an exploration of the reasons why people turn into stone. We today, sated as we are with reports and images of people crammed and locked into cattle trucks or forced to watch their children beaten to death before their eyes, can perhaps better understand what he was on about than most nineteenth-century critics. Indeed, an admittance that their hearts had been turned to stone by their experiences would often be more honest than attempts to convey the nature of the Nazi atrocities by those who have experienced these at first hand or delved into the archives.

What follows in Canto XXXIII is the heart of the episode. It touches us to the quick but should not for that reason cloud our understanding nor make us forget that the events are being mediated through Ugolino's own words. One son looks up and asks his father what is the matter. Ugolino does not answer. Instead he bites his own hand in grief. At which his children, misreading his action, say: "Father, it will be far less pain for us if thou eat of us" (61–62). Still he does not answer. Four days go by, and another child throws himself at his feet, cries out, "My father, why do you not help me?" (69), and dies.

As Freccero points out, there can be no doubt that here we are being presented with other signs, which, if properly understood, will counter the "bestial signs" we have encountered so far. Instead of the stone that is Ugolino, his children offer him bread, not literal bread, of course, but the bread of Heaven, which is the sacrifice of oneself for another. For Ugolino there is merely the pathos of their gesture, a sense that they have misread his anguished gnawing at his own arm as a sign of hunger. For us there is the sense, in that gesture of selflessness, of Christ's offer of his body as the true bread of the Heavenly City. For did not Christ say, after feeding the five thousand: "I am the living bread which came down from heaven: if any man eat of this bread, he shall live for ever: and the bread that I will give is my flesh, which I will give for the life of the world" (John 6:51)?

Behind Jesus' sacrifice lay another episode of father and son, the story of Abraham and Isaac. Here the son trusts the father as the father trusts God, and as God speaks to Abraham, so father and son can converse together. Ugolino speaks at length to Dante about what happened, but in response to his children's gesture he can only remain silent, even their words cannot turn that stony heart into flesh again. But even when he speaks to Dante, it is not out of understanding or remorse but only to bring tears to the pilgrim's eyes and so manipulate him that his later retelling of the story will be a kind of revenge by Ugolino on Ruggieri.

It is interesting in the light of this to compare the Monk's version of the Ugolino story with the English mystery cycles' versions of the Abraham and Isaac story. The Monk's Tale is sentimental because, for him, tragedy equals pathos; the cycle plays are moving yet dignified because they are part of a larger story that is, in the end, a comedy. (It may be that Chaucer, too, meant us to think of the Monk's tragedies taking place within the larger comedy of the *Tales* as a whole.) But there is more. In the difference of tone between the two lies much of the difference between the Middle Ages and the Renaissance with its aftermath, romanticism. Once this is understood it is possible to see that both Ugolino and those critics who see mere horror or pathos in the Dantean episode are looking at it from what we might call a post-Renaissance point of view. That is, they ask us to see it from a point of view in which individuals are merely themselves and nothing more; Dante the poet, on the other hand, and the authors of the mystery cycles see individual lives as part of a continuum, as embedded in a world that is ultimately meaningful, even if we mere mortals cannot hope to grasp the meaning.

But why should I, as a non-Christian, assent so readily to Dante's poem and to Dante the poet's point of view, and feel it to be much closer to reality than that of Ugolino or Dante's romantic critics? I think it is because Dante never preaches but is content to give a psychological account of the difference between the two cities. He asks us to see in the children's act of spontaneous selflessness not a mere sign of some higher truth, but an example of possible human response to horror, just as Aharon Appelfeld, in his wonderful novel *The Age of Wonders*, presents us not only with Jews who hurriedly married gentiles and covered over their tracks in the wake of the Nazi invasion of Eastern Europe, but also with some who proudly asserted their Jewishness and went to their deaths in dignified fashion. Both Dante and Appelfeld ask us to imagine a world where genuine community is possible because what drives people is generosity toward each other; and both insist on the fact that the alternative to speaking to each other is eating each other.

This perhaps helps resolve what has long been seen as the chief crux of the passage before us. "There he died," says Ugolino, ignoring his son's last words, and he goes on to recount how—always in silence—the other children also soon succumb. "Therefore," he concludes, "I gave myself, now blind, to groping over each and for two days called on them [now he speaks!] after they were dead. Then fasting had more power than grief" ("poscia, piu ch'l dolor, pote'l digiuno," 75). The question is whether the last line implies that Ugolino eventually died of hunger, which, rather than grief, has the power to kill, or whether then hunger overcame even grief, and he ate them. Ugolino stops abruptly at this point, and Freccero rightly refers us back to Francesca's "quel giorno piu non vi leggemmo avante" ("that day we read in it no further," V.138). Both sentences, he points out, are examples of the rhetorical figure of *reticentia*, a form of ellipsis designed to make us imagine more than language can convey. In both cases we are to imagine what follows, but in Francesca's case it is the act of love while in that of Ugolino it is an act of cannibalism. His present self may refuse to face this, yet his actions tell all, as Freud found when he said of one of his patients: "Her painful legs began to 'join in the conversation' during our analyses."[6] For when Ugolino had finished speaking, writes Dante, "with eyes askance he took hold of the wretched skull again with his teeth, which were strong on the bone like a dog's" (76–78). This is the final bestial sign. As in their lifetime Ugolino failed to respond to his children's appeal, would not or could not speak to them when they spoke to him, so after their death he reverts to that other, more primitive

6. *Studies on Hysteria*, vol. 3 (Harmondsworth, 1974), 217.

use of the mouth and tries to stave off his own death by feeding on them. Stone that he has become, he finally accepts literally their offer of food, even though they made it out of a misunderstanding of the signs he offered them, and so in eternity he is condemned to bite forever the head of his fellow-traitor.

That is the last we see of Ugolino, but what follows has retrospective force. Dante moves on along the ice and sees more figures locked in there. Only now do Ugolino's many references to tears acquire their full meaning, for this is the ultimate horror of Hell, that the most natural movement of sympathy in humans, the welling up of tears, is blocked as the ice freezes the water in their eyes. "Lift from my face the hard veils," cries out one of the sinners, "that I may give vent for a little to the misery that swells my heart, before the tears freeze up again" (110–11). The Italian says, "il duol ch'l cor m'impregna" ("the misery with which my heart is pregnant"), and we recall that Ugolino, too, was "pregnant" with grief but could not give birth to it. This failure to breed anything except death completes the series of oppositions round which these concluding cantos have been built: children-babble-speech-humanity-tears / beasts-stony hearts-false words-silence-impossibility of tears.

Dante begs the sinner to speak to him, saying that he will help him if he does so. When the soul has complied with his request, it repeats its prayer: "But now reach out thy hand here: open my eyes." "And I did not open them for him," Dante tells us, "and it was a courtesy to be a churl to him" (148–50). Modern scholars, in reaction against their romantic predecessors, have been quick to point out that Dante is quite right to act as he did and that there are good theological justifications for his actions. But I am not sure that we can read the poem quite so comfortably. In Canto V Dante had swooned at the end of Francesca's piteous tale; in XX he had wept at the sight of the false prophets so twisted in their bodies that their tears fell from their eyes down to their buttocks. There Virgil instructed him in one of the laws of Hell, rebuking him for his easy sympathy: "Qui vive la pieta quand'e ben morta" (28). Singleton translates this as "Here pity lives when it is altogether dead," but the punning line is perhaps better rendered as "Here piety lives when pity is quite dead." In Beckett's story, "Dante and the Lobster," the hero, quaintly called Belacqua, asks his Italian teacher the meaning of the line. She nimbly avoids the question, but it is one the story faces. Belacqua is, in fact, testing the teacher and challenging us to indict Dante for his callousness. It is in keeping with this that he should feel sympathy for the murderer he reads about in the paper and who is due to be hanged the following day, and for the lobster he has brought his aunt and which she is about to drop alive into her boiling pot. The aunt, like Virgil, is quick to condemn him: "You make a fuss and upset me and then lash into it for your dinner." Implicitly she rejects his pity as too easy and only a form of self-indulgence. Of course it is a shock to our postromantic sensibilities to think of empathy as ultimately selfish and unproductive, but there is much truth in what both the aunt and Virgil are saying. Pity, the sufferings of the gentle heart in sympathy for others, is, finally, a destructive sentiment, what brings Francesca to her present plight, and there is no place for it in Purgatory. (Graham Greene's finest book, *The Heart of the Matter*, is an extended exploration of precisely this self-destructive quality of pity.)

But is that the whole truth? The story suggests that Belacqua's response to the imminent death of the lobster is a better one than the aunt's. Just because we can never fully imagine the sufferings of another does not mean that we should not try. What the story suggests is that at least the awareness of our inability is itself a kind of life, whereas the stony heart of the aunt is not. And so I wonder whether those modern critics, armed with St. Augustine and St. Thomas, who criticise Dante the pilgrim for swooning over Francesca and praise him for his action in Canto XXXIII are entirely right. It may be that the pilgrim Dante's only way of getting through Hell is to make his heart stony, and that that is the lesson he learns between Cantos V and XXXIII. But the heart of the poet is not hardened. To write about the stony heart, you have to start with the language of *mamma* and *babbo*. Of course you cannot stop there. You have to be able to distinguish lies from truth, the lies we tell ourselves as well as the lies others tell us. But that is not done by hardening the heart or adopting a position of superiority. It is done by experiencing imaginatively what it means to refuse to enter the world of signs, the world of human speech. For, as Wallace Stevens understood, even "the absence of imagination had / Itself to be imagined." Dante the pilgrim will have to learn that while speaking like a child makes us vulnerable, it is also our only hope. Virgil, like all the virtuous pagans, may live a dignified and serene existence, but it is an existence without hope. Dante suggests, I think, that only by accepting how close we are to babyhood, to bestiality, can we find the springs of generosity that, with the right discipline, can lead to the founding of the City of God and the writing not just of the *Inferno*, but of the *Purgatorio* and the *Paradiso* as well.

That is a lesson every poet since Dante has had to learn for himself. We may argue about the validity or otherwise of this or that tradition, this or that poetic strategy, and no doubt both tradition and strategy are important to the poet. But prior to the choice of either comes the choice of what to do with the mouth, with the relation between food and utterance. To ignore that relation is to condemn oneself to a poetry without substance; to conflate the two is to condemn oneself to a poetry of mere indulgence. Somewhere between these two extremes every major modern poet has operated. The question we have to ask ourselves is a simple one, but upon its answer depends the trajectory of the poet's career: what kind of food do I most need?

# Four Late Poems of
# Lorine Niedecker

*James Kilroy*

GEORGIA O'KEEFFE'S paintings have drawn popular attention and critical regard not so much by their experimentation as by the startling force of what seems to be straightforward, realistic presentation of familiar flowers, animal forms, or landscapes. Of course, they are bold and original in conception, but their artistry does not call attention to itself, and symbolic or topical significance is never insisted upon. After years of study and apprenticeship, she left the artistic circle of New York in order to live and work in New Mexico; but years of steady, intense concentration on that rural landscape and on common subjects, informed particularly by her familiarity with contemporary artistic developments, earned her acclaim as a masterful painter.

Of twentieth-century American poets Lorine Niedecker deserves equivalent critical attention for producing works of immediate appeal but subtle technical innovation. Like O'Keeffe, she spent most of her working life away from the company of other artists, yet her work is in no sense primitive. A half generation younger than the painter, Niedecker adopted the techniques of modernist artists, particularly Pound, Williams, and the objectivists, in writing poems of common life and the apprehension of nature. Like O'Keeffe, Niedecker found in flowers not only objects of beauty but structures of great strength and emotive force. Names of flowers, even catalogs of types, she presents with the care and fervor of an amateur in botany. The flowers she most favors are not showy or delicate, but such tenacious specimens as commonplace weeds and the insectivorous Drosera, which had fascinated Darwin. She entitled one collection of her poems *T & G*, providing in footnotes two equally apt explanations for the initials: "Tenderness & Gristle (Lawrence Durrell)" and "Tongue & Groove (if you're a carpenter)." The plant prints of A. Doyle Moore accompanying that text record the fine veins and firm ribwork of common plants the beauty of which the poet likewise sought to convey. "Blue chicory" she once called her own poetry: familiar, pleasing in its simplicity, but persistent and strong:

Your erudition
the elegant flower
of which

my blue chicory
at scrub end
of campus ditch
illuminates.[1]

No mere modesty provoked this metaphor, but the opposite: a claim that her easily overlooked art in fact surpassed the sophistication of the work of more acclaimed poets by the strength of its forms, and because in its rough persistence it conveys fundamental perceptions about common life.

To say that Niedecker's life was unremarkable may not be fair, because she was reticent in discussing personal matters. But after graduating from Beloit College, she remained for the most part Wisconsin, particularly in Milwaukee and Fort Atkinson. (Her birthplace is less than fifty miles from O'Keeffe's.) Her life among her co-workers, her relations with her parents, and the difficulties of a woman trying to survive in harsh surroundings with little financial resources provide subjects for some of her best poetry. Her friendship with a few like-minded poets seems to have nurtured her, as did her reading, for she progressed in her art so remarkably that by her death in 1970 she had earned critical praise, and the respect of poets such as Basil Bunting. Early in her career she found in Louis Zukofsky's 1931 introductory essay to the objectivist issue of *Poetry* a statement of poetic principle that determined the course she would follow. Continuing friendship with him and his family sustained both the personal and the artistic aspects of her life.

The influence of William Carlos Williams is seen in the diction and rhythm of her early verse; in a letter to Kenneth Cox she described the intention of her first book as a "desire to get down direct speech—(Williams influence . . .)."[2] But the vivacity of perceptions of nature recalls Gerard Manley Hopkins more than that American poet:

Along the river
wild sunflowers

1. The edition cited for all quotations from Niedecker's verse throughout this essay is *From This Condensery: The Complete Writing of Lorine Niedecker*, ed. Robert J. Bertholf (Highlands, N.C., 1985).
2. "Extracts from Letters to Kenneth Cox," in *The Full Note: Lorine Niedecker*, ed. Peter Dent (Devon, 1983), 36.

```
over my head
    the dead
who gave me life
    give me this
our relative the air
    floods
our rich friend
    silt
```

The process of death nurturing life proves the union of the elements of nature: air, water, and earth; but the force of the poem comes from seeing that as a personal relationship, and from the sudden apprehension of the wild beauty of the flower.

Although remaining among farmers and tradesmen in rural Wisconsin allowed her to keep in touch with their language and thought, her profession necessarily separated her from them. A short poem on John James Audubon, who had similarly devoted himself to the exhaustive detailing of natural life, expresses the loneliness of the person who "works" the natural world artistically:

### Audubon

Tried selling my pictures. In jail
twice for debt. My companion
a sharp, frosty gale.

In England unpacked
them with fear:
must I migrate back

to the woods unknown, strange
to all but the birds
I paint?

Dear Lucy, the servants here
move quiet
as kildeer.

Assuming much of the responsibility for caring for a mother who was gradually becoming deaf, tending the house, and working at a variety of jobs were exhausting, far from intellectually satisfying. But she viewed herself and those with whom she worked with affection and humor. While employed as a proofreader in a print shop, she described her co-workers as "the folk from whom all poetry flows / and dreadfully much else." Despite their dullness she could even admire them:

> But what vitality! These women hold jobs—
> clean house, cook, raise children, bowl
> and go to church.
>
> What would they say if they knew
> I sit for two months on six lines
> of poetry?

At one point she even scrubbed floors in a Fort Atkinson hospital, apparently hiding from others her other work, the craft of verse. Her friend Jonathan Williams's photograph of her reveals the strength of her character: her face deliberately acknowledging the camera, hands stuffed in the pockets of a sensible coat, this dark figure against the piled snow seems durable and strong.[3]

The bulk of Niedecker's poetry consists of very short, untitled, and largely unpunctuated verses, which are terse but assertive. The most frequent subjects include natural change:

> Something in the water
>    like a flower
> will devour
>
> water
>
> flower

In the late 1950s she experimented with Oriental verse forms. In the series *In Exchange for Haiku* appears:

> Fog-thick morning—
> I see only
> where I now walk. I carry
>    my clarity
> with me.

As Niedecker matured as a poet, she progressed beyond terse and clever perceptions to greater subtlety and rigor. In "For Paul," a series of poems addressed to the son of Louis Zukofsky, she tackles more complex subjects; but the series is connected only by the one addressed. The best of her verse prior to its last period is distinguished by brevity and sharp wordplay:

> Now in one year
>    a book published

3. This photograph appears on the dust jacket of *The Granite Pail: The Selected Poems of Lorine Niedecker*, ed. Cid Corman (San Francisco, 1985).

and plumbing—
took a lifetime
to weep
a deep
trickle

The poems of Niedecker's final years, from the volume *North Central* to those published posthumously, are marked by an increased sureness and greater intellectual scope. Of these the longer poems deserve special attention; those poems "make my work worthy of mention," Niedecker wrote, disagreeing in this case with Charles Tomlinson, who had favored the short poems "as most do, I think."[4] Although she had earlier written series of poems linked by thought, she advanced, in her later years, to more challenging subjects and complex poetic structures, which are determined not by logical connections but by apparently disharmonious juxtapositions more common to visual art. This progression is best seen in two late poems on historical figures, "His Carpets Flowered: William Morris" and "Darwin,"and in her two longest poems on nature, "Paean to Place" and "Wintergreen Ridge."

For his aspiration to depict natural beauty in his fabric designs and his high regard for art, William Morris might well be regarded as a sympathetic figure. But Niedecker admits to Cid Corman that she could not read Morris's poems and that she would "probably weary of all those flowery designs in carpets, wall papers, chintzes." Nevertheless, reading his letters, she was struck by his personality: "as a man, as a poet speaking to his daughters and his wife—o lovely."[5] One must note in the last phrase "as a poet," for the contrast (and even conflict) between his artistic endeavors and his personal life forms the subject of Niedecker's poem. "His Carpets Flowered: William Morris" consists of three numbered parts, each focusing on discrete aspects of his life and career.

The poem begins in the middle of a description of a dream in which Morris's labor at manufacturing carpets is confused with his domestic life and his hopes to change society. Although the chronology is confused, as in a dream, the details are all accurate, and the text consists primarily of paraphrases and quotations from published letters and journals.[6] The fundamental issues are those that haunted William Morris: What if the

4. Letter to Kenneth Cox, 38.
5. "Extracts from *With Lorine: A Memorial: 1903–1970*," in *The Full Note*, 51.
6. See *The Letters of William Morris*, ed. Philip Henderson (London, 1950), xlvii, 75–78, 121, 145; and Philip Henderson, *William Morris* (New York, 1967), 42–43, 122, 216, 302.

changes in social structure that he fought for would not result in "better art"? Had he been wrong in insisting on "a few points of principle," which made the products of his firm so expensive that his business was unprofitable? Was he being compromised by his participation in employing others, becoming the one possessed as a result of possessing others? And at the center of the dream is a longing to escape: "O to be home to sail the flood." Such conflict between artistic, practical, and political endeavors and the desire for stable personal relations cannot be resolved. Likewise, the poem's second part, which records the young W. B. Yeats's reaction to Morris's lecture series on socialism, sets forth unresolvable problems. Yeats disagreed with the social program being proposed by saying that only a "change of heart" accomplished through religion, and not a violent revolution, would bring about the reform for which they hoped; that religious reform "must come, if come it did, with astronomical slowness, like the cooling of the sun, or it may have been like the drying of the moon." In the poem, Morris's response is evasive: he "rang the bell / for him to sit down." Such haunting uncertainties about the efficacy of one's program of social reform are not resolved even in the poem's concluding section. Instead, one further aspect of Morris's diverse activities is treated: his several voyages to Iceland, seen not only as the source of his poetic versions of the sagas, but as manifestations of his entire artistic achievement. Paraphrasing one of Morris's letters, the poem describes the physical ordeal of traveling across the rough terrain and shows how the oppressive landscape is relieved only by artistic vision: the black sand across which he travels is peppered in one place by a field of "sea-pink and bladder campion" so that the entire scene is transformed into a Persian carpet.

This final vision provides firm closure, but it is not arbitrarily imposed, for the carpet, a work of art, leads us back to three acknowledged, contrasting interpretations of the functions of art: as a vehicle by which the common life of the reader or apprehender can somehow be improved or enriched; as an attempt on the part of the artist to capture the forms of nature (which is what Morris saw the Persian carpetmakers as doing); and as the means of some consolation or relief in the life of the artist. Those contrasting but coexistent views have been established within the poem, as is the recognition that achieving them requires hard work and produces inevitable anxiety. Yet the frustration pervading all sections does not outweigh the celebration of beauty of either the carpet or the aspects of nature that it records.

Charles Darwin was for Niedecker, as for many modern writers, a haunting exemplar; references to his scientific observations, particularly those contained in his *Journal of Researches into the Natural History and Geology of the Countries Visited during the Voyage of H. M. S. 'Beagle'*, appear even in her early verse. The poem entitled "Darwin" explores both his intellectual endeavors and his attempt to reconcile traditional religious beliefs with the facts of evolutionary change as he discovered them. In just the first six words of the poem, which compose the entire stanza, those varied and conflicting aspects of his work are all suggested:

> His holy
>     slowly
>         mulled over
>     matter

The observations of natural life and geology in the Southern Hemisphere that Darwin recorded in the *Beagle*'s journal were slowly, and at times reluctantly, pursued. As is mentioned in the poem's fourth stanza, Darwin was delayed in Port Desire (the pun must have been irresistible) by calm winds, and by his own illnesses, possibly psychosomatic in origin. The labor of research was exhausting, and in a critical sense destructive: *mulled over* originally meant "ground," "pulverized." But it was "holy," sacred, the matter he studied, even if the conclusion to which he was led challenged Christian beliefs:

> 'Species are not
>     (it is like confessing
>         a murder)
>     immutable'

> As to Man
>     'I believe Man . . .
>         in the same predicament
>     with other animals'

The four parts of the poem that follow do not advance that realization, but they record a process of resistance to inexorable conclusions followed by a gradual accommodation. As in the previously mentioned poem, Niedecker makes extensive use of the actual letters of the title character to record these stages. In a letter to his sister Susan, Darwin had described the Andean peaks as "tossed about like the crust of a broken pie," and the *Journal* reports that he told how Chileans ate onions to help overcome shortness of breath. But the weight of the second section is on its conclusion, as was that of the first part: Darwin writes to his sister of his longing for the consolations of music, a most human admission of exhaustion and a desire to escape.[7] The third section begins, "FitzRoy blinked—" at the clinching evidence of seashells found on mountaintops, making the enterprise a "hell" to confront; but for Darwin, the evidence of constant geologic change seemed pieces of a puzzle—a "Paradise Puzzle"—which were beginning to fit together. The fourth section surveys the years of slow work, Darwin's continued studies of fossils and animals, particularly the destructive aspect of the insect-eating plant Drosera; such extended study only confirmed his dedication to science. His life of investigation is laconically summarized in only a few lines: Darwin "sailed out / of Good Success Bay / to carcass"—from the formative voyage of the *Beagle* to work on the carcass of Lyell's dead African cat, and from early promise to inevitable death. But the concluding statement of Darwin's scientific investigations is both balanced and confident:

> the universe
>     not built by brute force
>         but designed by laws
> The details left
>
>     to the working of chance
>     'Let each man hope
>         and believe
> what he can'

In such treatment of the historical record Niedecker complies with one of the dicta of her mentor, Louis Zukofsky:

> Try as a poet may for objectivity, for the past to relive itself not for his living the historical data, he can do only one of two things: get up a most brief catalog of antiquities (people become dates, epitaphs), or use this catalog and breathe upon it, so that it lives as his music. This latter action need not falsify the catalog.[8]

But in "Darwin" she does more than vivify the past, and something quite unlike what Zukofsky did in his poems. The poem's five parts remain fragments, pieces of evidence, not constituting a continuous narrative nor a progressively logical argument. However, the pieces are sufficiently

---

7. Niedecker's mistranscription—"I am ravenous / for the sound / of the pianoforte"— improves on Darwin's letter, "I shall be ravenous for the pianoforte." *Life and Letters of Charles Darwin*, ed. Francis Darwin (New York, 1887), 233.

8. Louis Zukofsky, "Ezra Pound," in *Prepositions* (Berkeley, 1981), 73.

*James Kilroy* 127

unified to justify the poem's firm conclusion: an acknowledgment of the inevitable conflict between the need to believe and those constraints imposed by the discovery of fact. The poem is a response to and an embodiment of the friction between contrasting impulses, which makes all its declarations strained and taut.

The flow of the longest sentences contrasts with the charged energy of the poem's first words, and the accentual meter throughout the poem conveys the strain of the title character's internal conflict. At its best, the insistent emphasis contrasts with the reluctance of the scientist to acknowledge the conclusions to which he is being drawn:

> Flightless cormorants
> Cold-sea creatures—
>   penguins, seals
> here in tropical waters

The poem echoes the scientist's process of discovery, questioning, hypothesizing, and repeating experiments, but in this case with a reluctance to conclude, because that last step undermines religious belief. Darwin remains a type, not a fully depicted character, making the poem other than a dramatic monologue; yet neither is he merely a puppet through which Niedecker can convey her own responses to the evidence of natural evolution. Zukofsky had seen the poet and scientist as alike in their attention to "inert and live things and relations," and in their insistence on "some concept of exactness of utterance," primarily in their attention to "number, measure and weight."[9]

Throughout "Paean to Place," Niedecker's control of those three elements—what is usually called *quantity* in verse—is striking. The opening stanzas set the form and meter of the poem:

> Fish
>   fowl
>     flood
>   Water lily mud
> My life
>
> in the leaves and on water
> My mother and I
>     born
> in swale and swamp and sworn
> to water

9. Zukofsky, "An Objective," in *Prepositions*, 7.

The usual punctuation marks, periods, commas, and semicolons, are dispensed with, and what Pound called "government of speed" is achieved by bold repetitions, assonance, and consonance. The gradual acceleration and deceleration of tempo within stanzas and the typography itself effect strong closure of each stanza, even when that does not correspond to the ending of a sentence.

The poem's subject is simply stated in the fourth and fifth lines above, with the pairing of "leaves" and "water" indicating the polar attractions of the poem: upward and downward. Her father is associated with the gravitational pull downward ("he seined for carp"; he "Knew what lay / under leaf decay") and the mother with flight upward ("canvasbacks / their blast-off rise / from the water"). The speaker herself is, then, a creature of both air and water:

> I was the solitary plover
> a pencil
>     for a wing-bone
> From the secret notes
> I must tilt
>
> upon the pressure
> execute and adjust
>     in us sea-air rhythm
> 'We live by the urgent wave
> of the verse'

The verb *to tilt* is derived from the Middle English: "to cause to fall," "to overthrow"; it suggests danger, leaning against formidable forces. Tilting upon the pressure, like striding surface tension, an ability attributed to water bugs in a previous stanza, approximates the effect of the poem, as it posits contrary, equally powerful forces against which the poet leans. The verse itself becomes a means of exploring resistive matter:

> All things move toward
> the light
>
> except those
> that freely work down
>     to oceans' black depths
>     In us an impulse tests
> the unknown

As these late poems reveal an insistence on precise expression, eschewing the confessional mode and the direct elicitation of emotion, they satisfy central tenets of Louis Zukofsky and George Oppen. Objectivist poetry, according to Oppen, reflects the poet's *sincerity*, the successful recognition of form, not merely a recording of outside phenomena. However, by the end of her career Niedecker had progressed well away from those poets she continued to admire. "Wintergreen Ridge," which she called "the best thing I've ever done," hardly resembles objectivist verse.[10] In fact, Niedecker disagreed with Charles Tomlinson's claim that the "music" of the poem's measure and the structure indicate her debt to Zukofsky: "It seems to me nothing could be further from the truth."[11]

"Wintergreen Ridge" progresses by associations among discrete observations, unified by the subject presented directly in the first two stanzas: the constant change seen in nature and man's place in that process:

> Where the arrows
> of the road signs
> lead us:
>
> Life is natural
> in the evolution
> of matter

The implications of that observation about life become increasingly more disturbing as the poem progresses through nearly three hundred lines, with the staccato effects of the short lines contributing to the intensity. Life is in essence no different from rock, all human constructions are temporary, and even the desire for endurance and transcendence through art is doomed. The strongest literary echoes here are not Zukofsky's verse, but the poems in W. B. Yeats's *The Tower*, which convey anxiety at the perceived chaos of the times and the relentless change seen in the universe. Like Yeats's "Nineteen Hundred and Nineteen," Niedecker's poem is composed of a series of episodes increasing in their intensity and culminating in the most disturbing visions.

As in "Paean to Place," contention between nature and humans is assumed from the start. Allowed only to observe the changing beauty and unknowable destructive forces around them, human beings constantly strive: "We are gawks / lusting / After wild orchids." But the foolishness of that effort is indicated by the word *gawk*, an awkward and even stupid person. If man is confined to such a small place in the universe, then the sign found in a natural preserve exhorting passersby not to pick the

10. Letter to Cid Corman, in *The Full Note*, 46.
11. Letter to Kenneth Cox, 38.

flowers—"Love and enjoy them / and leave them so"—must seem ironic. Yet such is the extent of human capacity: to love and enjoy the beauty of the world within the limits of time. Likewise, the women who "stopped bulldozers / cold" to save a flowering glen did something noble, but also futile, in their attempt to save botanical specimens "for all time." Even amid the beautiful foliage are destructive plants, specifically the Drosera, which traps and digests insects by secreting a deadly, sticky liquid. Well intentioned as the effort to conserve nature is, then, the relentless change, including the process of decay and destruction, cannot be impeded. The human being, inextricably placed within the world of struggle for survival, cannot preserve beauty that is forced by laws of nature to pass away.

Grim as is such a conclusion about the futility of efforts at conservation, it is "a pretty thing: Truth / 'a good to the heart,'" for, in the following sections, one is led to acknowledge that man's link to all of nature is as intimate as a family bond. Man is not truly separable from the rest of nature: animal, vegetable, and even mineral. While the poem becomes increasingly oppressive as it turns to personal matters, each acknowledgment of limiting natural laws is counterbalanced by a celebration of life. The memory of a mother's cry is followed by a recognition that grieving is cathartic, similar to a tree's shedding of leaves, and thus is a natural process. Even the most disturbing fact of temporality comes to be treasured:

> Nobody, nothing
> ever gave me
> greater thing
>
> than time
> unless light
> and silence
>
> which if intense
> makes sound

Each reminder of contemporary discord—"the grand blow-up— / the bomb," demonstrations against police, space-rockets, mind-altering drugs—is balanced by a description of the constant growth of plants and, most important of all, by their beauty: "the perfect order" of the water lily. Endurance within a world of unremitting change becomes the dominant subject of the final stanzas, and the sunflower its symbol.

"Wintergreen Ridge," like the three other late poems, shows Niedecker's affinities to Darwin in the close observation of nature, particularly in the concentration on the struggle for survival inherent in evolution. By placing man solidly in the course of natural change, regarding life as only a later stage in the evolution of matter, the poem pursues intelligently and equitably the most challenging implications of Darwinian theory, including its threat to religious belief. However, the force of the poem comes not only from such bold apprehension. A visual analogue, that contained in the title, best conveys the sustaining structure of the poem. One ridge of vegetation stands out in contrast to the fields before and beyond it. The product of men and women who sought to preserve it from some other kind of change, the field is no less a part of a changing and destructive natural world. Man, likewise, is both inseparable from the entire natural world and yet distinguishable from it in the human aspiration to understand and even to control nature. The poem, then, explores the ridges, the delineations, the contrasts between natural elements, just as a painting or a photograph might emphasize the dissonant relations between fields of light or color. It probes those ridges between human aspiration and natural limitations, between personal experience and immersion in nature. Within the poem no arguments are completed, no conclusions settled upon, yet the total effect gained from the series of subjects, each in some degree of contention or resistance against the other, is harmonious.

"Tilting upon the pressure" it was termed by Niedecker herself, this hazardous probing of contrasting elements. It appears not only in the relations among sentences and sections, but more forcefully in the very smallest units of stanzas and lines. The use of puns, internal rhymes, juxtapositions of trivial personal references with technical expression, and shifts from slang to abstract diction all convey the same contention. But the measure of each line and the stanzaic structures reflect the tight order achieved. In each of these four late poems, patterns of accentual meters are established at the start and sustained throughout. Because it has fewer accents than preceding lines, the last line of each stanza receives the greatest emphasis, and the final words of each poem acquire extraordinary resonance. Reconciliation of intense conflict is achieved in each case by a conclusion of great force, in terms of both meaning and aural effect. The single word "carpet" concludes "His Carpets Flowered." "Darwin" closes with a summary statement of its title character: "'Let each man hope / and believe / what he can.'" A vision of red Mars rising concludes "Paean to Place," with the imagined scene becoming an internal exploration of the mind, "with the persons / on the edge." In each of these poems, the last words resound with force and suggestion.

The very last words of "Wintergreen Ridge" present another flower of striking strength. But in these few lines the poem, which consists of fragments of striking disharmony, achieves a strong conclusion:

> Old sunflower
> you bowed
>
> to no one
> but Great Storm
> of Equinox

Introducing a new symbol in the last two stanzas is bold, and the direct address is unprecedented in the poem. But this final new fragment is a triumphant culmination. Admiration and a determination to emulate the sunflower are only implied, but the insistent rhythm gives the last words great force and conviction. Whether such an optimistic determination is realistic or not, the precision of the image and the force of the diction make the conclusion resonate. Poised against each other, as at the time of the equinox, are the natural forces of destruction and change; but even facing such fierce antagonists, the sunflower, symbol of fragile but tenacious human aspirations, does not bow.

# On Ambiguity, Modernism, and Sacred Texts

*Laurence Lerner*

I WANT IN this essay to look at the idea of poetic ambiguity, first as stated in recent literary theory, then as formulated by earlier theorists; and to suggest one or two conclusions for the reading of modern poetry. As a recent theorist I take Julia Kristeva, who writes as follows in "From one Identity to Another":

> I shall deal with a particular signifying practice which, like the Russian formalists, I call 'poetic language', in order to demonstrate that this kind of language, through the particularity of its signifying operations, is an unsettling process—when not an outright destruction—of the identity of meaning and speaking subject, and consequently, of transcendence or, by derivation, of 'religious sensibility'. On that account, it accompanies crises within social structures and institutions—the moments of their mutation, evolution or disarray.
>
> It is poetic language that awakens our attention to this undecidable character of any so-called natural language, a feature that univocal, rational, scientific discourse tends to hide—and this implies considerable consequences for its subject. The support of this signifying economy could not be the transcendental ego alone.
>
> It is of course Freud's theory of the unconscious that allows the apprehension of such a subject; for through the surgery practised in the operating consciousness of the transcendental ego, Freudian and Lacanian psycho-analysis did allow, not for (as certain simplifications would have it) a few typologies or structures that might accommodate the same phenomenological reason, but rather for heterogeneity, which, known as the unconscious, shapes the signifying function.
>
> Language as symbolic function constitutes itself at the cost of repressing instinctual drive and continuous relation to the mother. On the contrary, the unsettled and questionable subject of poetic language (for whom the word is never uniquely sign) maintains itself at the cost of reactivating this repressed, instinctual, maternal element.

This describes (and defends) the dissolution of semantic boundaries and the consequent unsettling of meaning and of the speaking subject. It is clearly related to Bakhtin's argument for the dialogic as opposed to the monologic text, and to Barthes's "Hunger of the Word" that

> initiates a discourse full of gaps and full of lights, filled with absences and over-nourishing signs, without foresight or stability of intention, and thereby so opposed to the social function of language that merely to have recourse to a discontinuous speech is to open the door to all that stands above Nature.

And it is clearly related, too, to symbolist poetics, to the rejection of argument and narrative as the unifying principles of poetic discourse, and the consequent musicalisation of language practised by Mallarmé and formulated by Valéry. The distinction between the symbolic (or referential) and the semiotic function of language, the former subverted and the latter freed by the "unsettling" practice of poetic language, corresponds to that between the traditional language of prose discourse and the musicalised language of poetry or (in Valéry's analogy) between walking and dancing. Poststructuralist theory often reads like an ex-post-facto statement of the theory underlying modernist practice.

Kristeva's view is stated in psycho-analytic terms, but it is by no means clear that these are necessary or even useful. Freud and Lacan may be needed for the apprehension of her theory of the dispersed subject, but they were not needed for the practice of symbolist poetry; and her statement of what psycho-analysis authorises, though it may be correct for Lacan (I am not competent to pronounce on that), is certainly not correct for Freud. Freud's project was not a licensing of the unconscious but an attempt to understand its operations, not a delight in hetero-geneity but an attempt to discover the mechanisms of displacement and rationalisation by which unconscious material is handled (Are *these* the "certain simplifications"? If so, we owe them to Freud himself). And Kristeva's last paragraph contains a good deal to argue about: it is surely possible to perceive (and to approve) a poetic activity that subverts the symbolic function of language, that uses the word not merely as a sign, without considering this an "instinctual drive" or a relationship to the mother. Though she *is* correct, surely, in seeing it as the rejection of social constraint (which the psycho-analytically inclined will no doubt regard as a rejection of the father): "We must analyse those elements of the complex operation that I shall call poetic language (in which the dialectics of the subject is inscribed) that are screened out by ordinary language, ie social constraint." This seems quite acceptable; and certainly it carries a lighter load of theory. The upheaval and dissolution of the signifying surface of language can certainly be seen as an example of antisocial behaviour, at least on the symbolic level: just as strong ego control screens out repressed impulses, so referential language screens out the tumultuous underside of words.

And what would be an example of this sort of poetic language? Kristeva herself is not rich in examples, but we do not need to look far:

> The river's tent is broken; the last fingers of leaf
> Clutch and sink into the wet bank. The wind
> Crosses the brown land, unheard. The nymphs are departed.
> Sweet Thames, run softly, till I end my song.
> The river bears no empty bottles, sandwich papers,
> Silk handkerchiefs, cardboard boxes, cigarette ends
> And other testimony of summer nights. The nymphs are departed.
> And their friends, the loitering heirs of City directors,
> Departed, have left no addresses.
> By the waters of Leman I sat down and wept. . . .
> Sweet Thames, run softly till I end my song,
> Sweet Thames, run softly, for I speak not loud or long.
> But at my back in a cold blast I hear
> The rattle of the bones, and chuckle spread from ear to ear.

This is dialogic language. The speaking subject is constantly unsettled, so that we cannot ascribe the lines to one coherent voice. Who is the speaking "I"? If it is a persona for the poet, it is a persona who so clearly deserves the term in its etymological sense that we can watch a series of masks being put on and taken off. The passage begins as conventional pastoral (autumn landscape, nostalgia, relief at being away from urban squalor) and modulates into satire rather more abruptly than is traditional in pastoral—though the movement from the idyllic to the satiric is conventional enough. Then the nostalgic voice misquotes a psalm, misquotes Marvell, begins to shift the register alarmingly.

It does not matter whether we say that there is a series of speakers, with no clear indication of who is who, or whether we say that the speaking subject is subverted and fragmented. The passage is full of devices of subversion, and if we read on, it grows even more dialogic, till the end is almost pure juxtaposition, with hardly any content remaining of what is juxtaposed:

> To Carthage then I came
>
> Burning burning burning burning
> O Lord thou pluckest me out
> O Lord thou pluckest
>
> burning

Decorum is abandoned, even attacked, as the conventional poetic moon shines bright on the Mrs. Porter of a coarse jazz ballad; and the language itself goes fuzzy as our attempts to identify speakers are disoriented. In Kriseva's terms we have upheaval, dissolution, and transformation; in Eliot's own terms, language is being forced, dislocated if necessary, to convey its meaning.

If the traditional forces of cohesion (narrative, argument, syntax) are abandoned, it seems natural to ask what replaces them. Or if we prefer to say that nothing replaces them, what sort of activity has now replaced coherent discourse? There are three possible answers.

The first is dream. That a poem should have the alogical structure of a dream is most apparent in surrealism, but there is an element of surrealism in most modernist poetry (or, if we prefer, surrealism is the isolating of one element in the complex of modernism). If dreams are interpreted psycho-analytically, as the working out, in symbolical form, of repressed processes, then the subverting of the transcendental subject (in Kristeva's terms) is also the subverting of the ego by repressed material. This too can be illustrated from *The Waste Land*, which has its dream sequences:

> What is the city over the mountains
> Cracks and reforms and bursts in the violet air
> Falling towers
> Jerusalem Athens Alexandria
> Vienna London
> Unreal

The second (already mentioned) is music. The symbolist idea of the musicalisation of language clearly attracted Eliot (witness his titles, *Preludes, Rhapsody, Five-Finger Exercises, Four Quartets*). It is not of course "word music" in the Tennysonian sense—though that may have more in common with Valéry's doctrine than at first appears—but the deploying of words for the chords formed by their overtones rather than for the logic of their meanings. Music, having no subject matter, cannot have logical structure.

The third is game. To see a poem as a language game removes all ethical content and all humanist purpose: this too has become a popular analogy in so-called "postmodernism," but since a game has rigid rules it may not be a good analogy for the chaos produced by the "unsettling process." Indeed, all three analogies are with rule-bound activities: game and music obviously so, and dreams too if we accept, with Freud, that they are disguises for forbidden but coherent wishes. And how could it be otherwise? If we look for a structuring principle, we must find something explicable, or it could not be a principle. But if we refuse to look for one, if we regard poetic language as a licensing of heterogeneity and nothing else, then it would strive toward the monkeys on the typewriters as its purest expression. Mere chaos, mere heterogeneity, could not be any kind of language.

I have so far used Kristeva's expression "poetic language," but it is obvious that what we are looking at is modernism. Kristeva seems uninterested in premodern forms of writing; when she cites earlier writers, she looks only for anticipations. We ought therefore to ask whether past poetry can be read in the light of modernist theories, whether the licensing of ambiguity that we are here considering has always been one of poetry's demands, but only recently admitted. The most famous attempt to do this is that of Eliot himself, in his claim that the English metaphysicals and the French symbolists wrote the same kind of poetry:

> It appears likely that poets in our civilisation, as it exists at present, must be *difficult*. Our civilisation comprehends great variety and complexity, and this variety and complexity, playing upon a refined sensibility, must produce varied and complex results. The poet must become more and more comprehensive, more allusive, more indirect, in order to force, to dislocate if necessary, language into his meaning.
>
> Hence we get something which looks very much like the conceit—we get, in fact, a method curiously similar to that of the 'metaphysical poets', similar also in its use of obscure words and of simple phrasing.
>
> Jules Laforgue, and Tristan Corbière in many of his poems, are nearer to the 'school of Donne' than any modern English poet.

There is a historical element in this argument, the grandiose and unsubstantiated claim that the "mind of Europe" (no less) suffered a dissociation of sensibility after Donne, from which the symbolists rescued us. We can treat this swagger with the contempt it deserves and concentrate on the element of the theory that avoids historical generalisation and concerns poetic language whenever it appears: the argument for difficulty. This has been the really influential part of Eliot's case, encouraging us to read Donne as if he were Rimbaud or Laforgue, Marvell as if he were Mallarmé. By now the matter has been exhaustively discussed by Renaissance scholars. The most famous reply is that of Rosamund Tuve, who claimed that the poetry of the metaphysicals should be related to their poetics, not ours, that images must be classified by logical function rather than by the content of the vehicle, that Donne does not use free association but complicated logic, that Renaissance poetry was not contrasted with rhetoric but parallel to it, and is therefore not discontinuous with prose in the way of symbolist poetry.

If I am warming up this old controversy, it is in order to shift its ground. As far as she goes, Tuve is unanswerable, but it is impossible to stop readers from using the practice of modernism to search for elements in earlier poetry that its own poetic did not admit. In doing this anew, I want to shift from ambiguity to the unsettling of the subject, and to look at the climax of Marlowe's Ovidian narrative, *Hero and Leander*:

> And now she lets him whisper in her ear,
> Flatter, entreat, promise, protest and swear;
> Yet ever as he greedily assayed
> To touch those dainties, she the harpy played,
> And every limb did, as a soldier stout,
> Defend the fort, and keep the foeman out;
> For though the rising ivory mount he scaled,
> Which is with azure circling lines empaled,
> Much like a globe (a globe may I term this
> By which love sails to regions full of bliss)
> Yet there with Sisyphus he toiled in vain,
> Till gentle parley did the truce obtain . . .
> And every kiss to her was as a charm,
> And to Leander as a fresh alarm,
> So that the truce was broke, and she, alas,
> Poor silly maiden, at his mercy was.
> Love is not full of pity, as men say,
> But deaf and cruel, when he means to prey . . .
> Seeming not won, yet won she was at length;
> In such wars, women use but half their strength.
> Leander now, like Theban Hercules,
> Entered the orchard of th'Hesperides . . .
> And now she wished this night were never done,
> And sighed to think upon th'approaching sun. . . .

On one level, this is straightforward narrative, but if, noticing the author's fondness for interpolated *sententiae*, we start to think about its attitude to love, explicit and implicit, and from that reconstruct the speaking subject or implied author, we shall soon find ourselves in trouble. There are probably three dominant views of sexual love in European literature, that which views it as a game, that which views it as war, and that which views it as the highest bliss (usually conveyed with a religious analogy): they are very different from—even incompatible with—one another, but all of them are present here. Love as a game appears in Hero playing "the harpy," letting him flatter, entreat, etc., and then not responding, and in the cynical aside, "In such wars, women use but half their strength"; it has already appeared at some length earlier in the poem, in Leander's ingenious courtship speech, in authorial asides like

> Maids are not won by brutish force and might,
> But speeches full of pleasure and delight,

and even, by analogy, in the word games played by the author ("a globe may I term this . . ."). Love as war provides the extended metaphor that runs through the passage, as well as the savage, disturbing couplets that form the climax ("So that the truce was broke . . ."). Love as bliss provides the image of sexual consummation as the "orchard of th'Hesperides," as religious imagery appeared earlier in Hero offering "up herself a sacrifice." Not just this passage, but the whole poem, shifts between contrasting, even incompatible, views of love, as it shifts between two views of Leander, the accomplished seducer, who makes the long and polished *carpe diem* speech (lines 199–294) with its elaborate conceits, its images for Hero's beauty, and its ingenious arguments in favour of "use"; and the naive and eager lover who when alone with Hero did not know what to do until "he suspected / Some amorous rites or other were neglected." To see this inconsistency as a flaw in the poem is to impose on it a criterion of organic coherence that it shows no interest in meeting. The delight in richness that underlies the description of Leander's beauty is closely related to the delight in variety that seizes every opportunity to drop into a mythological digression, and to the delight in inconsistency that sees the contradictions as all part of the fun.

It is a critical commonplace that *Hero and Leander* mingles the magnificent and the ironic, the sensuous and the comic. Such mingling could be described as an organic blending or as contradiction, and the terminology chosen will usually depend on the critic's allegiance (New Critic or Deconstructionist) rather than on any real difference in the perception of the poem. I am suggesting that, if we think carefully about the poem itself, contradiction is the more appropriate term. And that what it offers us is the unsettling of the narrator, a dispersed and not a coherent subject: it is perhaps a clearer example of such dispersal than anything in Donne.

But there is no linguistic disintegration, no semantic disarray, and certainly no licensing of the unconscious or reactivating of the instinctual, maternal element. All the alternative views of love are (or can be) consciously held; none of them is engaged in repressing the others. There is no need to use psycho-analytic language to describe this kind of dispersal of the subject, just as there is no forcing or dislocating of language.

Modernism can be seen either as a rejection of tradition, because poetry is no longer interested in logic and rhetoric, because it abandons coherence in a now incoherent world, or as the disengaging of one or two elements that have always been present in poetry—polysemy, and the unsettling of the subject. It is very difficult, perhaps impossible, to choose finally between these views.

Now I want to compare Kristeva's theory of ambiguity with another and earlier theory, that of William Empson. It too has a Freudian element, it too has a radical element, but it does not set out to license heterogeneity. On the contrary, Empson's theory of ambiguity can be seen as an almost frenetic attempt to sort out the unsortable, to bring order into the chaos that poetic language releases.

Empson's theory also differs from Kristeva's in that it is so richly and fully illustrated. There is no doubt of his theoretical concern, but it is the concern of a literary sensibility that thinks about poetry through actual poems. This makes it much harder to discuss, since most of his examples are so very complex that summary is unable to do justice to them. Here is a simplified version of a comparatively simple one:

> What murdered Wentworth, and what exiled Hyde,
> By kings protected and to kings allied?
> What but their wish indulged in courts to shine,
> And power too great to keep or to resign?

> Wentworth and Hyde may have wished merely to *shine*, to *shine in courts*, to *shine indulged* by king and courtiers, or to *shine indulged* by king and courtiers *in courts*; or they may have indulged their *own* wish to shine, or to shine in courts; or there may be a separate general reflection, putting commas after *wish* and *courts*, that the wish to shine is after all usually indulged in courts.

This is part of Empson's attempt to pursue his theory "into the very sanctuary of rationality":

> During the eighteenth century English poets were trying to be honest, straightforward, sensible, grammatical and plain; thus it is now my business to outwit these poor wretches, and to applaud them for qualities in their writings which they would have been horrified to discover.

It is clear that Empson's method, like Kristeva's, draws our attention to the feature of language "that univocal, rational, scientific discourse"— and we can add, Augustan clarity—"tends to hide." But Empson does much more than draw attention; he worries furiously at what he uncovers. By doing this, is he causing confusion or sorting it out? The question is important, but not easy to answer; and it will have the same kind of answer, I suggest, as the question whether Freud was the enemy or the defender of reason. In showing how much reason conceals from us in the way of hidden drives and unadmitted influences on our decisions, Freud is an irrationalist; but he revealed the strength of the irrational in order to understand and as far as possible to govern it ("where id was, ego shall be"). In the same way, Empson shows how much ambiguity lies hidden under the limpid surface even of Augustan poetry, but does this in order to explore more fully what is and isn't being said. No one takes very seriously Empson's classification of ambiguity into seven types, and it is difficult to know how seriously to take the classification into four types of equation in *The Structure of Complex Words*. But what we must certainly take seriously is the listing of the ambiguous senses, and the idea of an equation: that the best way to understand complex words (these are not of course such intellectually complex terms as *contingency* or *industrialism*, but the sort of word that will have a long entry in the *Oxford Dictionary*; and they are mainly found in poetry and in conversation) is to see them as stating equations between two elements in their meaning. Some of the equations Empson finds in (for instance) Shakespeare's use of *honest* or Wordsworth's use of *sense* are among the finest achievements of modern criticism, moving from particular ambiguities to a central insight into the poem or play as a whole.

The anti-humanism of much poststructuralist thought is well known and is stated explicitly by Barthes in a passage that links it with the language of modernism:

> These unrelated objects—words adorned with all the violence of their irruption, the vibration of which, though wholly mechanical, strangely affects the next word, only to die out immediately—these poetic words exclude men: there is no humanism of modern poetry.

A reading of *Writing Degree Zero* ought to be followed by a reading of *The Structure of Complex Words*. For Empson is certainly concerned with the Hunger of the Word, and its irruption into poetry; he is certainly aware that the control represented by univocality is shattered by the changeable structures that speakers are not fully aware of. But he would have dismissed as virtually meaningless the claim that meaning can operate as something "wholly mechanical." Empson is a deeply humanist critic, who believes that what he is exploring is the tensions within human and social attitudes. The reading of a poem, for him, is an attempt by the reader to discover what the author was saying (*actually* saying, of course).

This requires him to admit that our practice has always been wiser than our theory, and to claim "the human mind, that is the public human mind as expressed in a language, is not irredeemably lunatic, and can not be made so."

Humanism is traditionally an emancipation from religious authority, locating value in the human being as he is, not imposing a "higher" set of values to limit and deny experiences that we find fulfilling. The poststructuralist turn is to see humanism as simply a variant of the theological tradition that it believes itself to be rejecting, since both see the world as fixed and rational; and to reject them both in the interest of openness, subversion, and "a discourse filled with absences and over-nourishing signs." I suggest that Empson can teach us to interrogate this now fashionable view: his exploration of the absences and over-nourishing signs of complex words is a humanist project, committed to meaning, reason, and value.

And finally, as well as questioning the poststructuralist view of humanism, I want to question its view of religion. For this, let us go back much earlier for another version of the importance of ambiguity. Kristeva linked the symbolic, or referential, use of language with religion: poetic language is "knowingly the enemy of religion," and unsettles the religious sensibility. In this she echoes Derrida, who connects the metaphysics of the undeconstructed subject with God, and regards it as ultimately a theology. This is by no means the only possible view of religion, which can equally be seen as a subversion of rationality (*credo quia impossibile* is only the extreme version of that), and as a way of undermining the subject's confidence in his control over experience (the breaking of the will; Christ shall be my teacher). And it can certainly be seen as the subversion of univocal meaning.

The doctrine of the multiple meanings of Scripture goes well back into the Middle Ages, indeed back to the Talmud. Its most famous formulation asserts:

> Littera gesta docet, quid credes allegoria,
> Moralis quid agas, quo tendas anagogia.

Nicholas of Lyra, writing in the fourteenth century, is summing up a widespread belief, and though there are variants in the terminology, his classification is the standard one: that Scripture has a literal meaning (what happened), an allegorical, or typical, meaning (what you should believe—this means how you should link one historical or biblical event with another to see its significance), a moral meaning (what you are to do), and an anagogical meaning (what awaits us in the next life). This gave rise to some astonishingly complex explorations of ambiguity (as, for instance, a glance at St. Bernard's sermons on the Song of Songs makes instantly clear). The belief that Scripture has one clear meaning, which can be true or false, had to fight a long battle to get itself disentangled from this linguistic habit. Here is an example of the writing which that habit generated:

> But then this exitus a morte, is but introitus in mortem, this issue, this deliverance from that death, the death of the womb, is an entrance, a delivering over to another death, the manifold deaths of this world. We have a winding sheet in our mother's womb, which grows with us from our conception, and we come into the world, wound up in that winding sheet, for we come to seek a grave; And as prisoners discharged of actions may lie for fees, so when the womb hath discharged us, yet we are bound to it by cords of flesh, by such a string, as that we cannot go thence, nor stay there; we celebrate our own funerals with cries, even at our birth; as though our threescore and ten years life were spent in our mother's labour, and our circle made up in the first point thereof, we beg our Baptism, with another Sacrament, with tears.
>
> (Donne, "Death's Duel": Sermon preached at Whitehall, February 25, 1630)

Here is language that has been given its head and allowed to develop analogies with what seems uncontrolled fertility. We are moved between death as birth, and birth as a form of death; between literal and figurative meanings of womb, umbilical cord, shroud, tears; swept along by a linguistic restlessness that seems almost self-generated, as if the transcendental subject has abdicated. Of course he hasn't, since all the allusions, and all the word-play, are explicable, in a way that raises some of the central Christian paradoxes, and to that extent this is not modernism. But at the same time the subject *has* abdicated, since the didactic purpose of the sermon has quite ceased to control the generation of analogies: they spring up like tropical growth (if I may have a little word-play too), governed not by what is needed to make the meaning clear, but by a delight in fertility itself: and in that way this is very like modernism.

I have tried to show what can and what can't be done with Kristeva's theory of poetic ambiguity, and the more general modernist position to which it belongs. The fact that it is less literary than those of Valéry or Empson or Eliot is both a strength and a weakness. It is a weakness in that it never tackles the hard and rewarding task of looking at actual poems and observing whether they function as the theory suggests; but a strength insofar as much earlier poetry, though not using the linguistic strategies of modernism, does unsettle the subject—consciously and with delight.

By associating religion with ambiguity rather than with rational control, I propose that Kristeva's theory can be stood on its head. We can now see a good deal of modern literature as consisting of sacred texts. The critics and explicators are the biblical commentators, whose purpose is to show how richly the text generates meanings and also to sort out and understand those meanings. Modernism places more value on the generating and less value on the sorting than did biblical commentary, but there must always be both: polysemy requires the possibility of some interpretation, or we have the monkeys on their typewriters. To distinguish the subverting of order from the imposing of order is, I have suggested, not an easy task. I am not even sure how far it is, in the last analysis, possible.

Kristeva's view of poetic language emphasises the destructive element. If we think of ambiguity as an enhancing and enriching, we need not associate it with the mere overthrow of order, in discourse, in the psyche, in society. This could lead to a very different view of poetry, of the political dimension of poetry, and of religion.

# Poetry as
# Political Philosophy:
# Notes on Burke and Yeats

*Alasdair MacIntyre*

T O WRITE about Yeats in a volume honoring Donald Davie is an act
not of courage but of foolhardiness. For during the years in which
he directed the Yeats School in Sligo, Donald Davie must have
heard, let alone read, more words uttered about Yeats than any other
human being has ever been subjected to. There can be almost no con-
ceivable view to be taken about any poem of which Davie has not had to
hear the case for and the case against elaborated at a length that would
seem excessive anywhere but in Sligo. So to write about Yeats in partial
disagreement with Davie, as I am about to do, is perhaps more even than
foolhardiness. Yet it has been part of Davie's *magisterium* as teacher and
critic that he has often educated by inciting to disagreement. So that those
who disagree with him are in their very disagreement indebted. As I shall
be in writing about Yeats.

In the poetry that W. B. Yeats wrote in the decade between 1927 and
1937 one recurrent concern is the shedding of certain political illusions.
Any life that embodies truth requires, so Yeats asserted in his poetry, a
recognition that a coherent political imagination is no longer available.
Yeats was himself concerned to make a more particular and specific poetic
claim: that politics as understood by Edmund Burke could no longer
achieve imagined and embodied reality in the Ireland of that period. But I
shall suggest that the poetry which says this to us, and which said it to his
contemporaries, uses the local Irish condition as a symbol to assert more
generally that no coherent political imagination is any longer possible for
those condemned to inhabit, and to think and act in terms of, the modernity of the twentieth-century nation-state. The question to which, in the
end, although not perhaps in this paper, I want to find an answer is: Is
what Yeats says on this subject in this poetry true?

Questions about the truth or falsity of poetry are not often posed
nowadays. For in the compartmentalisations of modern culture, ques-

145

tions about truth and falsity, rational justification, and the like are allocated to philosophy and the sciences and more generally to the provinces of theoretical enquiry, while poetry is conceived of as an exercise of quite a different order. Theorizing about poetry is of course admissible; but that a poem *qua* poem might itself *be* a theory, let alone that a poem *qua* poem might provide for some particular subject matter the most adequate expression for some particular theoretical claim, these are thoughts excluded by our culture's dominant ethos.

I say "poem *qua* poem," because the notion that a poem may incidentally express a thought whose prose version makes a theoretical claim is acceptable and familiar. So those who write about Yeats's political theory and attitudes commonly supplement reference to his prose utterances by a use of quotation from the poetry which treats that quotation as if it were prose. I by contrast aim to discuss what the poetry shows us about politics *qua* poetry; such reference as I make to the prose will be only to elucidate the poetry, and Yeats's own political attitudinizing I shall exclude from attention almost altogether.

The poet who philosophizes *qua* poet—as Lucretius, Dante, Pope, Wallace Stevens, and Marianne Moore did—presents us with structures in which, although concepts and propositions may appear, they are subordinated to, and in key part derive their sense and significance from, images of greater or lesser complexity. It is in and through the image that poetic form and philosophical content are unified. The poetic claim for the primacy and necessary contribution of the image to understanding involves of course a view of the relationship of images to concepts that is itself philosophically controversial; and it cannot be argued for here. But some aspects of it need to be stated in outline.

Images are true or false, but not in the same way that statements are. Statements say or fail to say how things are; images show or fail to show how things are. Images are true insofar as they are revelatory, false insofar as they obscure, disguise, or distort. But the reality that an image represents more or less adequately is not one to which we have access independently of any exercise of imagination. Our perceptions are organized in and through images, and a more adequate imagination is one that enables us to see or envisage what we could not otherwise see or envisage.

A true statement remains true when conjoined with other statements, whether true or false. But an image conjoined with others may thereby either acquire new revelatory power or lose what it previously had. Images may be on occasion composed of statements, and statements may be true or false of realities constituted in key part by the imagination. For there are both human relationships and objects of attention in nature that could not exist without the constitutive work of imagination. So a land-scape or a sunset may be constituted as a structured object of attention; and so the community of a monastery or the society of a café or the complex relationships of a nation required imagination's work. One can-not be a monk or a member of café society without being able to imagine oneself as such; living the role of either is a form of imaginative acting out. And so too with the community of a nation: to be Irish or English, I must be able to imagine myself as an Irishman or an Englishman, something achievable in part by participating in the shared poetic utterance of the nation. Take away shared songs and poetry, shared monuments and architecture, shared imaginative conceptions of what is for *this* nation sacred ground and you at the very least weaken the bonds of nationality.

So nations to be real must first be imagined. And so too the loss of a coherent imagination can transform the kind of society that a nation is into something else. The poet and only the poet may be able to represent absolutely to us the incoherence or the sterility or both of the substitute images, the *ersatz* images, by which such a deprived form of political society may try to conceal from itself its condition. The poet may achieve a disclosure of this failed political imagination by putting the relevant images to the test, by using them in a poem and showing that when they are used with integrity what they disclose is imaginative incoherence or sterility or both. And it is just this, so I shall want to claim, that Yeats achieved for Ireland in some of his mature poetry. Those images that provided Yeats at once with part of his vocabulary and with part of his subject matter were, some of them at least, drawn from Burke and from Yeats's extended reflections on Burke. So that it is with Burke that we have to begin.

Burke was a thinker a large part of whose stock-in-trade, at least in his political philosophy, was images. Arguments and concepts do their work in his writings only with the aid of images. When he identifies what his images represent, he sometimes moves from speaking of "the state" or of "the commonwealth and its laws" to speaking of "society" as though the differences between these were insignificant. And his images were well-designed to obscure those differences. The habits of mind and action that the British state of his day, as he imagined it, prescribed exemplified for him the fundamental principles of social order itself. But this Burke could not have argued systematically without himself becoming just the kind of *theorist* (a term of condemnation for Burke) whose false abstractions (*abstract* is another such term) had on his view misled the French revolu-tionaries.

So in the self-imposed predicament of one who is a theorist against theorists Burke drew on the resources of the image-maker: British liberties are "an entailed inheritance," "a sort of family settlement."[1] In relying on established prejudices and the experience underlying them we avail ourselves "of the general bank and capital of nations and of ages" rather than each individual's "private stock of reason";[2] and in so doing we respect that "great primeval" contract "between those who are living and those who are dead and those who are to be born," which ordains for society and the state—Burke in one paragraph slides from speaking of the one to speaking of the other—the same divinely appointed order as that prescribed for nature.[3]

Images of inheritance, accumulated capital, and timeless contract and of these as reproducing the order of nature are juxtaposed to some very different types of image, which nonetheless reinforce Burke's overall thesis. One of these is of weight. The holders of a certain kind of extreme position are guilty of "levity" and "think lightly of all public principle"; governments are contrived so as not to "be blown down"; and the large property-users provide "the ballast in the vessel of the commonwealth."[4] Another set are images of natural growth. What "the British constitution" affords is "firm ground,"[5] the ground presumably on which grows "the British oak" in whose shadow silently repose "thousands of great cattle," while "half a dozen grasshoppers," those who agitate against the established order, mislead by the noise they make.

Burke's images are thus designed to secure the allegiance of the imagination to certain conceptions of stable continuity and hierarchical order, as well as an antipathy to any kind of theoretical reflection apt to produce scepticism about the credentials of the established order. By these means Burke invited the English to imagine or reimagine themselves as members of an order in which the hierarchies of authority embodied the wisdom of continuity and for whom any radical disruption of the relationships of power and property would be an unprecedented calamity. The English were thus invited to join with Burke in an act of collective self-deception. For what Burke's images masked and concealed were the radical discontinuities and disruptions, of both political and property relationships, which marked English history: the thefts by the large proprietors, both of the lands owned by the church and of the

1. *Reflections on the Revolution in France*, ed. C. C. O'Brien (Harmondsworth, 1968), 119–20.
2. Ibid., 183.
3. Ibid., 194–95.
4. Ibid., 155, 112, 141.
5. Ibid., 376.

common lands stolen by enclosure; the new invasive and destructive power of markets and of banks; the use of legalized terror to enforce new property relationships in the Black Act of 1723; the changed and increased polarization of power and property, described and condemned with gentle bitterness by Burke's fellow-Irishman Goldsmith. Burke was not the first maker of myths about the continuities of English history. The fabrications whereby the College of Heralds in the sixteenth and seventeenth centuries endowed the newly rich and powerful with fictitious ancient genealogies had the same function. But Burke was the greatest of these myth-makers.

He had his own immediate purposes in so writing; but the importance of his image-making transcends those purposes. Burke's imaginary England was a prototype in and for the modern world in the way in which it seemed to provide a much-needed mask to be worn by the modern state. The modern state, and those who inhabit and seek to uphold it, confront a dilemma. It has to present itself in two *prima facie* incompatible ways. It is, and has to be understood as, an institutionalized set of devices whereby individuals may more or less effectively pursue their own goals, that is, it is essentially a *means* whose efficiency is to be evaluated by individuals in cost-benefit terms. Yet at the same time it claims, and cannot but claim, the kind of allegiance claimed by those traditional political communities—the best type of Greek *polis* or of medieval commune—membership in which provided their citizens with a meaningful identity, so that caring for the common good, even to the point of being willing to die for it, was no other than caring for what was good about oneself. The citizen of the modern state is thus invited to view the state intellectually in one way, as a self-interested calculator, but imaginatively in quite another. The modern state presented only in the former light could never inspire adequate devotion. Being asked to die for it would be like being asked to die for the telephone company. And yet the modern state does need to ask its citizens to die for it, a need that requires it to find some quite other set of images for its self-presentation.

The attempt to resolve or dissolve this incoherence by a more adequate conceptualisation of the state is the conjuring-trick demanded of modern political theory: there is Rousseau's version of the conjuring-trick, there is Kant's, there is Hegel's, there is Mill's. But the conjuring-tricks all break down. It was the great insight informing Burke's work—one he himself could not have formulated, since he had to deceive himself as well as others—that where the conceptual resources of theory were bound to fail, since what was in fact incoherence could not be transformed into coherence, the image-making resources of rhetoric might succeed. What could not be transformed might be disguised. So Burke's work has had an importance other than and more general than he intended. But the political effectiveness of his rhetoric as a performance (and all rhetoric is performance) owed much to the fact that in it he reimagined not only the English, but also himself, so that among the images effectively authored by Burke there appear not only those of the British oak and the ballast in the ship of state but also that of Edmund Burke.

Burke, the spokesman for inherited property, himself inherited nothing, but near the start of his political career he purchased an English estate as one of the properties for his masquerade as a British, even an English, gentleman. The education he had received first in an Irish hedge-school, when still living among his mother's Catholic kin, and then from Irish members of the Society of Friends, had led on to the Anglican conformism of Trinity College, Dublin, and then at the age of twenty-one in 1750 to a quick exit to the larger stage of London. Here in *A Philosophical Enquiry into the Origin of Our Ideas of the Sublime and Beautiful* he argued that it is not the intellectual content of language, but the psychological force of the use of words that produces responses in action: "not clear, but strong expressions are effective" (V, 7). And Burke put this thesis into practice when he entered the House of Commons in 1766 as the political and financial dependent of the class that, by purchase of his estate, he aspired to join. Conor Cruise O'Brien has emphasized the ways in which Burke exhibited "Irishness."[6] But even he notes that Burke wrote "in the *persona* of an Englishman." And it was as an Englishman that for the most part he behaved and spoke. "Do you, or does any Irish gentleman," he asked a correspondent in a letter in 1773, in which he opposed the imposition of a tax on absentee landlords, "think it a mean privilege that, the moment he sets foot upon this ground, he is, to all intents and purposes, an Englishman?"

Burke's close friends were such Englishmen as Johnson and Reynolds. He planned to obtain a peerage for himself as an English, not an Irish, peer. Even on Irish matters he spoke as the English gentleman he had imagined himself into being. Arthur Young put him on his list of absentee landlords. And Burke argued in a speech in the Commons of 1785 that "independence of legislature had been granted Ireland; but no other independence could Great Britain give her without reversing the order of nature. Ireland could not be separated from England; she could not exist

6. Ibid., 23–41.

without her; she must ever remain under the protection of England, her guardian angel."[7]

So Burke deliberately discarded his Irishness, flouting both his Catholic and his Quaker teachers. He invented new images of England as a country in which his new image of himself could be at home. And in so doing he separated himself not only from the Irish, but also from the Anglo-Irish, whose Protestant ascendancy in Ireland he constantly, and to his credit, condemned. When Yeats reimagined Burke as an Anglo-Irishman, Yeats's Burke was, at least in that respect, a work of dramatic and distorting fiction. But so after all was Burke's English Burke.

Yeats read Burke copiously, if not carefully. He underlined passages as he read, and he drew upon Burke as a key source in his political speeches. But in so doing he reinvented Burke. Burke is spoken of in conjunction with Berkeley and less often with Swift and Goldsmith, but never with Johnson or Reynolds. Swift too, of course, became at Yeats's hands more emblematically Irish than he in fact was (*The Words Upon the Window-Pane*). But it was not just that Burke was added to a roll call of the great Anglo-Irish dead. Yeats also denied Burke any place in English thought: "We have in Berkeley and Burke a philosophy on which it is possible to base the whole life of a nation. That is something which England, great as she is in modern scientific thought and in every kind of literature has not" (*Speech on the Child and the State*, 1925).

Moreover in the same speech Burke was converted from image-making rhetorician to theorist, by way of a comparison with Berkeley: "Berkeley proved that the world was a vision, and Burke that the State was a tree, no mechanism to be pulled to pieces and put up again, but an oak tree that had grown through centuries." So Burke's image has become a generalization, the conclusion of a proof. And when Yeats uses Burke's images, he alters them by the way he selects from them. Images of inheritance remain; those of contract disappear; levity remains, but not the ballast in the ship of state. The tree becomes other than and more than the merely British oak. And Burke himself is added to the list as an image: "Burke with his conviction that all states not grown slowly like a forest- tree are tyrannies." But to these reordered Burkean images Yeats gave genuine poetic allegiance.

I speak of poetic rather than of political allegiance, since what Yeats said about politics in his poetry by means of these images was not

---

7. Quoted by John Mitchel, *The History of Ireland* (Glasgow, 1869), 164.

necessarily what he took himself to be saying, let alone what he actually said, thought, and felt in the realm of politics, as conventionally understood. It is particularly important not to read into the poetry of 1925–37 the tatterdemalion fascism that Yeats came to embrace during that period. For whatever Fascist states were, they were not "states grown slowly." Donald Davie, generally the most perceptive of readers, has seen Yeats's later fascism in "Blood and the Moon," a poem of 1928;[8] but the presence of Burke in that poem signals an antipolitics, not a politics, a rejection of the modern state as a possible work of the imagination. Davie is right of course in emphasizing that in "Blood and the Moon," as indeed elsewhere, Yeats rewrote and to a significant degree falsified Irish history; but this falsification does nothing to discredit Yeats's claim that whereas in the past the power that is expressed in blood and its spilling could be allied with wisdom, while now they are split apart. And the towers of the past, including the Anglo-Norman Thoor Ballylee, have become what the modern nation is: "Half dead at the top."

Goldsmith, aesthetically honey-sipping, Swift, "in sybilline frenzy blind," and Berkeley, as an alleged witness to the power of mind to dissolve the world, are three of Burke's companions in "Blood and the Moon." But Shelley too is numbered among his predecessors. The list is a catalogue of types of insightful mind, culminating with

> . . . haughtier-headed Burke that proved the State a tree,
> That this unconquerable labyrinth of the birds,
>                                           century after century
> Cast but dead leaves to mathematical equality.

Haughtier-headed? Perhaps the reference is to Thomas Hickey's portrait of Burke now in the National Gallery in Dublin. Certainly the adjective is intended to accentuate Burke's contribution of wisdom to "The strength that gives our blood and state / Magnanimity of its own desire," a magnanimity now lost. For in the third section "we," gathered where our blood-shedding ancestors were, "clamour in drunken frenzy for the moon." The politics that seeks to revive this past in the present is, as Davie recognizes, the politics of lunatics.[9] So in the final section of the poem the tower that was at the poem's opening "blessed" has become "Half dead at the top."

> For wisdom is the property of the dead
> A something incompatible with life; and power,

8. *Trying to Explain* (Ann Arbor, 1979), 165–73.
9. Ibid., 171.

> Like everything that has the stain of blood,
> A property of the living. . . .

"Blood and the Moon" is not, by the standards of Yeats's mature achievement, a successful poem. Too many disparate images are laid side by side, and there is no poetic intention clearly manifest in their conjunction. So the Burkean image of the state as a tree coexists with Yeats's comparison of the state to a tower, but the two images are brought into no particular relationship. The lack of coherence is a limitation of the poem and not itself a product of imaginative insight. Nonetheless the poem does give effective expression to Yeats's negative verdict on the politics of the Irish Free State.

What was the Irish reality that evoked from Yeats this type of negative response? It was the contrast between that in the movement for the making of Irish independence with which he had identified and that which the movement turned out to have made. On the one hand, there was the imaginary and imagined Cathleen Ni Houlihan and the real but equally imagined Padraic Pearse and Maud Gonne. Few potentially revolutionary movements have been as easily hospitable to poetry and to theatre as the Irish; fewer still have been as fortunate in the poetry and theatre which accepted that hospitality. At certain moments Irish politics had become transparently in key part a work of constitutive imagination, promising to restore traditional forms of communal order. Yet on the other hand, the end result of that work was a modern bureaucratic parliamentary state, the outcome of negotiated and calculated sets of accommodations in which the skills of bargaining had displaced the virtues of heroism. The Irish Free State had provided an arena for individuals to make what way they will and can in the world, an arena for individual calculation, ambition, and aggrandisement, in which success and failure have a measure that has remarkably little to do with the common good.

The predicament of the Irish Free State was that it had to present itself as meriting the allegiance of those whose political imagination had been formed in the movement that led toward Easter 1916 while at the same time functioning effectively as a form of imposed bureaucratic order. It confronted the problem of all modern postrevolutionary states, that of how to betray the revolution while appearing as its heir and guardian. And, that is to say, what it confronted was not in any way a problem peculiar to Ireland. It was indeed just one more version of that incoherence for the masking and disguising of which Burke's images were especially well-designed, the incoherence involved in the relationship of *the state as bureaucratic mechanism* to *the state as object of imaginative allegiance*.

The first great classic statement of these two aspects of the modern state was that by Marx in *The Eighteenth Brumaire of Louis Bonaparte*, who saw in the English Revolution of the seventeenth century and in the French Revolution of the eighteenth a sequence in which a stage of imaginative heroism, in which the historical actors were able to "sustain their passion at the poetic level appropriate to a great historic tragedy," was followed by one of "sober reality," the prosaic reality of bourgeois society. The politics of poetic imagination gave way to a quite other politics. Marx, however, misled his readers in two ways. He thought that he was describing the genesis of the peculiarly bourgeois state, when in fact it is the modern state as such that clashes with any politics of the imagination. And he failed to see that the "sober reality" of the modern state in good working order still requires an appeal to imagination, if only by way of disguise, an appeal which claims for the modern state that it is entitled to the same kind of imagination-informed allegiance appropriate for some at least of its antecedents and predecessors. Of course the continuing need for that appeal generates the incoherence that Burke disguised and Yeats diagnosed. What Yeats succeeded in showing, in the poetry in which he put Burke's images to work in specifically modern terms, was in part the failure of those and kindred images to mask or disguise (let alone remove) that incoherence in its modern Irish version, but also Yeats succeeded more generally in the course of exhibiting that particular Irish failure in revealing the incoherence of *any* specifically modern political imagination. The state can no longer be adequately imagined; and it can no longer function, therefore, as an object of allegiance to anyone educated into imaginative integrity.

"Blood and the Moon" is a significant part of Yeats's statement of this thesis, in spite of its flaws. It is effectively supplemented by and ought to be read in conjunction with two other poems or sets of poems. The first is the relatively simple proclamation of what Burkean thought cannot be accommodated to, but is necessarily opposed to, in "The Seven Sages." Goldsmith, Berkeley, and Swift are once again Burke's companions, but what unites them now is not that they are Irish, but that they are "four great minds that hated Whiggery." Goldsmith for once receives part of his political due as one who "sang what he had seen / Roads full of beggars, cattle in the field," although there is of course no reference to Goldsmith's corresponding indictment in "The Deserted Village" of the landed proprietors whom Burke had served and loved so well. Yet in this falsifying assimilation of Goldsmith, as of Swift and Berkeley, to Burke, Yeats is careful to note that their hatred of Whiggery was an attitude Yeats recognizes in them, whether they themselves did so or not. What was this Whiggery?

> A levelling, rancorous, rational sort of mind
> That never looked out of the eye of a saint
> Or out of a drunkard's eye.

And Yeats added immediately that "All's Whiggery now. . . ." So that he asserts a deep incompatibility between the dominant contemporary Whiggism of liberal individualist modernity and the Burkean view of things. That incompatibility Yeats ascribed to and saw as embodied in the one-sided personalities of the participants in the politics of the Free State. In "Parnell's Funeral" Yeats ascribed to Cosgrave and to de Valera the same lack—Parnell's heart. "Had Cosgrave eaten Parnell's heart, the land's / Imagination had been satisfied. . . ." O'Higgins is dead, and O'Duffy too has failed. Yeats at this time sees no leaders. And a fore-knowledge of the political failure that lay ahead was later to be ascribed to Parnell:

> Parnell came down the road, he said to a cheering man:
> 'Ireland shall get her freedom and you still break stone.'

Yeats's vision of Parnell was of course yet another falsification, but once again this does not discredit the use to which he put it in commentary upon what had made it the case that "All's Whiggery now. . . ." Yeats in his own conventional political attitudes perhaps never quite despaired of the possibility of finding leaders to replace the contemporary Whigs. But what he said in his poetry had a finality that is lacking in the attitudinizing of some of his later speeches. That finality is evident in the transition from the first version of what were at first entitled "Three Songs to the Same Tune," published in 1933, to the second version "Three Marching Songs," published in *Last Poems* (both sets to be sung to the same tune by Arthur Duff and so constrained to the same musical structure).

. Most obviously the order of the three songs is changed. The opening song of the later version corresponds to what is second in the earlier; the opening song of the earlier version is the final song of the later. These changes allow Yeats to emphasize a transformation of content. In the earlier version the second song declares a central theme of the whole: "Justify all those renowned generations" who made Ireland's past, "Defending Ireland's soul." The present generation are being summoned to complete the work of the past and so rescue it from failure:

Fail, and that history turns into rubbish,
All that great past to a trouble of fools. . . .

Yeats has not yet come to assert the resourcelessness of the Irish political present.

This is emphasized by the way in which in the earlier version the second song is linked to the first. That first song recounts the hanging of the singer's grandfather in a culture in which it has been the peculiar function of our grandparents to mediate the past to us. In the chorus the blame for trying to undo that in our present achievement, which could justify the past, is put upon fanatics, and the song of those who fight against such fanaticism is "The Tune of O'Donnell Abu," a song summoning the people of Donegal to victory over their enemies. Thus Yeats still looks for a reversal, for a possible victory. But in the later version it is quite otherwise.

The tune of O'Donnell Abu has disappeared from the poem. The chorus to the grandfather's song is about turning away from worldly resources to magical and not about any fight against fanaticism, and the theme of the poem in what has now become the first of the three songs is not the justification of the work of the dead, but the memory of that work: "Remember all those renowned generations. . . ." Consequently the line "Fail, and that history turns into rubbish" is changed from a warning to a prediction. In both versions the grandfather dies on the gallows for a cause. But in the later version it is a cause that is already lost.

What has any of this to do with Yeats's use of Burkean images? It is in what becomes the second section in the later version that these reappear, and the rewriting of the songs has prepared the way for and provided the necessary context for their use. It is Burke's tree, as an image of the state, that reappears and so does the levity that cannot resist the wind and so does that wind, which in Burke's version cannot blow down the firmly established state. But in Yeats's poem, there at the top of the tree is emptiness. "Great nations blossom above," but "What tears down a tree that has nothing within it?"

There is a deliberate reference back to "Blood and the Moon" where Yeats had asked: "Is every modern nation like the tower, / Half dead at the top?" But the lack of solidity is now ascribed to tree rather than to tower. So the modern nation-state can be conceived in Burkean terms only as a tree dead from half-way up and liable to be blown down by the winds of change. Yeats, having committed himself to the use of Burke's political image, has been compelled by his perception of Irish political reality to invert its use, so that the state is now to be imagined only as what has failed to flourish as a tree. The imagination either of the life of more traditional forms of community and social order or of the movement toward independence and a new restoration of those forms of community has given way to the Irish state of the twenties and thirties in which nothing coherent can be found for the imagination to represent, to express, or to constitute as an object of allegiance.

I suggested earlier that those features of the Irish state that allow Yeats to find only a negative and condemnatory use of Burkean images belong to it not as Irish, but as state. They are features of the modern state as such. And hence derives my thesis that Yeats reveals to us in the images of his mature poetry the imaginative poverty not of a particular regime or type of regime, but of the structure of every modern state. About this thesis, however, two final caveats need to be entered.

The first is about the political implication of the poetic claim that I have taken Yeats to be making. The imaginative sterility of the modern state certainly puts constraints on the possibilities of creative political action. But there are forms of institutionalized community in the modern world other than those of the state, and the preservation of and enhancement of certain at least of such forms of community may set tasks for a less barren politics, one very different from the conventional politics of the contemporary state.

A second caveat concerns the justification of my own claims: about what Yeats is saying, as a poet who is *qua* poet *a* political philosopher, about the problems confronting the modern state, and about the relationship between these. All that I have been able to do is to state a case in bare outline and to gesture toward the arguments required to support it. Those arguments would have to supply answers to questions that give expression to very different types of objection. There are those who would ask whether Yeats was not in fact blind to what they take to be the merits of the modern Irish state because of his aristocratic prejudices. And there are those who would ask whether Yeats failed to evaluate Irish realities correctly, because the language of his poetry was English and not Gaelic. That I do not answer these questions here does not mean that I do not recognize their relevance. This is a paper that sets an agenda for work yet to be done.

# Pound and Yeats:
# The Poetics of Friendship

## William Pratt

Pale hair that the moon has shaken
Down over the dark breast of the sea,
O magic her beauty has shaken
About the heart of me;
Out of you have I woven a dream
That shall walk in the lonely vale
Betwixt the high hill and the low hill,
Until the pale stream
Of the souls of men quench and grow still.

A READER ENCOUNTERING this brief lyric, entitled "He speaks to the moonlight concerning the Beloved," in a slim volume called *Exultations* published in London in 1909, might have imagined he was reading a poem by William Butler Yeats that had somehow strayed from its Irish author's third volume, *The Wind Among the Reeds*, published ten years earlier, in 1899. But in fact he would have been reading the fourth volume of poems by a young American recently arrived in London, whose ambition was to start a new literary Renaissance, and whose strategy for storming the heights of Parnassus was to imitate, translate, parody, or if need be plagiarize every good poet, ancient or modern, he could find. "Be influenced by as many great artists as you can" was his advice to other poets, "but have the decency either to acknowledge the debt outright, or to try to conceal it."[1] He would soon become much more adept at concealing his debts, but at the time Ezra Pound came to London, he declared openly that there was just one poet writing in English who was worthy of a younger poet's study, and that was Yeats.

Pound had arrived in London in 1908, fresh from Venice, where he had published his first volume of poems, with its title borrowed from

---

1. "A Retrospect," in *Literary Essays of Ezra Pound*, ed. T. S. Eliot (New York, 1954), 5.

Dante, *A Lume Spento* ("With Tapers Quenched," a phrase from Canto III of the *Purgatorio*, signifying burial without the rites of the church), and with a note to one of the poems saying that its mood had been appropriated from "Mr. Yeats in his 'Celtic Twilight,'" a mood of separation between a "corporal" self and an "aetherial" self. The poem was called "La Fraisne, or The Ash Tree," and the debt to Yeats was obvious enough:

> I have put aside all folly and grief.
> I wrapped my tears in an ellum leaf
> And left them under a stone. . . .

Pound had sent a copy of this first book to Yeats and was pleased to hear that Yeats liked it: "W. B. Yeats applies the adjective 'charming,'" he wrote to William Carlos Williams in 1908, and in the following year he was able to add, "I have been praised by the greatest living poet."[2] By then, Pound had succeeded in meeting Yeats, and a friendship had begun between the older poet and the younger poet that blossomed into one of the most fruitful in modern letters. The introducer had been Olivia Shakespear, a lawyer's wife and a writer herself (and, as we now know, Yeats's mistress for a time), who with her daughter Dorothy had attended Pound's lectures in 1909, and had taken him to one of Yeats's Monday evenings, in his flat at 18 Woburn Buildings, near Russell Square. It is remarkable how quickly their friendship ripened, considering that in 1910, in *The Green Helmet and Other Poems*, Yeats issued a warning to any poet who might dare to follow him too closely, in "To a Poet, who would have me Praise certain Bad Poets, Imitators of His and Mine":

> You say, as I have often given tongue
> In praise of what another's said or sung,
> 'Twere politic to do the like by these;
> But was there ever dog that praised his fleas?

Although the poet Yeats was addressing was his friend George Russell (AE), and the imitators were young Irish poets, it was Pound's good luck not to be taken for one of the "fleas."

But while it was Pound who initiated the friendship, it was Yeats who, more and more in the years that followed their first meeting, sought the advice of the younger poet, and in a few years they became collaborators, with Yeats depending on Pound as much as Pound had once depended on Yeats. The poetics of their friendship overcame all barriers, and allowed an established Irish poet in his mid-forties and an aspiring American poet

---

2. *The Letters of Ezra Pound, 1907–1941*, ed. D. D. Paige (New York, 1950), 7–8.

in his mid-twenties to influence each other, as they also influenced others, and so to shape a new poetic style in English. Yeats was moving from the softness of his Celtic Twilight period to the hardness of *Responsibilities*, which when it appeared in 1914 Pound hailed as "The Later Yeats," while Pound was transforming himself from an imitator to a critic and parodist of the Early Yeats, who in 1915 in his volume *Lustra* produced his own inimitable "The Lake Isle" in answer to Yeats's well-known "The Lake Isle of Innisfree":

> O God, O Venus, O Mercury, patron of thieves,
> Give me in due time, I beseech you, a little tobacco-shop,
> With the little bright boxes
>     piled up neatly upon the shelves
> And the loose fragrant cavendish
>     and the shag,
> And the bright Virginia
>     loose under the bright glass cases,
> And a pair of scales not too greasy,
> And the whores dropping in for a word or two in passing,
> For a flip word, and to tidy their hair a bit.
>
> O God, O Venus, O Mercury, patron of thieves,
> Lend me a little tobacco-shop,
>     or install me in any profession
> Save this damn'd profession of writing,
>     where one needs one's brains all the time.

Except for its title, there is nothing imitative of Yeats in this later poem; in fact, its style is quite opposite to that of the original "Innisfree" and deliberately plays off the gossipy intimacy of a gathering place in the city against the idyllic solitude of nature. Pound's flippant, irreverent invocation of the gods as "patron of thieves" is maintained until the final lines, when he suddenly becomes serious and changes the scene from a tobacco shop to a writer's study and directs the satire at himself and his own artistic endeavor. We are far from Innisfree, certainly, but not so far from other poems Yeats had written when he was changing his style from romantic to modern, making the transition that Pound of all readers was most alert to, as in one of the poems of *The Green Helmet* in 1910:

> All things can tempt me from this craft of verse;
> One time it was a woman's face, or worse—
> The seeming needs of my fool-driven land;
> Now nothing but comes readier to the hand
> Than this accustomed toil. When I was young,
> I had not given a penny for a song

> Did not the poet sing it with such airs
> That one believed he had a sword upstairs;
> Yet would be now, could I but have my wish,
> Colder and dumber and deafer than a fish.

What Pound's parody of "Innisfree" shows, beneath its air of ironic detachment, is a seriousness about the profession of poet amounting to despair, over the impossible demands it makes on him, linking him with Yeats in a way that is characteristically modern—the poet's self-criticism of his own art. By the time they wrote major poems in the new style, Yeats in *The Wild Swans at Coole* (1919) and Pound in *Homage to Sextus Propertius* (1919) and *Hugh Selwyn Mauberley* (1920), the figure of the poet as a failed hero and disillusioned idealist, struggling to create beauty despite the destructive materialistic tendencies of the age, had become a central subject for both poets. It was their serious view of literature as the most exacting of arts, "this craft of verse," "this damn'd profession of writing," that brought them together at a crucial period in each poet's development and caused them to produce the series of tragic-ironic self-portraits of the artist that placed them in the vanguard of modern poets. In a famous passage in his prose work *Per Amica Silentia Lunae*, in 1917, Yeats wrote, "We make out of the quarrel with others, rhetoric, but of the quarrel with ourselves, poetry," and went on to say that "the other self, the anti-self or the antithetical self, as one may choose to name it, comes but to those who are no longer deceived, whose passion is reality." And Pound in "A Retrospect," in 1918, said that "Mr. Yeats has once and for all stripped English poetry of its perdamnable rhetoric. He has boiled away all that is not poetic." Much later, in 1937, Pound would write that in the years from 1908 to 1914, "I was learning how Yeats did it," and what he learned was "mostly negative, i.e., he has stripped English poetry of many of its faults." Remarkably enough, Yeats credited Pound with doing much the same for him, when, at a dinner given in his honor by *Poetry* magazine in Chicago in 1914, he summed up what Pound had done for him in the five years of their friendship:

> We rebelled against rhetoric, and now there is a group of younger poets who dare to call us rhetorical. When I returned to London from Ireland, I had a young man go over all my work to eliminate the abstract. This was an American poet, Ezra Pound.[3]

3. An account of Yeats's speech appeared in the April 1914 issue of *Poetry* and is reprinted in vol. 2 of *The Uncollected Prose of W. B. Yeats*, ed. John P. Frayne and Colton Johnson (New York, 1975), 412–14.

Much of what Yeats and Pound exchanged in the years of their closest association, from 1909 to 1916, was frankly critical, a mutual effort to rid themselves of conventional habits of expression, to write more honestly, even to write of their own faults without embarrassment. Pound taught Yeats fencing to improve his health, and they engaged in verbal fencing matches to improve their style. As Yeats said in his remarks at the *Poetry* banquet in 1914, "The whole movement of poetry is toward pictures, sensuous images, away from rhetoric, from the abstract, toward humility." It seems that together Yeats and Pound taught each other as much about how *not* to write poetry as how to write it, taking their pleasure in what was hardest to do with words, making a subject of the pain of artistic endeavor in the pursuit of perfection. Yeats wrote in *The Green Helmet* in 1910:

> The fascination of what's difficult
> Has dried the sap out of my veins, and rent
> Spontaneous joy and natural content
> Out of my heart. . . .

And Pound wrote in *Lustra* in 1915:

> Go, my songs, seek your praise from the young
> and from the intolerant,
> Move among the lovers of perfection alone.
> Seek ever to stand in the hard Sophoclean light
> And take your wounds from it gladly.

Pound had come to Yeats as a younger admirer, ready to learn from an older poet; Yeats seemed to regard him at once as one of the "young and intolerant" from whom he too could learn. Early in 1910, Pound wrote to his mother of Yeats, "He is the only living man whose work has anything more than temporary interest—possible exceptions on the continent," and later that year, in his preface to *The Spirit of Romance*, he had already placed Yeats among the immortals, saying, "What we need is a literary scholarship that will weigh Theocritus and Yeats with one balance." Yeats, for his part, wrote to Lady Gregory at the end of 1910 about "this queer creature Ezra Pound, who has become really a great authority on the troubadours," and said with evident admiration that he "has, I think, got closer to the right sort of music for poetry than Mrs. Emery [the actress Florence Farr, adept at reading poetry aloud]—it is more definitely music with strongly marked time and yet it is effective speech." But Yeats went on, in a more critical vein, "However, he cannot sing, as he has no voice. It is like something on a very bad phonograph."[4] Though Pound and Yeats often read aloud to each other, privately each found fault with the other's vocal style, as we can gather from Pound's recollection:

> Years ago Yeats was struggling with my rhythms and saying they wouldn't do. I got him to read a little Burns aloud, telling him he cd. read no cadence but his own. . . . I had a half hour of unmitigated glee in hearing "Say ye bonnie Alexander" and "The Birks o'Aberfeldy" *keened*, wailed with infinite difficulty and many pauses and restarts to *The Wind Among the Reeds*.[5]

If they admired the music in each other's poetry, it was for the way it was written rather than the way it was read.

In 1911, Yeats met Pound in Paris for the first of several excursions they took together on the Continent. They went to the Sorbonne, to Versailles, and to Notre Dame, and Yeats's response to the cathedral was memorably recorded much later in Canto LXXXIII:

> and Uncle William dawdling around Notre Dame
> in search of whatever
>                 paused to admire the symbol
> with Notre Dame standing inside it

In 1912, the relation between them became more professional, when Pound, as foreign editor of the newly founded *Poetry* magazine in Chicago, asked Yeats to submit some poems. Yeats obliged with five of his new poems, "The Realists," "The Mountain Tomb," "To a Child Dancing upon the Shore," "A Memory of Youth," and "Fallen Majesty." Pound accepted them, but made slight changes in the wording of three of the poems before sending them off to Harriet Monroe for publication. He deleted three superfluous words ("as it were") from "Fallen Majesty," changed an "or" to a grammatically preferable "nor" in "The Mountain Tomb," and corrected Yeats's grammar again in "To a Child Dancing upon the Shore" by substituting "him" for "he." When he showed these fairly trivial but justifiable changes to Yeats, their friendship was sorely tested, since Yeats was offended and took them all back for further revision. In the end, however, Yeats accepted Pound's deletion in one poem and rewrote the other two, retitling one of them "To a Child Dancing in the Wind." When Pound finally sent the poems to Chicago, he told Harriet Monroe that "peace reigns on parnassus."[6] This incident gives us the only docu-

---

4. *The Letters of William Butler Yeats*, ed. Allen Wade (New York, 1955), 543.

5. *Letters of Ezra Pound*, 180.

6. Richard Ellmann, "Ez and Old Billyum," in *Eminent Domain: Yeats Among Wilde, Joyce, Pound, Eliot and Auden* (New York, 1967), 67.

mentation that has turned up so far of what Pound did to improve Yeats's poetry, and it seems to have been practical criticism of the sort he offered to many of his contemporaries. What seems exceptional is that he offered it as readily to an older, established poet as he did to younger writers like Joyce and Eliot and Hemingway. Yeats may have bristled at first, but eventually he came to respect Pound's editorial judgment so much that he asked Pound to become his private secretary.

As Yeats wrote to his father in the summer of 1913:

> Next winter I am taking a secretary though I shrink from the expense, believing that I shall be able to bear the expense because I shall be able to write. When my sec comes at the end of October you will find me a better correspondent as he will answer business letters.[7]

That Pound served as much more than a stenographer for Yeats is clear from another letter Yeats wrote the same year to Lady Gregory:

> My digestion has got rather queer again, a result of sitting up late with Ezra and Sturge Moore and some light wine while the talk ran. However, the criticism I got from them has given me new life and I have made that Tara poem [probably "The Two Kings," published in Poetry in 1913 and Responsibilities in 1914] a new thing and am writing with new confidence having got Milton off my back. Ezra is the best critic of the two. He is full of the middle ages and helps me get back to the definite and concrete and away from modern abstractions. To talk over a poem with him is like getting you to put a sentence into dialect. All becomes clear and natural.[8]

In order to seclude themselves for serious work, Yeats invited Pound to spend the winter with him at a cottage he had rented near London, and in November 1913 the two poets betook themselves to Stone Cottage, Coleman's Hatch, in the Ashdown Forest of Sussex. Pound's view of the enterprise was not very optimistic, as he wrote to his mother before going there: "My stay in Stone Cottage will not be in the least profitable. I detest the country. Yeats will amuse me part of the time and bore me to death with psychical research the rest. I regard the visit as a duty to posterity."[9] However, the experience seems to have been the cementing of friendship between the two poets, for Pound wrote in December to William Carlos Williams: "Yeats is much finer *intime* than seen spasmodically in the midst

7. *Letters of W. B. Yeats*, 584.
8. Quoted by Ellmann in *Eminent Domain*, 66.
9. *Letters of Ezra Pound*, 25.

of a whirl. We are both, I think, very contented in Sussex."[10] Pound had formed another valuable literary friendship with Ford Madox Ford, the novelist and editor of the *English Review*, whom he saw often in London, and Ford (then Hueffer) invited the two poets over to his cottage at Slough for a week in late December (1913). Of this encounter Pound wrote one of his most amusing letters to his mother:

> Am down here for a week with the Hueffers in a dingy old cottage that belonged to Milton. F.M.H. and I being the two people who couldn't be in the least impressed by the fact, makes it a bit more ironical. . . .
> Yeats reading to me up till late Sat. evening, etc. . . .
> Have written about 20 new poems.
> 3 days later:
> Impossible to get any writing done here. Atmosphere too literary. 3 "Kreators" all in one ancient cottage *is* a bit thick.[11]

While Yeats was correlating Lady Gregory's collection of Irish myths and folklore with the folklore and religion of other countries during part of this time, he and Pound were writing poems, and Pound was editing *Des Imagistes*, the first anthology of Imagist poems. Yeats suggested to Pound that he get in touch with a promising young Irish author then living in Trieste, as a result of which Pound wrote to James Joyce for the first time, asking to see some of his work. But before Joyce had time to reply, Yeats had unearthed a poem from Joyce's *Chamber Music* called "I Hear an Army Charging" and showed it to Pound. Pound liked it so much that he wrote again to ask Joyce for permission to include the poem in *Des Imagistes*, and Joyce obliged. This first contact between Joyce and Pound was of crucial importance to Joyce's career, since it led to the serial publication of *A Portrait of the Artist as a Young Man* in the *Egoist* magazine in 1914, when Pound was serving as one of the editors, and in time to serial publication of *Ulysses* in *The Little Review*, for which Pound was then foreign editor. Thus Yeats was able to help both Pound and Joyce, and he was especially generous with Pound when, that same winter at Stone Cottage, he received a prize of fifty pounds from *Poetry* for "The Grey Rock," a poem Pound had sent in for him, and publicly requested Harriet Monroe to give forty pounds of it to Pound, "because," as he said in his open letter to her, "although I do not really like with my whole soul the metrical experiments he has made for you, I think those experiments

10. Ibid., 27.
11. Ibid., 28.

show a vigorous creative mind."[12] Pound commemorated Yeats's generous act by buying a new typewriter "of great delicacy," along with some statues from his sculptor friend, Henry Gaudier-Brzeska.

It was in January of 1914 that Yeats and Pound joined other poets in London for a dinner in honor of the older English poet, Wilfred Scawen Blunt, at which Pound read a verse tribute and presented a statue by Gaudier, and Yeats made a short speech in praise of Blunt, in the course of which he spoke of the changes then occurring in English poetry, declaring that "we are now at the end of Victorian romance—completely at an end. . . . Every year some part of my poetical machinery suddenly becomes of no use. As the tide of romance recedes I am driven back simply on myself and my thoughts in actual life."[13] He spoke of younger poets who were in rebellion against romanticism, especially of Ezra Pound, who, he said, "has a desire personally to insult the world" (with Pound no doubt smiling in the audience). Two months later, at the *Poetry* banquet in Chicago, Yeats was more complimentary of Pound, saying, "Much of his work is experimental; his work will come slowly, he will make many an experiment before he comes into his own," and then reading two of Pound's poems that he believed were "of permanent value," "The Ballad of the Goodly Fere" and "The Return." He called "The Return" "the most beautiful poem that has been written in the free form, one of the few in which I find real organic rhythm. A great many poets use *vers libre* because they think it is easier to write than rhymed verse, but it is much more difficult."

Pound's poem had appeared in 1912 in *Ripostes,* the sixth collection of his poems, and the one in which his new Imagist style was most evident. For Yeats, it was the poem he continued to admire most of all of Pound's work, not only for its masterful use of free verse, but for its vision of the ancient gods returning to earth. Yeats used it many years later in the preface of the revised edition of *A Vision,* and he said in 1929, in *A Packet for Ezra Pound,* after explaining how his wife's automatic writing had brought him the vision of history as a complex interaction of cones and gyres:

> You will hate these generalities, Ezra, which are themselves, it may be, of the past—the abstract sky—yet you have written "The Return," and though you but announce in it some change of style, perhaps, in book and picture it gives me better words than my own.[14]

12. *Letters of W. B. Yeats,* 585.
13. Excerpts from Yeats's speech were quoted in the *Egoist,* February 2, 1914, 57.
14. *A Vision,* reissued with the author's final revisions (New York, 1966), 29.

Yeats's use of Pound's poem may seem remarkable, when he had written so many fine visionary poems himself, but it does bear a more than superficial resemblance to his own "The Magi," written during the period of Yeats's closest association with Pound and published in 1914 in *Poetry*. Pound praised it for its "quality of hard light" and quoted it as an example of Imagism by a poet who was not an Imagist, maintaining that "a passage of *imagisme* may occur in a poem not otherwise *imagiste*" and indicating that Yeats was in sympathy with the new poetic style. Setting the poems side by side helps to clarify the similarity between them:

### The Return

See, they return; ah, see the tentative
    Movements, and the slow feet,
    The trouble in the pace and the uncertain
Wavering!

See, they return, one, and by one,
With fear, as half-awakened;
As if the snow should hesitate
And murmur in the wind,
    and half turn back;
These were the "Wing'd-with-Awe,"
Inviolable.

Gods of the winged shoe!
With them the silver hounds,
    sniffing the trace of air!

Haie! Haie!
    These were the swift to harry;
    These the keen-scented;
    These were the souls of blood.

Slow on the leash,
              pallid the leash-men!


### The Magi

Now as at all times I can see in the mind's eye,
In their stiff, painted clothes, the pale unsatisfied ones
Appear and disappear in the blue depth of the sky
With all their ancient faces like rain-beaten stones,
And all their helms of silver hovering side by side,
And all their eyes still fixed, hoping to find once more,

Being by Calvary's turbulence unsatisfied,
The uncontrollable mystery on the bestial floor.

Different as these poems are in their rhythms and sounds, they display a marked similarity of imagery and tone, for both depict a group of super-human figures seen as ominous and thrilling apparitions, described as "troubled" and "unsatisfied" in their bearing, as if they expected some momentous change and were impatient for it to take place. Both poems are prophetic, and the prophecies are dark although alluring. The key color word in both is "silver," which blends with the stormy atmosphere to give a tone of coldness and harshness to the apparitions. What these gods and Magi appear to be foretelling is a time of adversity for men, perhaps the end of civilization as we know it and the beginning of another epoch controlled by gods rather than men.

Probably no two poems by Yeats or Pound are closer than these short lyrics, and the praise each gave to the other's poem would indicate the affinity they felt. Yeats's poem appeared in the May 1914 issue of *Poetry*, along with a number of his poems that were published at the same time in *Responsibilities*, notably "To A Friend Whose Work Has Come to Nothing," "The Peacock," and "A Coat," all poems exemplary of the change in Yeats's style from early to later. Pound had been the first to speak of "The Later Yeats," giving that title to his review of *Responsibilities* in the same issue of *Poetry*, and calling Yeats "so assuredly immortal that there is no need for him to recast his style to suit our winds of doctrine," but noting "a manifestly new note in his later work" that younger poets "might do worse than attend to." Pound said the new note had become audible as early as 1910 in *The Green Helmet*, and "since that time, one has felt his work becoming gaunter, seeking a new hardness of outline." Besides praising "The Magi" and "A Coat," he spoke highly of "the poems on the Irish gallery," meaning "September, 1913" and others composed by Yeats in his indignation over the failure of Ireland to raise a public subscription for a gallery in Dublin to house Hugh Lane's collection of French impressionist paintings. Pound commented approvingly that "we find this author certainly at *prise* with things as they are and no longer romantically Celtic."

It is likely that Yeats composed all these poems Pound admired while the two were staying at Stone Cottage in the winter of 1913–14. We may conclude this from their publication soon afterward in *Poetry*, and also from a much later source of evidence, Pound's *Pisan Cantos*, where "The Peacock" is quoted as part of the evocation Pound gives of the ancient cottage, and the creative interaction of the two poets, for which the peacock may well have been a symbol:

The Peacock

What's riches to him
That has made a great peacock
With the pride of his eye?
The wind-beaten, stone-grey,
And desolate Three Rock
Would nourish his whim.
Live he or die
Amid wet rocks and heather,
His ghost will be gay
Adding feather to feather
For the pride of his eye.

Pound colors the scene in his memory, and adds a tone of hilarity to the creation of the poem, doubtless unnoticed by Yeats in the fervor of his invention:

so that I recalled the noise in the chimney
as it were the wind in the chimney
but was in reality Uncle William
downstairs composing
that had made a great Peeeeacock
in the proide ov his oiye

proide ov his oy-ee
as indeed he had, and perdurable

a great peacock aere perennius
or as in the advice to the young man to
breed and get married (or not)
as you choose to regard it

at Stone Cottage in Sussex by the waste moor
(or whatever) and the holly bush
who would not eat ham for dinner
because peasants eat ham for dinner
despite the excellent quality
and the pleasure of having it hot.

well those days are gone forever
and the traveling rug with the coon-skin tabs
and his hearing nearly all Wordsworth
for the sake of his conscience but
preferring Ennemosor on Witches

did we ever get to the end of Doughty:
The Dawn in Britain?
                    perhaps not
Summons withdrawn, sir.)

It was in April of 1914 that Pound married Olivia Shakespear's daughter Dorothy, and Yeats told his father in New York that he must hurry home for the wedding. The Pounds chose to honeymoon in Stone Cottage, and the following winter Yeats, who was past fifty but still a bachelor, came to join them there. In all, the poets spent three highly productive winters together, Pound publishing his first collection of Chinese translations, *Cathay*, and an anthology of new poems by contemporary poets, *The Catholic Anthology*, which included T. S. Eliot, a recent discovery of Pound, as well as Yeats's poem, "The Scholars." Yeats invited Pound to edit a selection of passages from the letters of his father, John Butler Yeats, for the Cuala Press in Dublin run by Yeats's sisters, and Pound was glad to oblige, since he was given to quoting phrases from the elder Yeats's letters in his own letters and essays. Yeats explained in one of his letters his reason for asking Pound to do it: "I thought he would make the selection better than I should. I am almost too familiar with the thought, and also that his approval, representing as he does the most aggressive contemporary school of the young, would be of greater value than my approval, which would seem perhaps but family feeling."[15] Pound was also spending much of his time deciphering the manuscripts of Ernest Fenollosa, and finishing his translation of Japanese Noh plays. In 1916, the Cuala Press published *Certain Noble Plays of Japan: From the Manuscripts of Ernest Fenollosa, Chosen and Finished by Ezra Pound*, with an introduction by Yeats. Yeats gave as his reason for including these Oriental dramas in a normally Irish series that "I have asked Mr. Pound for these beautiful plays because I think they will help me to explain a certain possibility of the Irish dramatic movement." Yeats had found in Pound's Noh plays a new way of conceiving of theatre, and wrote a play about his mythical Irish hero Cuchulain on the model of the Noh. In introducing it, Yeats claimed that "I have invented a form of drama distinguished, indirect and symbolic, and having no need of a mob or press to pay its way—an aristocratic form." This play was *At the Hawk's Well*, the first of Yeats's plays for dancers and masks, and instead of being staged at the Abbey Theatre in Dublin, as his earlier plays had been, it was played in a London drawing room to an invited audience. Yeats conceded that popu-

---

15. *Letters of W. B. Yeats*, 606–7.

lar drama must be realistic, but since he preferred poetic drama, he saw in the Japanese court theatre a new potentiality: "In the studio and in the drawing-room we can found a true theatre of beauty."

Pound not only supplied the model for this new drama of Yeats, but he found a Japanese dancer to act in it, helped to stage the play at Lady Cunard's house in London, and even had something to do with the guest list. We know from one member of the audience, T. S. Eliot, what effect the play had on him:

> Yeats was well-known, of course; but to me, at least, Yeats did not appear, until after 1917, to be anything but a minor survivor of the '90's. (After that date, I saw him very differently. I remember clearly my impression of the first performance of *The Hawk's Well* in a London drawing room, with a celebrated Japanese dancer in the role of the hawk, to which Pound took me. And thereafter one saw Yeats rather as a more eminent contemporary than as an elder from whom one could learn.)[16]

Pound spoke of the play as "new Theatre, or theatreless drama," and applauded Yeats's departure from the conventional stage. Yeats was satisfied enough with the result of his experiment to write another Cuchulain play along the same lines, *The Only Jealousy of Emer*, which he produced in 1919.

But poetry was still Yeats's main interest, as it was Pound's, and in 1917 Pound became foreign editor of *The Little Review* and provided a new outlet for their work. A large group of Yeats's poems appeared in the June 1917 issue of the magazine, including "The Wild Swans at Coole," which would become the title of his next collection, and such memorable poems about his unrequited love for Maud Gonne as "A Deep-Sworn Vow" and "Broken Dreams." In *The Little Review*, Yeats was in the company of the best of the younger generation, Joyce and Eliot as well as Pound, and he clearly belonged with them. When finally he married in October 1917, he took as his wife Georgie Hyde-Lees, the close friend and cousin-in-law of Dorothy Shakespear Pound, and fittingly, Ezra was his best man. Yeats trusted Pound with the arrangements for the wedding, but when he asked him to send a telegram to Lady Gregory at Coole Park, he stipulated that the message should be "*not* one that will be talked about in Gort for the next generation."

In 1918, Pound published a book of essays called *Pavannes and Divi-*

---

16. "Ezra Pound (1946)," quoted in *Ezra Pound: A Collection of Essays*, ed. Peter Russell (London, 1950), 25.

*sions,* which contained "A Retrospect," his fullest summary of the changes that had taken place in English poetry in the previous decade. He spoke especially of the difference Imagism had made in realistic presentation, economy of language, and rhythmical variety, but used Yeats as his chief example of the new spare style, saying, "He has become a classic in his own lifetime and *nel mezzo del cammin.* He has made our poetic idiom a thing pliable, a speech without inversions," and testified to "the lines of Yeats that ring in my head and in the heads of all young men of my time who care for poetry." In 1919, Yeats published *The Wild Swans at Coole,* with its theme "That the heart grows old," and that

> The living beauty is for younger men:
> We cannot pay its tribute of wild tears.

Yeats made poetic capital of the painful contrast between his aging body and his youthful mind, casting himself as "A weather-worn, marble triton / Among the streams." But when he received the Nobel Prize in 1923, Yeats looked at the medal, which depicted a young poet listening to the Muse, and reflected, "I was goodlooking once like that young man, but my unpracticed verse was full of infirmity, my Muse old as it were; and now I am old and rheumatic, and nothing to look at, but my Muse is young." How he had transformed his Old Muse into a Young Muse is partly explained in a note appended, in 1924, to his essay "Blake's Illustrations to Dante," where he says that "some seven or eight years ago I asked my friend Mr. Ezra Pound to point out everything in the language of my poems that he thought an abstraction, and I learned from him how much further the movement against abstraction had gone than my generation had thought possible."[17]

Pound was now writing his longer poems about poets, *Homage to Sextus Propertius* (1919) and *Hugh Selwyn Mauberley* (1920), in which he cast himself in a similar, prematurely aging role, as a neglected poet who thinks he will

> have, doubtless, a boom after my funeral,
> Seeing that long standing increases all things
> Regardless of quality,

and who writes his own mock-epitaph:

> He passed from men's memory in *l'an trentiesme*
> *De son eage;* the case presents
> No adjunct to the Muses's diadem.

17. *Essays and Introductions* (New York, 1961), 145.

The figure of the poet as a self-admitted failure, "out of key with his time," who

> strove to resuscitate the dead art
> Of poetry: to maintain 'the sublime'
> In the old sense,

bears a strong resemblance to the poet as Yeats was depicting him at that time:

> Whether we have chosen chisel, pen or brush,
> We are but critics, or but half create,
> Timid, entangled, empty and abashed,
> Lacking the countenance of our friends.
>               ("Ego Dominus Tuus," in *The Wild Swans at Coole*)

In fact, some of the sections of Pound's *Mauberley* are a poetic condensation of certain passages in Yeats's *Autobiography*, for in "The Tragic Generation," Yeats gave an account of the downfall of his fellow-poets in the Rhymers' Club, some of whom Pound describes poetically: "how Johnson (Lionel) died / By falling from a high stool in a pub" and "Dowson found harlots cheaper than hotels." Yeats had survived the weaknesses of his generation of poets by singular devotion to his art and learned to make great poetry out of human frailty: "A poet writes always of his personal life, in his finest work out of its tragedy," he said in 1937 in "A General Introduction for My Work." And Pound learned from Yeats's experience as well as his own to view the poet as a man whose gift intensifies the pain of human existence even as it shapes it into art:

> Beneath the sagging roof
> The stylist has taken shelter,
> Unpaid, uncelebrated,
> At last from the world's welter.
>               (*Hugh Selwyn Mauberley*, X)

What Pound liked to refer to as the "hardness" of the new poetic style was not simply a sharper imagery but the feeling of pain endured, and poetry, for both Yeats and Pound, was a discipline of the emotions to endure the pain and suffering that are a necessary part of life, a willingness to face the worst life could offer without sentimentality or self-delusion:

> The rhetorician would deceive his neighbours,
> The sentimentalist himself, while art
> Is but a vision of reality.
>               ("Ego Dominus Tuus")

After 1920, Yeats and Pound saw each other much less frequently, for Yeats was increasingly occupied with Irish politics, and Pound moved from London to Paris and on to Rapallo. Their paths met only when Yeats traveled to Italy to see Pound, as he did in 1924, when the two poets toured Sicily together, Yeats being enchanted with the Byzantine mosaics at Monreale and in the Palatine Chapel in Palermo, and Pound recalling later that Yeats asked him to speak some poetry aloud in the old Greek amphitheatre at Syracuse, to which he responded by quoting a line from Homer in Greek. It was in 1928 that Pound published two new Yeats poems in his magazine, *Exile*, along with his own Canto XXIII. Yeats's poems were "Sailing to Byzantium" and "Blood and the Moon." Yeats's Byzantium imagery owed something to his tour of Sicily with Pound:

> O sages standing in God's holy fire,
> As in the gold mosaic of a wall . . .

and when Yeats later published his "Crazy Jane" cycle in *The Winding Stair and Other Poems* in 1933, he made his only direct borrowing from Pound. Two lines of "Those Dancing Days are Gone" read:

> I carry the sun in a golden cup,
> The moon in a silver bag.

In a note to these lines, Yeats wrote, " 'The sun in a golden cup' . . . though not 'The moon in a silver bag' is a quotation from the last of Mr. Ezra Pound's *Cantos*." Yeats was always troubled by Pound's *Cantos*, though he found much to admire in them, and he always regarded Pound as one of the artists most sensitive to the age, an accurate barometer of the time of the "widening gyre" of European civilization. In a note to his play, Fighting the Waves, published in 1934 in a collection called *Wheels and Butterflies*, Yeats speculated that "Europe is changing its philosophy" and saw it reflected especially in the later work of Pound and Joyce and Virginia Woolf:

> Certain typical books—*Ulysses*, Mrs. Virginia Woolf's *The Waves*, Mr. Ezra Pound's *Draft of XXX Cantos*—suggest a philosophy like that of the *Samkara* school of ancient India, mental and physical objects alike material, a deluge of experience breaking over us and within us, melting limits whether of line or tint; man no hard bright mirror dawdling by the dry sticks of a hedge, but a swimmer, or rather the waves themselves.[18]

18. *The Variorum Edition of the Plays of W. B. Yeats*, ed. Russell Alspach (New York, 1969), 569.

In this view, Yeats saw Pound as one of the writers who intuitively expressed the fragmentation and disunity of the age, which Yeats himself mirrored in *A Vision* and later poems, but with the intent of countering them in his poetry, posing a unity of art against the disunity of the world. The difference is well illustrated by a comparison of "Sailing to Byzantium" with Canto XXIII, which is rather like comparing a painting with a mosaic, since Yeats's poem expresses a desire to transcend earthly existence, in perfectly controlled stanzas, while Pound's expresses a similar desire, but in lyric fragments of free verse. It could be said that the themes of the two poets continued to run parallel, while their forms increasingly diverged.

Yeats recognized how complementary the two poets were, as men and as artists, when he wrote his *A Packet for Ezra Pound* in 1929. By then, he was in his mid-sixties, and had come to Italy with his wife and children for his health. After battling for some years in the Senate of the new Irish Free State, Yeats wrote to Olivia Shakespear in 1928: "I am tired, I want nothing but the sea-shore and the palms and Ezra to quarrel with, and the Rapallo cats to feed after nightfall."[19] He found Rapallo "an indescribably lovely place" to live, and as for company, he said, "I shall not lack conversation. Ezra Pound, whose art is the opposite of mine, whose criticism commends what I most condemn, a man with whom I should quarrel more than anyone if we were not united by affection, has for years lived in rooms opening on to a flat roof by the sea."[20] What they talked about was poetry, as before, but also about religion and politics, and on each subject they held a few points in common but many points in contrast. Yeats tactfully advised Pound to steer clear of politics: "Do not be elected to the Senate of your country. I think myself, after six years, well out of that of mine. Neither you, nor I, nor any other of our excitable profession, can match those old lawyers, old bankers, old business men, who, because all habit and memory, have begun to govern the world." Unfortunately, Pound did not follow Yeats's advice to stay away from politics; if he had, he might have avoided much of the controversy of his later years. As for religion, Yeats and Pound were unorthodox believers, but believers nevertheless, as Yeats went on to say:

> I have been wondering if I shall go to church and seek the company of the English in the villas. At Oxford I went constantly to All Souls' Chapel, though never at service time, and parts of *A Vision* were thought out there. In Dublin I went to Saint Patrick's

19. *Letters of W. B. Yeats*, 746.
20. "A Packet for Ezra Pound," in *A Vision*, 1–2.

and sat there, but it was far off, and once I remember saying to a friend as we came out of Sant' Ambrogio in Milan, "That is my tradition and I will let no priest rob me."

In the end, Yeats made up his mind to avoid worship services at Rapallo: "I shall haunt empty churches and be satisfied with Ezra Pound's society and that of his traveling Americans." Pound, for his part, was as much opposed to organized religion as Yeats, though in his *Guide to Kulchur* in 1938 he recalled saying to Yeats: "Anticlericalism is no good (it being known between us fairly well what we did and did not believe). I can see a time when . . . we will have to join the Monsignori against Babbitt." And Yeats had replied, "But CONfound it! In my country the church IS Babbitt."[21] Pound, like Yeats, took the tolerant view of Christianity of a liberal Protestant, allowing him to borrow freely from its tradition without any obligation to subscribe to its doctrines. "I cd. be quite a 'good catholic,'" Pound wrote, "if they wd. let me pick my own saints and theologians."[22] From the viewpoint of his later, more orthodox Anglo-Catholicism, Eliot placed both Yeats and Pound among the modern heretics in his *After Strange Gods: A Primer of Modern Heresy* (1933), and it was certainly a reasonable view of their unorthodox beliefs—although to be fair to them, it should be said that they both presented notable images of Christ in their poetry, Pound in his early "The Ballad of the Goodly Fere" and Yeats in his later "Two Songs from a Play," while Eliot never presented Christ directly in his poetry, even in his later period.

But poetry absorbed most of their attention at Rapallo in 1928 and 1929, and Yeats wrote with open admiration of Pound's collected early poems, the *Personae* of 1925, and more critically of the *Cantos*, which Pound was just bringing to the number of thirty, about a third of the whole. Of the *Personae* Yeats wrote:

> One is a harder judge of a friend's work than of a stranger's because one knows his powers so well that his faults seem perversity, or we do not know his powers and think he should go our way and not his, and then all in a moment we see his work as a whole and judge as with the eyes of a stranger. In this book just published in America are all his poems except those Twenty-seven Cantos which keep me procrastinating, and though I had read it all in the little books I had never understood until now that the translations from Chinese, from Latin, from Provencal, are as much a part of his original work, as much chosen as to theme, as much

21. *Guide to Kulchur* (New York, 1938), 155.
22. Ibid., 189.

characterized as to style, as the vituperation, the railing, which I
had hated but which now seem a necessary balance. He is not
trying to create new forms because he believes, like so many of his
contemporaries, that old forms are dead, so much as a new style, a
new man.

Yeats frankly admitted that he could not yet understand the *Cantos*,
though he knew there was much fine poetry in them:

> I have often found there brightly printed kings, queens, knaves,
> but have never discovered why all the suits could not be dealt out
> in some quite different order. Now at last he explains that it will,
> when the hundredth canto is finished, display a structure like that
> of a Bach Fugue. There will be no plot, no chronicle of events, no
> logic of discourse, but two themes, the Descent into Hades from
> Homer, a Metamorphosis from Ovid, and, mixed with these,
> mediaeval or modern historical characters. He has tried to produce
> that picture . . . where everything rounds or thrusts itself without
> edges, without contours—conventions of the intellect—from a
> splash of tints and shades: to achieve a work as characteristic of the
> art of our time as the paintings of Cezanne . . . as *Ulysses* and its
> dream association of words and images, a poem in which there is
> nothing that can be taken out and reasoned over, nothing that is not
> a part of the poem itself.

So Yeats gave his fullest view of Pound's work in *A Packet for Ezra Pound*,
and though Pound reacted irritably to it in a letter, saying that "if Yeats
knew a fugue from a frog, he might have transmitted what I told him in
some way that would have helped rather than obfuscated *his* readers," [23] it
remains a generally helpful and favorable opinion of Pound's achievement up to that time. To it, Yeats added only a few words in his introduction to *The Oxford Book of Modern Verse*, which he edited in 1935, saying that
he found "more style than form" in Pound's poetry, but that Pound had
"more deliberate nobility and the means to convey it than any contemporary poet known to me."

Pound was less fair to Yeats in those years, as we know from the
account Yeats gave in his preface to *The King of the Great Clock Tower*, the
play he published in 1934, where he recounted the humiliating experience
of going "a considerable journey to get the advice of a poet not of my
school who would, as he did some years ago, say what he thought." After
inviting Pound to dinner at Rapallo, Yeats said he told Pound, "I am in my
sixty-ninth year" and "probably I should stop writing verse, I want your

23. *Letters of Ezra Pound*, 293.

opinion of some verse I have written lately." According to Yeats, Pound did not even ask him to read it aloud, as would have been their custom in earlier years, but took the manuscript away without comment, and "next day his judgment came and that in a single word 'Putrid.'" Certainly Pound's rudeness was uncalled for, and Yeats could only take consolation in the relative success of the play. It strained the friendship between the two poets, and they did not meet again, except briefly in London in 1938, when Pound was on his way to the United States in a futile attempt to try to keep his native country out of the impending Second World War—a war in which Pound would ill-advisedly implicate himself on the side of the Italian Fascists, leading to his imprisonment eventually in a mental hospital in Washington. It is the dark side of Pound's career, his thirteen years in St. Elizabeths, and yet he made literary capital of it, for he wrote the later Cantos there, which, despite their controversial nature, contain many brilliant poetic passages that are a major part of his whole achievement. Among the best of them are his reminiscences of the friendship with Yeats during the London years, some forty years earlier, and a few are of encounters in Rapallo in the later years:

> "Sligo in heaven" murmured Uncle William
> when the mist finally settled down on Tigullio
> (Canto LXXVII)

The friendship between the two men lasted in the younger poet's mind long after the older poet's death in 1939, and Pound did try to make amends after the fact for the breach he had caused. The last word in the poetics of their friendship was spoken by Pound, when he placed Yeats among the secular saints of his poetic Paradise, along with Ford and Joyce:

> Lordly men are to earth o'ergiven
> these the companions:
> Fordie that wrote of giants
> and William who dreamed of nobility
> and Jim the comedian singing:
> "Blarney Castle me darlin'
> you're nothing now but a StOWne"
> (Canto LXXIV)

It was poetry that drew them together, and it is their poetry that remains as the chief record of their friendship and of their achievement as writers. During the twenty years of their closest friendship, from 1909 to 1929, they learned from each other, criticized each other, borrowed from each other, and shaped each other's poetic style, fashioning, each in his way, a kind of Achilles' shield for confronting and reflecting their age, a destructive period in Western history, where the poet himself, whether Yeats or Pound, is a tragic actor in the midst of catastrophic changes, struggling for a unifying personal vision in a time of cultural disintegration. Yeats's apocalyptic vision of his time was expressed in many different ways, nowhere more strikingly than in the early "Valley of the Black Pig":

> The dews drop slowly and dreams gather: unknown spears
> Suddenly hurtle before my dream-awakened eyes,
> And then the clash of fallen horsemen and the cries
> Of unknown perishing armies beat about my ears.

Near the end of his life, Pound reached far back in his memory for a final echo from Yeats, when he wrote, in the notes for one of the last Cantos, CVII:

> That I lost my center fighting the world.
> The dreams clash and are shattered—
> And that I tried to make a paradiso terrestre.

Thus the poetics of their friendship is preserved in the terrestrial paradises of their poetry, and however different they may sound, some echo will always be heard of their singing together.

# Bards, Boardrooms, and Blackboards: John Ashbery, Wallace Stevens, and the Academicization of Poetry*

## Claude Rawson

JOHN ASHBERY is perhaps the most highly regarded living poet in America. He is, in more ways than one, the heir of Wallace Stevens, and like Stevens some three decades ago is acquiring a belated minority following in Britain. He is in many ways a critics' poet, like many modern and postmodern masters, the product of a culture whose reading is shaped in the seminar-room and which accepts "explication" (even defeated explication, which is a permanent invitation to more explication) as an essential constituent of its reading experience. This need not imply inauthenticity. It is a natural (and by no means the ugliest) product of the hegemony of university English departments over the literary consciousness of the more affluent regions of the anglophone world, and (as Alvin Kernan showed some years ago)[1] deeply rooted in the economics of (especially) American publishing, which have identified even for imaginative writers the profitability of the teacherly text. In Britain, English departments, like everything else, are fewer and smaller than in the United States, and to this day form a smaller proportion of poetry's reading public. This may have something to do with Ashbery's relatively late recognition there, though these correlations are doubtless not simple.

The phenomenon of an academicized literary idiom is wider and older than the institutional hypertrophy of literary studies that it nowadays reflects. Its roots lie partly in an earlier modernism, in the works of Joyce, Eliot, and Pound, whose principal writings precede the rabbitlike pro-

* An earlier version of this essay, entitled "A Poet in the Postmodern Playground," appeared in the *Times Literary Supplement*, July 4, 1986, on the publication of John Ashbery's *Selected Poems*. It is reprinted here by kind permission of the editor.

1. Alvin B. Kernan, *The Imaginary Library: An Essay on Literature and Society* (Princeton, 1982).

liferation of literature departments since World War II, and certainly weren't written for the classroom or initially much read within it. Some features of these writers may in some ways be thought of as late incarnations of the ancient idea of the learned poet. One variant of this is the poet whose learning shows not in his mastery of earlier poets but in his adoption of the style of professors, a narrowing of the old ideal to classroom dimensions which occurred quite early in this century and was not confined to university poets. It appears fully formed, and in a manner Ashbery was to assimilate, in Stevens's "Notes Toward a Supreme Fiction" (1942), whose very title mimics academic discourse, while a still earlier poem is actually called "Academic Discourse at Havana," though it first appeared in 1923 as "Discourse in a Cantina at Havana" and acquired its "academic" label in 1929.

That there is derision and indeed self-derision in such scholarly gesturing does not diminish its academic character. Stevens spoke jeeringly of poets of a certain kind as "introspective exiles, lecturing" (he may have meant Eliot, in 1918),[2] but it's a truism that academic and mock-academic often come to the same thing. This is not only because deriding the academic is the academic community's favourite tribal custom. It is also that, in the high self-conscious mix of postmodern Shandyism, the ubiquitous element of parody, instead of implying rejection, tends to cherish what it mimics along with the mimicking self.

Ashbery's best-known poem, "Self-Portrait in a Convex Mirror," takes its title from a famous painting by Parmigianino, but is as much of an "Academic Discourse" as any Stevens poem that announces its nature in its heading: its form is that of a lecture or treatise on that painter. Like Stevens's "Notes," it is an extended exploratory statement of aesthetic principles, and has something of the same centrality in his oeuvre and the same authority as a doctrinal key. It is difficult to be sure whether it's the intrinsic power of these poems or our culture's sensitised receptivity to the academic that has contributed most to this "classic" status. Certainly the volume containing and named after "Self-Portrait" is the one that first established Ashbery as a major figure, winning the three big book prizes (Pulitzer, National Book Award, National Book Critics Circle Award) for 1976.

Perhaps predictably, Ashbery's poem goes even further than Stevens's in its half-joky apparatus of professorial pretension, citing authorities ancient (Vasari) and modern (Sydney J. Freedberg, author of *Parmigianino:*

---

2. For a fuller discussion of this supposition, see my article "Wallace Stevens's 'Le Monocle de Mon Oncle,'" *Studi Americani* 13 (Rome, 1967): 417–62, esp. 422–23, 444–46.

*His Works in Painting* [Harvard, 1950]), and affecting a pedantic gusto for periodizing pronouncements or the explanatory aside or afterthought:

> The words are only speculation
> (From the Latin *speculum*, mirror).

The donnish parenthesis functions here as a didactic counterpart to the poetic *trouvaille*, a small leap of discovery that settles, somewhat limply, into punning congruence with the poem's principal image. It's interesting that Ashbery's didactic flourishes, like Stevens's before him, often strain to transpose themselves to a nondidactic wavelength of poetic epiphany. Few poets have been more self-consciously self-repeating than Stevens. And perhaps none has so confidently claimed, or with more didactic insistence, that repetition and the endless restatement with variations are of the essence of the imaginative quest, a hovering that precedes the homing in:

> One of the vast repetitions final in
> Themselves and, therefore, good, the going round
>
> And round and round, the merely going round,
> Until merely going round is a final good,
> The way wine comes at a table in a wood,

a return of the table to its original element, festively celebrated with wine. Such "mere repetitions" in Stevens's "Notes" are a key to the structure of entire poems, to their "circular" rather than linear progression to discovery. But they operate insistently in local ways, with words repeated and repeated and each repetition a nudge toward perceptual finality. The manner easily turns to mannerism, in Ashbery as well as in Stevens. In Ashbery's early poem "Two Scenes" the line "Destiny guides the water-pilot, and it is destiny" shows the pedagogue's emphatic manner put, rather clumsily, to tentative or exploratory purposes. The repeated word purports to be an advance on the first usage, a redefined confirmation of insight, enacting the process of discovery as well as its product. It's as though "What oft was *Thought*" were shown labouring toward the "ne'er so well *Exprest*" in a blackboard demonstration, while purporting to be surprised by joy.

Ashbery has frequented the world of art scholarship and earned his living in the college classroom, unlike Stevens, who after studying at Harvard neither had nor sought close connections with the university world. And Stevens's exercises in didactic delivery sometimes resemble a philosophy seminar hammed up in a businessmen's boardroom. It's amusing to see this feature rubbing off on Ashbery, whose experience of boardrooms must be considerably less even than Stevens's exposure to pedagogues. This comes over in poems like "Decoy," whose entire form suggests parody of public speaking ("We hold these truths to be self-evident: / That ostracism, both political and moral, has / Its place in the twentieth-century scheme of things"), or "Soonest Mended," where there seems at times to be self-conscious mimicry of a public man's commencement address ("the learning process is extended in this way, so that from this standpoint / None of us ever graduates from college").

But it also occurs in Ashbery's many poems of more straightforwardly aesthetic exploration, with their repetitious precisions and their pleasure in the prim revolving of platitude:

> The mark of things belongs to someone
> But if that somebody was wise
> Then the whole of things might be different
> From what it was thought to be in the beginning, before an angel
> bandaged the field glasses.

The idiom, the "doctrinal" content, the quaint angel image, are recognisably Stevensian, unlike the metrical spillage of the long last line, which is the kind of thing critics like to ascribe to the influence of Whitman. And it's true that America's most un-Whitmanian poets, Stevens and Ashbery no less than Pound, have often felt obliged more or less ostentatiously to make their "pact" with Whitman. But what such lines imitate is a surface garrulity, not the driving rhapsodic delight. Whitman's metrical capaciousness turns in Ashbery into a fussy exercise in extended pointmaking ("Now all is different without having changed / As though one were to pass through the same street at different times"), just as Whitman's expansive enumerations turn elsewhere in Ashbery (in the list of rivers in "Into the Dusk-Charged Air," for example) into self-indulgent pieces of low-pressure variation.

Stevens is metrically more restrained, more "classical," but Ashbery's loping Whitmanian lines merely open out into a more relaxed version of Stevens's discursive prosiness. (There is nothing of the pedagogue or boardroom orator in Whitman's garrulities.) This effect is already visible, in a small incipient way, in "Two Scenes":

> This is perhaps a day of general honesty
> Without example in the world's history
> Though the fumes are not of a singular authority
> And indeed are dry as poverty.

This goes back to the Stevens of *Credences of Summer,*

> This is the last day of a certain year
> Beyond which there is nothing left of time,

whose definitional tautness is pointedly slackened in Ashbery, in a traducing that out-Stevenses Stevens's own lecturese.

Ashbery's formative involvement with professional art criticism has of course left other marks on his poetry than this predisposition to pedagogic utterance. The strong painterly interests he shared with his close associate Frank O'Hara, "poet among painters," derived much of their stimulus from the abstract expressionists. That influence might be expected to tend away from the academic, and is reflected most fully perhaps in an interest in randomness, in vitality of surface, and in some strong energies of colouring. Both poets are variously "painterly" (though Ashbery, as Marjorie Perloff has pointed out, affects to play down the visual aspect of his art and claims to be "much more audio-directed," with John Cage as a seminal influence).[3] But their pictorialism tends to be sharply though often unconventionally "representational," and strongly anchored in narrative. The "story" element in Ashbery comes over in fragmented and nonsequential ways, but the fragments have a strong power of visual evocation and a startling precision of outline even in their most surreal effects:

> Behind the steering wheel
>
> The boy took out his own forehead.
> His girlfriend's head was a green bag
> Of narcissus stems.

This is painterly, but hardly abstract expressionist. Its visual counterpart is Magritte.

Ashbery has always been interested in surrealism and Dada. He once began a doctoral dissertation on Raymond Roussel, and his works reflect a fascination with Roussel, Reverdy, and other writers in the surrealist tradition. He seems to know French better than most American poets, especially than Stevens, and seems correspondingly less addicted to peppering his poems with snippets from that language. Stevens was in his way a painterly poet, too, though surrealism may not be what first comes to mind when we think of Stevens's pictorialism. Yet even here the connections are close, and early. Ashbery's "Illustration" is written in an

---

3. Marjorie G. Perloff, "'Transparent Selves': The Poetry of John Ashbery and Frank O'Hara," *Yearbook of English Studies* 8 (1978): 171–96, esp. 172.

idiom of aesthetic *bizarrerie* that recalls one of Stevens's most delightful early styles:

> A novice was sitting on a cornice
> High over the city. Angels
>
> Combined their prayers with those
> Of the police, begging her to come off it.
>
> One lady promised to be her friend.
> "I do not want a friend," she said.
>
> A mother offered her some nylons
> Stripped from her very legs. Others brought
>
> Little offerings of fruit and candy,
> The blind man all his flowers.

Readers of Stevens's *Harmonium* poems "The Plot against the Giant" and "Cy Est Pourtraicte, Madame Ste Ursule, et les Unze Mille Vierges" will recognise the ingredients: a more or less scabrous episode sharply and elegantly sketched, the dandy-decorative "slight lyric grace" hardened by a grasp of ugly realities, the festive offerings of flowers coyly fraught with bawdy meanings, devotional proprieties lightly but uncompromisingly defiled.

One might, on the basis of this evidence, propose an analogous progress in both poets from early "dandy" lyric to the more extended and abstract meditations on imagination and reality in the later work. In fact this "later" manner is to some extent already present in the early Ashbery. A second part of "Illustration" moves on to reflections on what the narrative may be thought to illustrate, and reads like a pastiche of middle or late Stevens:

> Much that is beautiful must be discarded
> So that we may resemble a taller
>
> Impression of ourselves. Moths climb in the flame,
> Alas, that wish only to be the flame:
>
> They do not lessen our stature.
> We twinkle under the weight
>
> Of indiscretions.

It's perhaps the first of several minimalist variations on Stevens's theme of the "major man" and occurs earlier in Ashbery's than in Stevens's work. Ashbery's progress in one sense replicates Stevens's progress from early to late, but his own early phase also picks up where Stevens left off. When

Ashbery's *Some Trees*, which contains this poem, came out in 1956, Stevens's *Collected Poems*, published in 1954 on Stevens's seventy-fifth birthday, had only recently made available within a single book a sense of the older poet's entire progress, and Stevens's death in 1955 provided an additional context for inclusive overviews of his oeuvre. It is striking to see, not only in "Illustration" but in "Two Scenes," many features of the older poet's middle and later style.

Where Ashbery from the start differs from Stevens is in a recurrent atmosphere of menace, a violence of feeling or of natural process. This may be sensed in the surreal lyricisms of "Glazunoviana," which ends, like "Sunday Morning," in the massive melancholy of a movement of birds, but a melancholy of explosive rather than elegiac suggestion:

> In the flickering evening the martins grow denser.
> Rivers of wings surround us, and vast tribulation.

It is also conveyed in fragmentary hints of narrative ("Popular Songs," "A Boy") and in a more fully formed state in the story of the novice in part 1 of "Illustration," which ends in a lurid finale of sexual exposure and suicide:

> With that, the wind
> Unpinned her bulky robes, and naked
>
> As a roc's egg, she drifted softly downward
> Out of the angels' tenderness and the minds of men.

It's not often that Ashbery gives us a completed narrative. In "The Instruction Manual" the speaker, seeking escape from humdrum labour, imagines a rose-coloured novelette set in Guadalajara, a variation on Stevens's Latino-exotic dreamlands. But "A Long Novel," also from *Some Trees*, is neither long nor a novel. Nor, however, is it a Borgesian compression of a large narrative into a few paragraphs, as you might expect instead, but an elusive anecdotal surface concerned with speculative aesthetics rather than any story of human lives.

The professed anecdote is favourite ploy in Stevensian poetics. Stevens himself has six poems entitled "Anecdote," one of which, "Earthy Anecdote," opens the *Collected Poems*. They tend to be fully formed little fables, not fragmentary like Ashbery's, but in the best-known, "Anecdote of the Jar," both suggestions of "Anecdote" (story, informal chat) are subverted: the narrative is nugatory, and the poem's spare and resonant proposition of aesthetic principle is no more informal or chatty than "Notes Toward a Supreme Fiction" are scribbled jottings.

Ashbery's poems are not called "anecdotes," but their titles often suggest anecdotal chatter caught in mid-flow: "And You Know," "Soonest

Mended." And the poems themselves, while not telling full-formed stories, are full of narrative intimations that erupt into the discourse with a surreal, unsettling urgency in precisely that idiom of innocent colloquial triviality: "The funniest little thing . . . That's how it all began." A poem like "What Is Poetry," whose title does announce aesthetic discourse, proceeds much more in the anecdotal mode than do Stevens's "anecdotes":

> Beautiful images? Trying to avoid
>
> Ideas, as in this poem? But we
> Go back to them as to a wife, leaving
>
> The mistress we desire?

Such analogies seem flip, but they are not foreign to formal arts of poetry. Pope's *Essay on Criticism* has several:

> *Wit* and *Judgement* often are at strife,
> Tho' meant each other's Aid, like *Man* and *Wife*. . .
>
> A Muse by these is like a Mistress us'd.

Ashbery's procedure, however, is not that of illustrative or conclusive analogy but of suggestive narration, incipient and open-ended, its propositions about art as open as the outcome of any speculative event: "It might give us—what?—some flowers soon?"

The snatches of gossip imply the insufficiency of formal stories. They explore instead the discontinuity of events or of our perception of events, suggesting an intermittent "eavesdropping" on a "private language," the "rejected chapters" of a novel. He speaks in "The New Spirit" of "an open field of narrative possibilities. Not in the edifying sense of tales of the past that we are still (however) chained to, but as stories that tell only of themselves." In fact, his stories aren't always free of "allegory," and their openness to "possibility" is (as in Stevens or in Borges) definable against rather than free from "tales of the past."

Thus, a note of mystery-story menace or hints of an unexpounded sexual drama chat their way across a poem, detached from their conventional novelistic context, though inevitably calling such a context to mind in its very absence:

> A man in her room, you say.
> I like the really wonderful way you express things. . . .

The effect hovers uncertainly between the fraught and the flip. The poem from which this example comes is called "Unctuous Platitudes," but that

self-violating title is another blind, harshly at odds with the limpid delicacy of lyrical probing which is in fact the poem's dominant note:

> I like the really wonderful way you express things
> So that it might be said, that of all the ways in which to
>
> Emphasize a posture or a particular mental climate
> Like this gray-violet one with a thin white irregular line
>
> Descending the two vertical sides, these are those which
> Can also unsay an infinite number of pauses
>
> In the ceramic day. Every invitation
> To every stranger is met at the station.

The air of platitude in the last line is perhaps lapidary, not especially "unctuous," but lapidary, as another poem says, with a "special, lapidary /
Todayness." And since the meaning is by any standard opaque rather
than obvious, the suggestion of "platitude" is itself, as the postpeople say,
deconstructed. Titles in Ashbery regularly exist in a kind of adversarial
tension with the rest of the poem. What the invitations to strangers met at
stations really evoke are not truisms but the shadowy convergences of
mystery-plots. Their strange potency comes from the fact that the general
proposition is made to carry an urgency of particular events, like
Gulliver's descriptions of war, but transposed from Swift's overexplicit to
an inexplicit (suspenseful or "mysterious") mode. These closing lines are,
in a specific sense, story-lines, but stripped of context and generalised to a
kind of pregnant meaninglessness. Suggestions of "anecdote" are again,
as in Stevens, subverted, but subverted by incompleteness rather than by
a belying of informality.

"Rivers and Mountains" is a "mystery-poem" whose narrative surface
misleads expectation in the way that some of Ashbery's titles do:

> On the secret map the assassins
> Cloistered, the Moon River was marked
> Near the eighteen peaks and the city
> Of humiliation and defeat. . . .

The lines are remarkable for evoking not one but at least two narrative
styles that conventionally presuppose conclusive explication: that of the
suspense thriller and, more surprisingly, that of traditional allegory (add
initial capitals, and "the city / Of humiliation and defeat" might have come
out of Bunyan, though Auden is in this as in other things an intervening
influence). The free-floating preoccupation with narrative style, "not
events" but "rather . . . their 'way of happening,'" is nowhere more

evident than here, since the idiom of allegory offers no allegory, only an atmosphere of doom, and the mystery-plot is never unravelled.

Ashbery reports that when he was asked by Kenneth Koch whether his poems had "hidden meanings," he said no, "because somebody might find out what they were and then the poems would no longer be mysterious." The reply belongs with the statement about Parmigianino's "Self-Portrait" that its "secret" is that there is "no secret," and thus with the poetics of *surface*, which, as Marjorie Perloff says, Ashbery has derived from action painting.[4] It can also be read as an extreme formulation of the old modernist dogma of the irreducibility of poems to meanings, and it contains an element of Dada tease. Narrative has become a form of play, "almost / very important" in the words of Frank O'Hara. In "Rivers and Mountains," there is a sinister atmosphere of Kafkaesque menace. But there is also an Auden-like feeling that deadly conspiratorial doings are not far removed from schoolboy adventure, and the withholding of explanation has something of the "I shan't tell you" of children's play.

The detective- or mystery-story has enjoyed a rather solemn vogue in postmodern letters. The new novelists in France, Orton and Fowles in England, Vonnegut and Pynchon in America, have exploited it as a structural frame for experiments with the well-made plot and enquiries into the play of artifice in art. Borges has been cited as an analogue to the Ashbery of "Rivers and Mountains."[5] But if Ashbery can be said to share with all these writers a feeling for violence subjected to stylish containments, he hardly ever plays with the structure of the suspense plot, only with fragments of its surface. "Story" is for him, in Perloff's words, "a point of reference, a way of alluding, a source . . . of parody,"[6] though even "parody" is a misleading term to the extent that it suggests stylistic reversal rather than dislocation.

In her recent book *The Dance of the Intellect* Perloff speaks of "the return of story in postmodern poetry."[7] I doubt whether "story" had receded from poems in the way she implies, and whether its present prominence is confined to the "postmodern." Ashbery's methods invite comparison, for example, with the "secret narrative" element in some recent British

4. Ibid., 178.

5. David Shapiro, *John Ashbery: An Introduction to the Poetry* (New York, 1979), 84–85.

6. Perloff, *The Dance of the Intellect: Studies in the Poetry of the Pound Tradition* (Cambridge, 1985), 161.

7. Ibid., 155. Despite some disagreements on particular points, I am greatly indebted to Marjorie Perloff's various studies of Ashbery and his associates, including, in addition to the works already cited, *Frank O'Hara: Poet Among Painters* (New York, 1977), and *The Poetics of Indeterminacy: Rimbaud to Cage* (Princeton, 1981).

poetry, hardly postmodern, where the undisclosed or partially disclosed event also exerts an unsettling pressure of feeling. One difference is that Ashbery's narratives seem "fractured"[8] to a point where disconnection or randomness goes beyond a mere sense of information withheld, whereas in the poems of Andrew Motion or perhaps of Tom Paulin the idea of a chain of events hovers over the poem even if we can't reconstruct it. I suspect too that in these British poets the implied narrative acts in a "lyric" way, as a carrier of personal feeling in a manner similar to what Wordsworth had in mind when he said that in the narrative of "lyrical ballads" the feeling "gives importance to the action and situation" and not the other way round. Motion's narratives are, unlike Wordsworthian ballads, implied rather than overt, with the "secrecy" supplying part of the emotional charge. I suppose that Ashbery would have no truck with such "lyrical" purposes. His focus is on a bravura artifice, a depersonalised surface crackling with "possibility," a brilliant randomness in which the analogy with action painting asserts itself with special force, and should not be underestimated merely because the paint strokes take an auditory anecdotal form.

8. The word is David Shapiro's, *John Ashbery*, 36.

# Stendhal's Mirror and Yeats's Looking-Glass: A Reconsideration of *The Tower*

## C. K. Stead

IN DONALD DAVIE'S still marvellously readable, challenging, and rewarding book, *Articulate Energy*, W. B. Yeats appears from time to time as the modern poet who, almost alone, holds to "the conscious mind's intelligible structure"[1] against the chaotic "realism" of the modernists—a realism that for Davie is signalled by the breakdown of traditional syntax. The poet who (as Yeats liked to put it) withdraws into the quicksilver at the back of the mirror, merely reflecting the chaos that lies about him, is abandoning one of the sacred duties of art—to impose order. In *The Tower* we see the Yeatsian order imposed in two separate but related ways. These poems can be described as "philosophical." That's to say their "thinking" is apparently orderly, purposeful, and of a generalising nature. And the poet's deliberation is also apparent in the forms he uses. These poems are demonstrations of craft-skill in the very highest degree. No one who has tried to write poetry—or perhaps I should say no one who grew up writing poetry at a time when everyone experimented with verse forms—can be indifferent to this aspect of the later Yeats; and it is especially evident in the three verse sequences, "The Tower," "Meditations in Time of Civil War," and "Nineteen Hundred and Nineteen."

Yet these are also highly subjective poems. The persona and the poet are always close and often indistinguishable. Yeats's response when he reread the whole collection was surprise at what he saw as the revelation of his own bitterness. Here speaks the "sixty-year-old smiling public man," a man troubled by the "absurdity" of

> —this caricature,
> Decrepit age that has been tied to me
> As to a dog's tail;

a poet wondering whether he should

---

1. *Articulate Energy* (London, 1955), 124.

> bid the Muse go pack,
> Choose Plato and Plotinus for a friend
> Until imagination, ear and eye,
> Can be content with argument and deal
> In abstract things.

Yeats is present in the volume as the man who has loved and lost Maud Gonne and who continues to remember that loss with varied and powerful emotions; as a husband late in life and father of young children; as a man who has taken up residence, or summer residence, in a tower situated in countryside he has already made his own in poetry; as a man recording and commenting on a violent phase in Irish political history; as a man anxious about the future of Western civilisation; as a man trying to order his mind while he comes to terms with the onset of old age and what it means. And it's not just that the man, Yeats, is in the poems; he's in them as poet, asking (for example) in verse whether he should stop writing verse. This is a twentieth-century version of Wordsworth's "egotistical sublime." If one grows tired of anything in Yeats, it's likely to be the first person singular.

Yeats often expressed dissatisfaction with the realist tradition, citing Stendhal's description of a novel as "a mirror dawdling down a lane." He rejected most modern fiction because he felt it satisfied Stendhal's requirement. But what if the alternative to Stendhal's objective, perambulating mirror should be merely the poet staring into his own? Part of my argument will be that the poetry in Yeats was at war with the philosopher. It was the philosopher who resented and rejected Stendhal's realist mirror, but the poet had need of it if he wasn't to go wildly astray in total subjectivity.

Yeats's System (as he called it), set out in the book he called *A Vision*, might be seen as an attempt to break out of the Berkeleyan solipsism. It was, at least, a broadening of the view, giving pseudo-scientific patterning to the movements of history, the rise and fall of civilisations, and even to the changing fortunes of individual men and women, by relating them to the mathematical precision of the stars and planets.

The apparent objectivity of all this (leaving aside the question of its truth, or its value) is undermined by wild rhetorical assertions of total subjectivity—as in part 3 of "The Tower" for example:

> I mock Plotinus' thought
> And cry in Plato's teeth,
> Death and life were not
> Till man made up the whole,
> Made lock, stock and barrel

Out of his bitter soul,
Aye, sun and moon and star, all,
And further add to that
That, being dead, we rise,
Dream and so create
Translunar Paradise.

(I will come back to those lines.) Or the lines from "Blood and the Moon" about Berkeley:

And God-appointed Berkeley that proved all things a
      dream,
That this pragmatical, preposterous pig of a world, its
      farrow that so solid seem,
Must vanish on the instant if mind but change its
      theme.

Nevertheless, within that subjectivity, or Berkeleyan solipsism, the poet's view could be large or small. The prison of the self could be ample or confining; and in the years in which the poems of *The Tower* were written, Yeats went all out for amplitude. So he could be disappointed lover, or Irish republican, or paterfamilias, on a larger stage. Or he could very occasionally absent himself altogether in favour of "history." One such occasion, signified by the absence of the first person singular, is the poem "Leda and the Swan":

A sudden blow: the great wings beating still
Above the staggering girl, her thighs caressed
By the dark webs, her nape caught in his bill,
He holds her helpless breast upon his breast.

How can those terrified vague fingers push
The feathered glory from her loosening thighs?
And how can body, laid in that white rush,
But feel the strange heart beating where it lies?

A shudder in the loins engenders there
The broken wall, the burning roof and tower
And Agamemnon dead.
                          Being so caught up,
So mastered by the brute blood of the air,
Did she put on his knowledge with his power
Before the indifferent beak could let her drop?

Yeats, as I've said, is absent from the poem, except that his fingerprints are everywhere. The form, however, is unusual. It's a sonnet. I can think of one other Yeatsian sonnet—"While I from that reed-throated whisperer" at the end of *Responsibilities*, which has a much more extraordinary and sinuous syntax, and which, being a personal statement, seems to belong to its form. What's odd about "Leda and the Swan" is that Yeats drops the first person singular but uses the form that seems most to call for it—the sonnet being traditionally a personal expression of love or piety.

Nevertheless, formal constraints always brought the best out of him as a poet. "Difficulty is our plough," he told Margot Ruddock;[2] it gets us "down under the surface." The "difficulty" in this poem was to compress an action exactly into the octave, and its implications into the sestet.

Zeus as swan rapes Leda—that is described in the octave with a curious, almost cold precision, part pictorial, part dramatic, part psychological. The problem for me—and I don't believe I can be unusual in this— is that in the mythology the form the god takes for this invasion of the human universe is that of a bird; and what Yeats's poem does is to bring the mythological event up close, making it so real, or plausible, it becomes very nearly *de*-mythologised.

Birds were important to Yeats. Like Maud Gonne, he kept many in cages. They were caged in his poems, too, as emblems. ("Another emblem there!" as a swan goes over in one of the Coole Park poems.) Zeus in disguise is not the only swan in *The Tower*, and certainly not the only bird. Along with the swans go crows, daws, peacocks, water hens, moorhens, hawks, owls, starlings, parrots, and nightingales; then there are unspecified "wild birds and caged birds," "passing birds," "birds of the air." There are also phoenixes; there are the "brazen hawks" and "the innumerable clanging wings that have put out the moon" in "The Tower"; and there is that famous golden bird Yeats was to become when he had shaken off his mortal dress. And when he wanted to present himself negatively, he chose a scarecrow for image—something that frightens the birds from their song.

The soul is likened to a swan in one of these poems. But in the sonnet Zeus as swan is decidedly not incorporeal. He's a very birdy god—an almost believable avian rapist, worthy of Alfred Hitchcock. The physical details—Leda's "thighs caressed / By the dark webs," her "terrified vague fingers" that try to push the "feathered glory" away, her "loosening thighs," her body "laid in that white rush"—these can be almost repellent, or absurd, or distasteful exactly in the degree to which Yeats's skill has made them real.

2. *Ah, Sweet Dancer: W. B. Yeats—Margot Ruddock: A Correspondence*, ed. Roger McHugh (London, 1970), 81.

But if by the end of the octave the mind of a reader can be delicately poised between admiration and distaste, the opening two and one-half lines of the sestet must, I think, swing the balance entirely in the poem's favour. They are among the great lines of modern poetry, and they tend to gather to them all that's positive in one's response to the octave and neutralize all the latent negatives:

> A shudder in the loins engenders there
> The broken wall, the burning roof and tower
> And Agamemnon dead.

This is Ezra Pound's method of the "luminous detail"—so little standing for so much—and it probably derives directly from the opening lines of Canto IV:

> Palace in smoky light,
> Troy but a heap of smouldering boundary stones.

The sonnet moves now to its conclusion, which takes the form of a question—not the strongest way to finish a poem, but the form is sustained perfectly, and any slight downturn in energy can be justified (if it needs justification) as a kind of postcoital lowering.

Modern criticism has learned partly from dealing with Yeats that a purist insistence that the text in isolation must yield up all its meaning won't do. It doesn't help to complain about it—it's simply a fact that all the poem "means" is not in the text. The fullness of its meaning is found in reading other Yeats poems, and in reading his prose work. So we find "Leda and the Swan" has a place in the book he called *A Vision,* where it heads a section called "Dove or Swan." There Yeats tells us:

> I imagine the annunciation that founded Greece as made to Leda, remembering that they showed in a Spartan temple, strung up to the roof as a holy relic, an unhatched egg of hers; and that from one of her eggs came Love and from the other War.

Eggs came from the rape. One produced Helen of Troy. They also produced those two huge abstractions of which Helen is symbol or focal point—Love and War.

Yeats's use of the word "annunciation" signals the pattern he is constructing: new civilisations are initiated by divine intervention. Leda is to the Graeco-Roman culture what the Virgin is to the Christian. In each case the god implants the seed of the new in the mortal body of a woman. What is born lasts two thousand years. Our own civilisation is about to end. As Yeats has it in "The Second Coming" (another poem ending in a question):

> And what rough beast, its hour come round at last,
> Slouches towards Bethlehem to be born?

If you are at all of a (Dr.) Johnsonian and literal disposition, as I am, you have to keep reminding yourself that all this is intellectual and symbolic. One is not required to struggle toward literal belief, nor even, I think, to a whole-hearted suspension of disbelief in the rape of Leda by a feathered Zeus. One must, in fact, see through the feathers to the abstract idea—that the new civilisation, simply *because* it's new, must appear to the old in the guise of rapist and destroyer. Leda is victim in the poem; she is being invaded by the new and therefore the unknown. In its power there may be a kind of glory (both words occur in the poem), but she tries vainly to push it away. This brutal quality of historical inevitability was something that fascinated Yeats. To itself the Rough Beast of the future may be beautiful; to us it will appear with "a gaze blank and pitiless as the sun."

I suggested that in its attention to detail the poem seems to go dangerously close to de-mythologising its subject and thus rendering it absurd. Once our extended reading has put the idea back into the event, the poem is protected against our literalness. But solving one problem can immediately produce another. Yvor Winters complains as follows:

> If we are to take the high rhetoric of the poem seriously, we must
> really believe that sexual union is a kind of mystical experience, that
> history proceeds in cycles of two thousand years each, and that the
> rape of Leda inaugurated a new cycle. . . . But no one save Yeats
> has ever believed these things, and we are not sure that Yeats really
> believed them.[3]

Although Winters is often unfair to Yeats and misrepresents him by overstatement, there is an element of truth in this objection that I think it's wrong to dismiss out of hand. A kind of "high rhetoric," to use Winters's phrase, *is* carrying us along over some very strange intellectual territory.

My response is first to acknowledge that I can't take Yeats's "System" seriously. But I'm prepared in some degree to entertain it, as one entertains a fiction. His history is, if you like, his narrative structure—a narrative in which the characters are half-human, half-abstract. I suppose this has always been the case in poetry that dealt with mythological figures. What is new here is the degree of self-consciousness. It's as if Yeats has produced both a primitive mythology and a modern commentary on it.

Yeats called the spiritual presences, who spoke to him through the

3. Yvor Winters, *The Poetry of W. B. Yeats* (Denver, 1960).

mediumship of his wife, his Unknown Instructors. When he offered to give up the rest of his life to expounding the truths they were conveying, they replied, "No. We have come to give you metaphors for poetry." But if the metaphors were for poetry, what was the poetry for? Not, evidently, simply a vehicle for these arcane truths—or Yeats's offer to expound them would have been accepted. How then do we answer Winters if he argues that we either take Yeats's "silly ideas" (as he calls them) literally or condemn the poetry to a self-enclosed, self-referential function—metaphors for the sake of poetry, poetry for the sake of itself?

I think one can argue that the psychological truth of these poems resides in the notion of historical inevitability, and that's something one can accept without getting tangled up in details of gyres and cones and two-thousand-year cycles. As we age and the world ceases to be the one we were born into, history appears more and more as an unwelcome force. It alters the rules of lifemanship we grew up with; it changes the look of everything that established our notion of normality; and worse, it reminds us that we will shortly be removed altogether from the scene. Leda and the Swan can be seen, each of them, as part of the human psyche as it comes to terms with time and change. One represents an onrushing eagerness to embrace the future—to establish (in the famous concluding line of another modern sonnet) "new styles of architecture, a change of heart."[4] The other resists, fears, experiences horror, or what has been called lately "the shock of the new," but is forced to recognize necessity.

And history as rapist is what makes the underlying psychology of this apparently impersonal sonnet engage and interlock with that of the personal, first-person poems of *The Tower*, where Yeats laments what time has done to his body, and resolves to prepare his mind, or his soul, for what remains of life. A man learns historical necessity by the decline of his own powers.

The sonnet concludes with a question: "Did she put on his knowledge with his power . . . ?" If you look at three variously representative critics of Yeats—Yvor Winters, Richard Ellmann, and Helen Vendler[5]—you will find they don't agree at all on what to make of this question, and that

---

4. W. H. Auden, "Petition," in *Collected Shorter Poems 1930–44* (London, 1950), 120.

5. "Put on" must mean "take on," "assume," "acquire." Yvor Winters says the question implies she did put on his *power*, and he asks, "In what sense? She was quite simply overpowered." Richard Ellmann (*Yeats: The Man and the Masks* [London, 1949], 246) says the poem is asking, "Could power and knowledge ever exist together in this world?" Helen Vendler (*Yeats's Vision and the Later Plays* [Cambridge, Mass., 1963], 107) says the poem is asking "whether a special knowledge attaches to the conferred power of artistic creation."

perhaps signals a weakness. Ideally, I think, such an emphatic poem as this is should not end on something that produces uncertainty. Nevertheless, I have to say that when I look long and hard at the poem, the meaning at that point doesn't seem to me unclear.

The two key words in the question are "knowledge" and "power." The god's power has been displayed in the poem. If his knowledge is also there, it must be knowledge of the future he's engendering:

> The broken wall, the burning roof and tower
> And Agamemnon dead.

Did Leda also see into the future at the moment of consummation? That I think is the question the poem asks but doesn't answer.[6] But again (if that is what the question means) it connects the poem with Yeats himself as a victim of time. In old age *he* has had a vision of the future. In another of his favourite dicta, "It is only at the moment of darkness that the owl of Minerva descends." Wisdom arrives too late to be of use.

*The Tower* as a collection (to go back to the beginning) opens with "Sailing to Byzantium." Here the "I" who speaks is not quite the literal Yeats of "The Tower" or "Meditations in Time of Civil War"; it's a mythical Yeats, a persona, but very close indeed to the real man. In marvellously packed lines he evokes the natural world of time and change, of procreation and death, in which he feels himself to be nothing but a scarecrow; he bids that world farewell and prays to be purged of his physical existence in "God's holy fire":

> Consume my heart away; sick with desire
> And fastened to a dying animal
> It knows not what it is; and gather me
> Into the artifice of eternity.

In the final stanza he declares that after purging in the holy fire he will become a golden bird singing to lords and ladies of Byzantium of past, present, and future. Does he mean that after death he will become his poetry? It seems so—except that we all know Yeats believed not only in the soul's immortality but also in strange and various reincarnations. Perhaps he did want to be a golden bird. As so often in Yeats, the statement may seem equivocal. If we lean on it too literally, it will say, "Ease off. I'm only a metaphor." But the moment we lessen our pressure on its meaning it begins again to strut about and put on airs like a *real* statement.

But what stays powerfully with the reader is not the final stanza but

6. In an earlier version of the poem Yeats had the line "Did nothing pass before her in the air?"

those opening images of teeming nature, and then the astonishing force and directness of the self-characterisation: "sick with desire / And fastened to a dying animal." It's an image that makes most confessional poetry of the 1960s look pale.

Immediately after "Sailing to Byzantium" comes the title poem, "The Tower," and it opens with lines that seem to follow directly from the preceding poem:

> O heart, O troubled heart—this caricature,
> Decrepit age that has been tied to me
> As to a dog's tail.

He goes on to assert that his imagination is more "Excited, passionate, fantastical" than ever, and his ear and eye more alert, yet they ("imagination, ear and eye" are repeated) must give up poetry and be content with philosophy—"Choose Plato and Plotinus for a friend."

There is a puzzle in this. If imagination is active and ear and eye alert, why must poetry be given away? In the end it isn't. Plato and Plotinus are sent packing and poetry seems to reassert itself, but why should the question have arisen? This poem was written in Yeats's sixtieth year. He was in reasonably good health (he had in fact thirteen years to live). He was at the height of his fame and of his powers; he was a Nobel Prize winner, an Irish senator, a family man, and (most important) he was writing more authoritatively than ever. So what was the source of this insistence on age and incompetence?

It was undoubtedly connected with sex, perhaps specifically with sexual performance. "Sick with desire" seems to make that clear, as does a letter to Olivia Shakespear in which he says some of the poems of *The Tower* were written in a mood "between spiritual excitement and sexual torture." The torment came, no doubt, partly from a sense of, or a fear of, declining sexual competence, and from the very widely held belief (or perhaps one should say the very common *recognition*) of a link between sexuality and creativity. So when he says he must "Choose Plato and Plotinus for a friend," the word "friend" half-suggests, as it often does in Yeats, "lover."

All this is familiar enough, I suppose, in the history of art and literature. But in the case of Yeats there was the additional recognition of how much he had denied himself in his youth, and how that denial had sprung from a romantic conception of the spiritual bond between himself and Maud Gonne—a bond she had treated with indifference. In the later years of his life his early years of self-imposed celibacy seemed to weigh on him sometimes, as if it had all been a folly and a waste.

In the opening poem of the sequence called "A Man Young and Old"—a poem called "First Love"—the young man believes the woman he loves has "A heart of flesh and blood"; but when he lays his hand on her breast, he finds "a heart of stone." This is reminiscent of the "hearts with one purpose alone" in "Easter 1916" that are "enchanted to a stone"; and it contrasts surprisingly with what Leda experiences, raped by the Swan who is a god, or even an abstract idea, but whose "strange heart" she feels beating. Maud Gonne had become abstract, more idea than woman; conversely, the ideas that had come to Yeats through the mediumship of his wife seemed to possess not merely wisdom, but flesh and blood.

In a letter written at the time these poems were being composed Yeats tells Olivia Shakespear—his mistress of those early years when his passion for Maud was still at its height—that he had come on two early photographs of her (Olivia). He has been struck by her beauty, and by the fact that he took so little of what she offered. And he says, "One looks back to one's youth as to a cup that a mad man dying of thirst left half-tasted."[7] This in turn becomes one of the poems of "A Man Young and Old":

> A crazy man that found a cup,
> When all but dead of thirst,
> Hardly dared to wet his mouth
> Imagining, moon-accursed,
> That another mouthful
> And his beating heart would burst.
> October last I found it too
> But found it dry as bone,
> And for that reason am I crazed
> And my sleep is gone.

"The Tower," as we've seen, begins and ends with personal declarations—part I asking what the aging man is to do with himself, part III making his public/poetic last will and testament and committing his soul to school itself finally in the great traditions of art and literature. In between comes part II, a curious, apparently leisurely, not consistently well-turned perambulation around the countryside of Ballylee—thirteen eight-line stanzas invoking real and mythological characters associated with the region. We meet the aristocratic Mrs. French; the beautiful peasant girl Mary Hynes; the blind poet Raftery who made Mary into his Helen as Yeats did with Maud; the local men who were driven mad by Mary's beauty, or by Raftery's songs of her beauty; then there's the man-

7. *The Letters of W. B. Yeats*, ed. Allan Wade (London, 1954), 721.

at-arms and his troop who once occupied the tower; and finally Hanrahan, Yeats's own fictional creation.

Toward the end of this section the poet calls together the ghosts of these various characters because he has a question to put to them—in fact he has announced in the very first stanza of part II that he is going to ask them something. The question when it comes in stanza 11 is this:

> Did all old men and women, rich and poor,
> Who trod upon these rocks or passed this door,
> Whether in public or in secret rage
> As I do now against old age?

It seems a curiously empty question after such a build-up; and almost at once, without waiting for an answer, Yeats dismisses them all, except Hanrahan:

> Go therefore; but leave Hanrahan,
> For I need all his mighty memories.

And now comes the heart of part II, which makes all the rest of it seem like a beating about the bush, or a strategy of obfuscation—because Hanrahan, the one fictional character, appears to be another of those disguises for Yeats himself. He's addressed as "Old lecher with a love on every wind"; and in the final stanza he's asked:

> Does the imagination dwell the most
> Upon a woman won or woman lost?
> If on the lost, admit you turned aside
> From a great labyrinth out of pride,
> Cowardice, some silly over-subtle thought
> Or anything called conscience once;
> And that if memory recur, the sun's
> Under eclipse and the day blotted out.

This is the real question—the question behind the question—and the answer is clear enough: imagination dwells more on the woman lost than the woman won. Here for the first time—I think for the only time—Yeats sees his failure with Maud as being of his own making. She rejected him, of course. But he accepted the rejection, complied with it, built a mythology around it, made out of it something like a profession and a career. The old man, in the strength and confidence of his maturity, sees the young man's acceptance of defeat as something springing from cowardice, conscience, pride and, he says, as if for a moment he has become Yvor Winters, "silly over-subtle thought." So when memory recurs, it brings darkness, gloom, despondency.

It's not a particularly well-turned stanza. But to my ear it comes in some ways nearer to the feel of truth than almost anything else Yeats wrote on the subject of Maud Gonne. It's an important moment in his poetry—a brave denial of such a large part of the rhetorical and emotional structure of what he had written previously on the subject.

When I first read "The Tower" as a young man (this was in the 1950s, and of course I'm referring to a number of readings), the whole poem seemed to gather in strength toward the final section, and especially toward the marvellous closing lines—"Now shall I make my soul / Compelling it to study," and so on—and I don't think I gave much thought to how Yeats got there. But if, as the present occasion surely requires, I am to apply the kind of rigour that Donald Davie's criticism has taught us to bring to such matters, how can I overlook the fact that Yeats gets there via that final stanza of part II which seems to question the whole Maud-mythology and everything that goes along with it? And doesn't that moment of realism and self-reproach provide at least one measure—a very important one—by which what follows must stand or fall?

Pride, cowardice, and an over-subtlety that he allowed himself to call conscience—these, Yeats acknowledges, more than Maud herself, were what stood in the way; and these in turn permitted the romantic self-denial, the heroic celibacy, the elevation of Maud into an Irish Helen. Now the "Old lecher with a love on every wind," blown about by alternating gusts of exaltation and bitterness, acknowledges the folly of it.

Pride is the first of the faults acknowledged. But in part III it's as if he forgets his moment of truth, or sets it aside. His pride is what he bequeaths to the young; and pride is the first quality of the people he claims as his own:

> Pride like that of the morn
> When the headlong light is loose,
> Or that of the fabulous horn,
> Or that of the sudden shower
> When all streams are dry,
> Or that of the hour
> When the swan must fix his eye
> Upon a fading gleam
> Float out upon a long
> Last glittering reach of stream
> And there sing his last song.

How can any sensitive reader be immune to the beauty of that? But how can I (once I've thought of it) avoid asking in what way pride is *like* early morning light, or *like* the horn of plenty, or *like* a sudden shower of

rain, or *like* the hour when the swan dies? Whatever pride is *like* apart
from itself, it seems to me it's not like any of these things. And of course
the swan there is not a swan at all but W. B. Yeats taking his cue from Zeus
and wearing feathers. The swan singing his last song is the poet writing
his last verses.

Next we turn to his faith, and it's as if the renewal of pride has licensed
a new intellectual extravagance, beyond anything we've seen from Yeats
up to this point:

> And I declare my faith:
> I mock Plotinus' thought
> And cry in Plato's teeth,
> Death and life were not
> Till man made up the whole,
> Made lock, stock and barrel
> Out of his bitter soul,
> Aye, sun and moon and star, all,
> And further add to that
> That, being dead, we rise,
> Dream and so create
> Translunar Paradise.

I've read some pretty flushed defences of those lines. The best is
probably Ellmann's. It's not good enough, Ellmann says, to object that
these lines are "philosophical nonsense." In that way Ellmann contrives
to acknowledge that they *are* "philosophical nonsense" but to insist it
doesn't matter. The lines are, he goes on, "a dramatic cry of defiance
against those who would denigrate man or subject him to abstractions like
death, life, heaven or hell, God, Plotinus's One, Plato's Good or eternal
ideas."[8]

I'm all for rescuing humanity from its own self-terrorising abstractions—including, if you like, God, heaven, and hell. But how are we
rescued from death by the mere assertion that we ourselves invented it? If
for just a moment you can stretch your credulity to the limit and accept
that all that Yeats names—everything in fact—is invented by the human
imagination, how then are the facts of human life altered? If we invented
birth and death, we're still therefore born, and we still die. And if we've
invented something called "Translunar Paradise" (which suggests to me
something like a transcendental fun-park), I'm not sure that means—even
to Yeats—that we *have* it, or *go* there.

8. Richard Ellmann, *The Identity of Yeats* (London, 1954), 225.

Is it possible to see the lines as heroic? I suppose it must be, and that's what they aim to be. If I were in a mood to make an entirely positive summary of the poem, it would go something like this: The "Old lecher," "derided by" age, which is "a sort of battered kettle at the heel," acknowledges that youth was wasted in romantic dreams, refuses to lament, asserts his pride, declares his faith in the poetic imagination and in the Anglo-Irish stock from which he comes, and determines to go forward boldly as a poet, not retreat into philosophy—though he will at the same time school his soul in indifference and so prepare it for death.

Locked up in "The Tower" there is very obviously a modern confessional poem asking to be let out. If it had been, what would it have said? Perhaps that the opening of the gates of sex late in life can lead to an excess of desire, as if to make up for all that has been missed. That with this discovery of appetite come renewed energy and strength. That the suppression of appetite has been a suppression of one's full powers, disguised as sensitivity and scrupulousness. That the loved object could indeed have been won, and thus rendered more real, less abstract, more ordinary, if those powers had been released earlier. Now, released late, they are served by a body that has begun to fail. Age would be less terrible if youth had not been sacrificed to heroic dreams.

Some of that—I think a good deal of it—is in the poem, half-buried, half-uncovered, half-confronted, and then all swept aside by a marvellously theatrical conclusion that revives the dream more forcefully than ever. The sensitive pride of youth is acknowledged and blamed; but then a new, bold, nonchalant, elderly pride is asserted in its place. The folly of youth is admitted, but then a more extravagant folly is celebrated. It's as if Yeats will challenge the facts of life and death by a display of heroic will. I enjoy the challenge. But I also know that the facts of life and death won't be bullied; and I think in this poem Yeats fails to face them. Gesture has replaced thought; or the bold gesture has replaced the timid one. Yeats invokes the blind poets Homer and Raftery, and that's perhaps appropriate. He is blind himself in this poem, because in the end he shuts his eyes.

If by rhetoric in the modern pejorative sense that Yeats himself used we mean an eloquence that is in some degree empty, language in excess of what is being said, then "The Tower" is for me rhetorical, and I prefer "Nineteen Hundred and Nineteen," a less masterful, less seductive poem, but one that does, I think, look bravely at the facts of the world we occupy.

In "Sailing to Byzantium" Yeats prayed to be gathered into "the artifice of eternity" where he would become a golden bird. Eternity was an artifice because, as "The Tower" asserts, it and everything else is created by the mind of man. In both poems Yeats seems to be twisting about in a web of recognition and counter-assertion. The recognition is that death is absolute and that the traditional palliatives are false—invented by the mind of man. The counter-assertion is that it is one of the glories of the human mind to create the reality it desires. Eternity may be an artifice, but that's no reason why Yeats should not enter it singing and become a golden bird. The problem is perhaps the old one of those who send God off the field of play and immediately bring on a substitute. If the imagination becomes God, everything it creates must be real, and in fact there is nothing it doesn't create. That seems to be Yeats's philosophical position—one that stands, I suppose, as an assertion, or rude gesture, against alternative realist philosophies.

The world view presented in the poem "Nineteen Hundred and Nineteen" is very bleak, and it contains no compensating assertions of the power of the poetic imagination, or the heroic will, to make things better. It begins by looking squarely at the fact that the traditional notion of the eternity of art is an illusion.

> Many ingenious lovely things are gone
> That seemed sheer miracle to the multitude.

Even the great Athenian sculptures didn't survive. Nor did the great peace of the nineteenth century, which was thought to have rendered armies merely decorative.

> Now days are dragon-ridden, and the nightmare
> Rides upon sleep.

Later sections of the poem acknowledge that the dreams of youth have not been fulfilled, that an apt image of modern public life is "the weasel's twist, the weasel's tooth," and that mockery is what the time seems most readily and pertinently to call forth. Finally comes an apocalyptic vision of the future, one in accordance with Yeats's idea that our era must soon come to a violent end.

My approval of "Nineteen Hundred and Nineteen" as against "The Tower" doesn't come from a temperamental pessimism or an appetite for large negatives. But this poem, although parts of it draw heavily on the historical overview of *A Vision*, has about it so much less of the Yeatsian bluster and so much more of what one senses to be hard, even harsh, reality. That engagement with realities gives the language more solid work to do. It gives a more compacted poetic texture, a greater linguistic density. What I'm saying here, I think, is not just something about "style." It's something about "philosophy" (in the broadest sense) as well, and how the two interact and express each other. When Yeats allows the realist in himself more room, when he gives a little more attention and credence to Stendhal's perambulating mirror and a little less to the Berkeleyan looking-glass, then there is correspondingly more grit, or salt, and less wind in his style. And perhaps what makes *The Tower* as a whole the marvellous book it is, is not the philosophy, not the heroics, not the vision, but the solid background of Irish place and circumstance that Yeats was too good a poet ever to abandon.

But something else in "Nineteen Hundred and Nineteen" helps to give it a sense of balance and of truth. Section 2 calls up an image of Loie Fuller's Chinese dancers—that memory as an image of the movement of history. What, seen close up, is violence and destruction—days that are dragon-ridden—from the perspective of eternity is a graceful dance. Loie Fuller's dancers also made a dragon, but it was "a floating ribbon of cloth."

> All men are dancers and their tread
> Goes to the barbarous clangour of a gong.

If this is a statement of faith—that there is, after all, some coherence, some pattern, even beauty in what happens in the world at large—it's a faith that is modest in scope and doesn't conflict with the negatives. The clangour of the gong is "barbarous"; nevertheless, the movements are a dance.

The image of the dance brings us finally to "Among School Children," which is one of the great Yeats poems. It stands in much the same relation to "Leda and the Swan" as "A Prayer for my Daughter" does to "The Second Coming"—the personal, even domestic statement as against the impersonal, symbolic one.

I offer two observations: first, that in all but its conclusion this poem is simpler than the commentaries suggest. Its subject—like "Sailing to Byzantium" and "The Tower"—is simply and consistently *age*. Yeats's diary entry for March 14, 1926, reads:

> Topic for poem—School children and the thought that [life] will
> waste them perhaps that no possible life can fulfill our dreams or
> even their teacher's hope. Bring in the old thought that life
> prepares for what never happens.[9]

My second point is that insofar as it's a difficult poem the difficulty

---

9. A. Norman Jeffares, *Commentary on the Collected Poems of W. B. Yeats* (London, 1968), 299.

can't be entirely overcome or explained away. The poem makes a huge and uncharacteristic leap into its final stanza, but that leap makes it a great poem.

The poem is about a visit to a school. Children make the "sixty-year-old smiling public man" more than ever conscious of his age. His image of himself is again the scarecrow, making the children, by shadowy implication, birds—"those dying generations at their song," which he sails away from in "Sailing to Byzantium." Here he tries by smiling to be a *"comfortable* scarecrow." In his mind he has the image of Maud, daughter of the Swan—of Zeus in fact, because he equates her with Helen. Maud's once "Ledaean body" is now wasted like his own, her face

> Hollow of cheek as though it drank the wind
> And took a mess of shadows for its meat.

What mother of one of these children, he wonders, would think it all worthwhile if she could see her child in old age. He thinks of the great philosophers—Plato, Aristotle, Pythagoras. By the time their fame was achieved they were like him, "Old clothes upon old sticks to scare a bird."[10]

So far the poem is elegant, benign, its tone beautifully balanced. It is what Yeats called it—his "curse on old age"—but a mellow, wry, accommodating curse.

But in stanza 7 the complexities set in:

> Both nuns and mothers worship images,
> But those the candles light are not as those
> That animate a mother's reveries,
> But keep a marble or a bronze repose.
> And yet they too break hearts—O Presences
> That passion, piety or affection knows,
> And that all heavenly glory symbolise—
> O self-born mockers of man's enterprise.

"Both nuns and mothers worship images." He's at a Catholic school, being shown around by a nun, so the thought has its feet on the ground of the poem. But what are the images both nuns and mothers worship? To the fond mother the child is not simply itself. It is also an image of what it may become, and in this the child is to the mother what the statue of

---

10. "Here is a fragment of my last curse on old age. It means that even the greatest men are owls, scarecrows, by the time their fame has come." (This is followed by a quotation of a version of stanza 6.) *The Letters of W. B. Yeats,* 719.

Christ or the Virgin is to the nun—a symbol and a focus of hope for the future. And the young lover too once worshipped a "Ledaean body," an image rather than a woman. These worshipped images represent hope. They invoke a future. The notion of "heavenly glory" is only a more grandiose version of the lover's dream of consummation and the mother's dreams for her child. They are "self-born mockers of man's enterprise" because they are trapped in time. The imagined consummations—of religion, of love, of family life—lie always somewhere ahead. Tomorrow never comes. Or as Yeats says in that note sketching the idea for the poem, life prepares us for what never happens. Desire looks forward, and imagination—that imagination he has been celebrating in this book—is its servant. But it is in the present that life is lived; and it's the present that those desires cloud. Life passes in a wishful haze, and we wake—if we wake at all—to find ourselves wise old scarecrows. Once again, "It is only at the hour of darkness that the owl of Minerva descends."

And so we take a leap into the final stanza, which is a sort of visionary resolution:

> Labour is blossoming or dancing where
> The body is not bruised to pleasure soul,
> Nor beauty born out of its own despair,
> Nor blear-eyed wisdom out of midnight oil.
> O chestnut-tree, great-rooted blossomer,
> Are you the leaf, the blossom or the bole?
> O body swayed to music, O brightening glance,
> How can we know the dancer from the dance?

Here labour is no longer *hard* labour; it blossoms or it dances "naturally," effortlessly. Here beauty and wisdom occur without pain or effort. And the two images of this marvellous ease and naturalness are the chestnut tree and the dancer. The tree doesn't imagine a future, and neither does the dancer. One blossoms, the other dances, and both are integrated, whole, unified, and beautiful.

Keats says somewhere (also using the image of a tree): "If poetry come not as naturally as the leaves to the tree it might as well not come at all." That Zen-ish attitude to poetic composition is quite alien to the Yeatsian deliberation and labour; yet here at the end of "Among School Children" Yeats seems to celebrate a similar notion of natural, unforced, easeful flowering or burgeoning. In fact it seems to me that the poem by a kind of inner logic has forced Yeats to reverse the direction of thought that is characteristic of most of the poems of *The Tower.* Instead of aspiring beyond the world toward "Translunar Paradise" or some new incarnation, aspiring to leave the world of "dying generations" to become a golden bird singing in an immortal city, Yeats finds his images of perfection—dancer and tree—in the mortal world and in nature.

I say the poem forced him to this because if you think about it, how could it be otherwise, given the stanzas that go before? Byzantium and the golden bird of art are only Yeatsian variants of those images that nuns, lovers, and mothers worship. They too are "self-born mockers of man's enterprise." The extraordinary thing is that, after a long hesitation in the process of composition, Yeats had the courage to follow that logic and to make what seems like a blind leap into the final stanza—a leap that, at least philosophically, very nearly cancels out all the poems that go before; and it's the courage of that leap that produces the curious exaltation in the closing lines. The way out of the trap of time is neither backward into memory nor forward into desire. It is in the moment itself. It is in being, not in becoming.

When I stand back from what I've been saying about these poems, the implications are something like this: I judge the poems as *poems*. That's to say I'm a person expert in a poetic tradition, and through that, in language—and to the best of my ability—I judge the poem as a linguistic event. But strengths and weaknesses in language reveal something that can be expressed in terms of "philosophy" or of a world view. What I discover in *The Tower* is, I think, that the poems are in some degree at war with the poet. They resist some of the things he asks them to do. Another way of putting this is to say that the poet in Yeats is at war with the philosopher, or that the language of poetry contradicts the language of philosophy. Or again, that some of the things Yeats wants to believe don't stand up when put to the test of poetic language. He can force them through in rhetorical gusts; but when the cloud clears, the world is unchanged. He sees that it's unchanged, and his language reflects what he sees. The report of Stendhal's mirror conflicts with that of Berkeley's looking-glass. Yeats the man might have preferred Berkeley and the freedom to dream; but Stendhal's mirror wouldn't go away. It went on dawdling along its lane, showing him what he called "this pragmatical, preposterous pig of a world," and because of that the realist he disliked so much finds in the best of his poems an equal voice, or even at times gets the upper hand.

# Some Presences on the Scene:
# A Vista of Postwar Poetry

*Charles Tomlinson*

B Y "SOME presences on the scene," I wish to indicate a handful of writers who, impinging on our postwar literary world, offered varying possibilities to the poet. They made something new available, or they made something old that we had forgotten about, re-available. The people I shall be discussing are all practitioners, though besides poems, some of them wrote criticism. I want to see how both their poems and their critical effort worked against the determinism of circumstances as we emerged, or sought to emerge, from a period of chaos, and as we sought to restabilize what Eliot had once called "the mind of Europe." That Donald Davie is one of these presences and that others should have been enthusiasms he and I have shared, would seem, perhaps, appropriate to the present occasion.

Some of my presences are Americans whom we did not really learn about until well after the war—Yvor Winters, William Carlos Williams, and George Oppen. For, after 1945, London was no longer the unchallenged literary capital of the English-speaking world, and English poets were to become far more attuned than previously to what was going on in New York and in California. One of my climactic moments is 1966— the year when Basil Bunting published *Briggflatts*, perhaps the most successfully ambitious poem of some length since *Four Quartets*. Much, of course, has happened since then, but a great deal of it will not go on reverberating into the future for as long as Bunting's poem, though the publication of George Oppen's *Of Being Numerous* a year later and of his *Collected Poems* in 1972 still leaves us a lot to think about. Indeed, those two books might well prove a good antidote to the excessive attention we have given to greatly gifted but showier and more ego-bound figures like John Berryman and Robert Lowell. But that is to anticipate a theme to which I shall be returning later.

"Presences on the scene" (it will soon be obvious) implies that those presences, and the qualities they stand for, were in some measure a condition for the release of my own poetry. *Release* as against blockage. By 1945, one of the principal voices that threatened to block the release of the individual voice among younger poets was that of Dylan Thomas. Not all younger poets, of course. You could, even after that date, if you were like the youthful Ted Hughes, homogenize Thomas into a high rhetoric of your own, as you reflected of man that

> Though he bends to be blent in prayer, how
>     loud and above what
> Furious spaces of fire do the distracting devils
> Orgy and hosannah, under what wilderness
> Of black silent waters weep.

If you were not Ted Hughes and were prone to worry about the use of words like "furious"—sure to conjure up a whole supporting cast of alliterative intensifiers—or if verbs like "orgy" and "hosannah" seemed unlikely vessels to *contain* what you wanted to say, you would need to go on listening to the healthful silence a little longer. Such diction implies a certain tone of reading voice, and with a writer lacking Hughes's craggy yet nervous manner of reading, tone could easily degenerate into the actorish flummery of Dylan of the golden voice—a voice people were always wanting to play you their records of, and a voice that was sure to be delivering itself on the Third Programme when poetry was on the air, the listeners' mental purchase blurring into the waves of sound:

> And from the windy west came two gunned Gabriel,
> From Jesu's sleeve trumped up the king of spots . . .
> Rose my Byzantine Adam in the night . . .
> By waste seas where the white bear quoted Virgil
> And sirens singing from our lady's sea-straw. . . .

If it was manners you wanted and not mannerisms, this sort of thing wasn't going to take you far. If it was a certain resistance in words that seemed to offer you a medium in which you could (as it were) sculpt your meaning, this playing with words as if they were plasticine might seem regressive. On the one hand, you could hear in the puns, echoes of the night world of Joyce's *Finnegans Wake*, on the other a sort of prophetic overplus always pretending to be saying a little more than it could actually articulate and, as here, not quite sure of the degree of seriousness that was intended. Thomas, of course, was a highly talented poet and could write far more compellingly than this, but his more loosely violent rhetoric, with European chaos and actual war as its background, gave the excuse to less expert practitioners to posture as J. F. Hendry did:

Cast in a dice of bones I see the geese of Europe
Gabble a skeleton jigsaw and their haltered anger
Scream a shark-teeth frost through splintering
    earth and lips.

When in 1952 Donald Davie published his *Purity of Diction in English Verse*, one knew that the *rappel à l'ordre* had come and that part of what he had to say was an indictment of a decade and more of poetic bad manners of this kind. Davie is the first of my positive presences. His book pressed home the realisation that poetry need not be merely a string of metaphors and that the poetic habits of a number of neglected Augustans—Goldsmith, Cowper, Langhorne, Charles Wesley, and the hymn writers—had lessons for us today in the 1950s. They might help the practitioner to a fuller consciousness of the way poetry could define with accuracy, could denote as well as connote, could work as much by a honed clarity of diction as by attempting to trail clouds of metaphorical glory.

The significant critics—for the poets, at any rate—are those who, in Arnold's phrase, assist in making "an intellectual situation of which the creative power can profitably avail itself." Suppose one tries to measure Davie's impact on the fifties, in this respect, with the earlier impact of another poet-critic, namely, T. S. Eliot. Eliot reopened negotiations with the English seventeenth century, particularly with the metaphysical poets and also with the dramatists' way of writing, so that Webster, Tourneur, and Middleton could be models for his own and other poets' work. Now when Davie came on the scene, there was reason for feeling that Eliot's revaluation of the seventeenth century had, to some extent, run its course, that metaphorical modes of writing based on a stage rhetoric had indeed entered a phase of decadence. Davie's own reopening of negotiations with the eighteenth century, as in Eliot's case, grew out of his practice as a poet. Thus his interest in diction before metaphor, or diction as counterbalance to metaphor, was born of an effort at establishing poetic clarity, and this effort often focussed on a very specific and practical attention to certain words. Hence Davie's illuminating example in *Purity of Diction* of Sir John Denham's lines on Cowley, lines that compliment Cowley on his having learned from classical literature and that make their point largely through diction:

Horace's wit and Virgil's state
He did not steal, but emulate!
And when he would like them appear,
Their garb, but not their cloaths, did wear.

Davie comments on this example: "It had not occurred to the reader that the distinction between 'garb' and 'clothes' was so fine yet so definite." This kind of distinction, which is to be found time and again in certain Augustan poets, was one that recommended itself to Davie as both critic and poet. In his first pamphlet of verse, published by Fantasy Press in 1954, appears a poem called "At Knaresborough." Here, the poet meets someone—a fellow Yorkshireman—who guesses from his accent that he also comes from Yorkshire. The man wants to push the poet into a rather false kind of intimacy, and the latter resists that immersion in those exaggerated feelings prompted by shared origins:

> 'Broad acres, sir.' You hear them in my talk,
> As tell-tale as a pigment in the skin.
> Vowels as broad as all the plain of York
> Proclaim me of this country and your kin.
>
> And, gratified to have your guess endorsed,
> You warm to me. I thaw, and am approved.
> But, to be frank, the sentiment is forced,
> When I pretend, for your sake, to be moved.
>
> To feel so little, when his sympathies
> Would be so much engaged (he would have said).
> Surprised the poet too. But there it is,
> The heart is not to be solicited.
>
> Believe me, sir, I only ply my trade,
> Which is to know when I am played upon.
> You might have moved, you never shall persuade.
> You grow too warm. I must be moving on.

This poem is not dense in metaphor, though what metaphors there are take point from the clean, unforced diction:

> You warm to me. I thaw, and am approved.

In

> You might have moved, you never shall persuade.
> You grow too warm. I must be moving on.

there is a tough and plain distinction between "being moved" and "moving on." After that fine line "The heart is not to be solicited" (it is prostitutes who solicit feeling) comes the declaration

> Believe me, sir, I only ply my trade,
> Which is to know when I am played upon.

Poets are vulgarly supposed to be "creatures of feeling." And here is Davie refusing to be merely a creature of feeling. His trade, unlike the prostitute's, is both to feel and to discriminate feeling. It was the discrimination part that seemed particularly tonic in the poetic climate of the early fifties. Here was an oeuvre that was to prove in its growth and extent to be at once a defence of poetry and a defence of reason.

"A defence of reason." That phrase brings to mind the title of a book Davie had certainly read before writing *Purity of Diction—In Defense of Reason* by Yvor Winters. Winters is the second presence on my scene and an American one. In 1950 he inscribed a copy of his selected poems, *The Giant Weapon*, for Davie, and through Davie's early work, both poetic and critical, Winters is filtered for the first time into the British atmosphere, although his book *In Defense of Reason* had appeared in America in 1947 and parts of it ten years earlier.

I first read this book in 1953, a year after the publication of *Purity of Diction* and the very year of Thomas's death. That scenario of self-destruction in which Thomas was *our* principal protagonist found a curious parallel in Winters's pages in the suicide of his friend, the poet Hart Crane. The readiness of American poets to kill themselves or to court self-destruction—Crane, Berryman, Roethke, Plath, Sexton, Jarrell, Delmore Schwartz, Lowell—is a subject that had exercised Winters's mind in the wake of Crane's death. For this death seemed to him to confirm his belief that the surrender to impulse and the divine right of self-expression—even taking it as far as self-immolation—were attitudes not only firmly embedded in American culture, but given philosophical sanction (so he thought) in the work of Emerson. And Winters argued, rightly or wrongly, that what he took to be the moral determinism of writers like Emerson (and Poe, Whitman, and Henry Adams were for him in the same boat) was a continuing component of American modernism, of that modernist fragmentation of form exemplified by Pound and Eliot and of which Eliot's *Waste Land* was the principal specimen. This was heady stuff to come across in 1953. I have, of course, overcompressed Winters's arguments, and you will hardly take as proven that T. S. Eliot was an exponent of the divine right of self-expression. Winters, however, virtually argues that he was, and that the despair of *The Waste Land* represented precisely the self-expression that has run out of steam and, as in Crane's case, could easily veer toward suicide. Be that as it may, I have never been able to feel that Winters was altogether wrong about certain features of Eliot's outlook. When, in *In Defense of Reason*, he claims that "Eliot's position is one of unmitigated determinism," the passage he has in mind is the following from *After Strange Gods*. Eliot writes there:

> No sensible author, in the midst of something that he is trying to write, can stop to consider whether it is going to be romantic or the opposite. At the moment when one writes, one is what one is, and the damage of a lifetime, and of having been born into an unsettled society, cannot be repaired at the moment of composition.

Winters replies to this with Johnsonian trenchancy. First he summarises: "At the moment when one writes, one is what one is: one has, in other words no power over that moment; one must surrender to one's feelings and one's habits at that moment if one is to achieve sincerity." And now comes the Johnsonian bit:

> Yet at what point in a poet's career does this become true? If it were true at the age of sixteen, the poet would develop but little beyond that age; and if the poet at the age of sixteen is to be encouraged to improve his literary habits, why should not the poet at the age of forty-six? Obviously one will not change one's literary habits between moments of composition; one will change them if at all in writing. And if one's conversion to Catholicism and to classicism is worth a flourish of the pen, it is worth risking a few years of unsatisfactory composition in order to form new habits. I am reasonably certain that both Aquinas and Aristotle are on my side in this matter. Eliot's position is one of unmitigated determinism.

When I say this was heady stuff to come across in 1953, I mean that it forced one to think and it helped one, not ultimately to unseat T. S. Eliot, but to counter attitudes that had seeped into literary culture by that date. I had on my shelves an anthology containing an essay by a then famous poetry reviewer, G. S. Fraser, a quite powerful maker of reputations and promulgator of attitudes. It was entitled "Apocalypse in Poetry" and contained the following plangent, almost winsome expression of "unmitigated determinism." "The obscurity of our poetry," wrote Fraser, "its air of something desperately snatched from a dream or woven round a chime of words are the results not of disintegration in ourselves, but in society." Winters taught one how to reply to that sort of thing. He also wrote brilliantly about the power of the short poem and led one with new insight to Ben Jonson, Fulke Greville, Ralegh, Gascoigne, Paul Valéry. There were few critics who could write as challengingly as he did when he said things like, "A race that has lost the capacity to handle abstractions with discretion and dignity may do well to confine itself to sensory impressions, but our ancestors were more fortunate, and we ought to labor to regain what we have lost." So much for Winters the critic.

What of Winters the poet? His presence showed itself, I think, in Davie's poetry, a point not touched on in the recent book of essays edited by George Dekker, *Donald Davie and the Responsibilities of Literature* (1983). Winters's influence carried over into Davie's often taut stanza patterns at that phase in the fifties. To read Winters's verse then—and Davie had handed on to me his copy of *The Giant Weapon*—was to experience the sense of an often tragic nobility not readily found in much contemporary verse. I recall particularly his "John Sutter," that narrative of the ruination of the powerful Sutter by the Californian gold-rush when his lands were overrun and his patriarchy overthrown:

> I was the patriarch of the shining land,
> Of the blond summer and metallic grain;
> Men vanished at the motion of my hand,
> And when I beckoned they would come again.
>
> The earth grew dense with grain at my desire;
> The shade was deepened at the springs and streams;
> Moving in dust that clung like pillared fire,
> The gathering herds grew heavy in my dreams.
>
> Across the mountains, naked from the heights,
> Down to the valley broken settlers came,
> And in my houses feasted through the nights,
> Rebuilt their sinews and assumed a name.
>
> In my clear rivers my own men discerned
> The motive for the ruin and the crime—
> Gold heavier than earth, a wealth unearned,
> Loot, for two decades, from the heart of Time. . . .
>
> With knives they dug the metal out of stone;
> Turned rivers back, for gold thro' ages piled,
> Drove knives to hearts, and faced the gold alone;
> Valley and river ruined and reviled;
>
> Reviled and ruined me, my servants slew,
> Strangled him from the figtree by my door.
> When they had done what fury bade them do,
> I was a cursing beggar, stripped and sore.
>
> What end impersonal, what breathless age,
> Incontinent of quiet and of years,
> What calm catastrophe will yet assuage
> This final drouth of penitential tears?

Davie—if I am correct in seeing the influence of Winters in his earlier work—was surely instinctively right to direct his own tone more to the conversational end of the poetic gamut. Winters, at a time when it was growing increasingly usual for poets to come on with their doublets all unbraced, suggested other and more dignified possibilities. All the same, a prolonged exposure to Winters's verse—and the constriction one hears in some of his own pupils points the danger—does perhaps lead one to feel what Hopkins felt about Tennyson, that there is a deal of Parnassian in him. Not for nothing was Winters a translator of Leconte de Lisle.

At about the same period when I was reading *The Giant Weapon*, I came upon the poetry of Keith Douglas. The first I'd known of it was an extremely intelligent review of the posthumous *Collected Poems* of this young poet, dead in the war, by Ronald Bottrall in *The New Statesman* for October 13, 1951, and a quotation from that review stayed with me a long time. This quotation caused me to sense that, although Winters was a maturer poet than Douglas ever had survived to become, you could be as formally exact as Winters but more supple and still draw on the body of traditional verse Winters set such store by. The poem in Bottrall's review was called "Time Eating," and the passage he quoted went like this:

> But as he makes he eats; the very part
> where he began, even the elusive heart,
> Time's ruminative tongue will wash
> and slow juice masticate all flesh.
>
> That volatile huge intestine holds
> material and abstract in its folds:
> thought and ambition melt and even the world
> will alter, in that catholic belly curled.

Douglas's way of writing about the war was the opposite of Hendry's "Cast in a dice of bones I see the geese of Europe / Gabble a skeleton jigsaw . . . " where the attempt to be apocalyptic, with its slackly literary rhetoric, comes between the writer and any possibility of either taking possession of the experience or being possessed by it. You feel that Douglas's use of words is marvellously adequate to his experience and to measuring it, that his metaphors and his irony are turned toward the definition of that experience and not toward any self-congratulatory expression of righteous indignation, or any show of personality that would excite the reader into feeling with the writer some ennobling palpitation of which they might *both* be proud. On the contrary:

> Three weeks gone and the combatants gone,
> returning over the nightmare ground
> we found the place again, and found
> the soldier sprawling in the sun. . . .
>
> Look. Here in the gunpit spoil
> the dishonoured picture of his girl

who has put: *Steffi. Vergissmeinnicht*
in a copybook gothic script.

We see him almost with content,
abased, and seeming to have paid
and mocked at by his own equipment
that's hard and good when he's decayed.

But she would weep to see to-day
how on his skin the swart flies move;
the dust upon the paper eye
and the burst stomach like a cave.

For here the lover and killer are mingled
who had one body and one heart.
And death who had the soldier singled
has done the lover mortal hurt.

In a fine "Homage to Keith Douglas" (*Stand*, vol. 6, no.4, 1964-5), Geoffrey Hill takes issue with the way Wilfred Owen's "Anthem for Doomed Youth" slides off the thing being written about into an over-gorgeous rhetoric. "The poetry," he says, "applies a balm of generalised sorrow at a point where the particulars of experience should outsmart that kind of consolation." And Hill says of this sort of art that its "artifice is only-too-adequate to engulf purpose," contrasting it with Douglas's refusal of a rhetoric of generalised sorrow and his particular sense "of the unique and alien existence of a man destined for, or engaged in battle."

Hill's phrase about a certain kind of artifice being "only-too-adequate to engulf purpose" supplies me with my next transition. Hill's phrase recalls something that the American poet William Carlos Williams said on an earlier occasion: "The goal of writing is to keep a beleaguered line of understanding which has movement from breaking down and becoming a hole into which we sink decoratively to rest." Williams's diction and his avoidance of "artifice . . . only-too-adequate to engulf purpose" resulted during the sixties in a renovated sense of how nakedly poetry can declare itself. The presence of Williams was quite slow in making itself felt. He had been at work since the beginning of the century, but it wasn't until 1963, the year of his death, that he finally found a British publisher.

From the sixties up to the early seventies there ensued a marvellous phase for English poets and English readers to get a fuller measure of what had been going on in the Williamsite camp, opposed in so many ways, as it was, to the American modernist we had *all* been taught to respect, namely, T. S. Eliot. This phase of a new awareness of Williams's side of American poetry was made possible here by the imaginative publishing of MacGibbon and Kee, Fulcrum Press, Calder and Boyars, Cape Goliard, and Centaur Press. Between 1963 and 1967 we got most of Williams's available poetry in somewhat higgledy-piggledy order, the *Collected Later Poems* coming two full years before the *Collected Earlier Poems.*

Prior to Williams and in some ways dependent on him, Charles Olson's *The Maximus Poems* had slipped through in 1961. The year 1965 saw Robert Creeley's *Poems 1950–1965* and also Ed Dorn's *Geography.* In 1972, the impetus already slackening, Fulcrum brought out a scrappy but welcome *Collected Poems* of George Oppen—three years before the New Directions *Collected* appeared in New York. It is my intention not to offer a hasty comment on each of these volumes, but to register them—there were many others—as a composite presence and evidence of a time when a particular kind of American poetry seemed to have altered the specific gravity of the literary atmosphere in England. The immediate result, of course, was the usual derivativeness that follows the introduction of any fresh literary mode, and for a time, we got a lot of breathless imitations of Williams and Creeley, all innocence and hurry.

On a more intelligent level, a dramatic confrontation of literary modes had already appeared in Thom Gunn's *My Sad Captains* of 1961. Gunn, always an elaborately formal poet, had gone on to study under Yvor Winters at Stanford University and to be confirmed, one might have supposed, in the use of ever more stringently traditional forms. But, no: *My Sad Captains* is split into two distinct rhetorics; half the book is in regularly rhyming stanzas, half in a diction and a disposition of sentences broken irregularly across the line endings owing much to Williams.

What was it that Williams brought belatedly to English poetry, often through poems he had written in the twenties and thirties but only now to be got at and read? One was surprised, I suppose, at the way Williams could reduce the gap between direct statement and poetic statement, and how in the best poems—for Williams is a very uneven writer—intense personal excitement can be conveyed without heavyweight expressionist insistence, the poet's personality lost (as it were) in its object. It is as if Williams had learned to fit his words accurately to the moment-by-moment progress of the happening he was a part of—a part of, rather than master of, as a more rigid formal approach might have implied:

> I must tell you
> this young tree
> whose round and firm trunk
> between the wet

pavement and the gutter
(where water
is trickling) rises
bodily

into the air with
one undulant
thrust half its height—
and then

dividing and waning
sending out
young branches on
all sides—

hung with cocoons
it thins
till nothing is left of it
but two

eccentric knotted
twigs
bending forward
hornlike at the top

If Williams's lineation, as in "Young Sycamore," gives you the shapely
graph of an experience, his asymmetrical movement like the panning of
some extraordinarily sympathetic movie camera can be true to the heterogeneity and the detritus of the American scene.

Morning

on the hill is cool! Even the dead
grass stems that start with the wind along
the crude board fence are less than harsh.

—a broken fringe of wooden and brick fronts
above the city, fading out,
beyond the watertank on stilts,
an isolated house or two here and there,
into bare fields. . . .
                         —Firewood, all lengths

and qualities behind patched
outhouses. Uses for ashes.
And a church spire sketched on the sky,
of sheet-metal and open beams, to resemble
a church spire— . . .

There is more art in this than meets the eye, and it has taken longer than one would have thought possible to meet the English eye. My generation was ill-prepared for it. We at first put up a resistance of the kind that, for a time, kept Americans like Lowell at a distance from Williams. In a sympathetic essay of 1961, "William Carlos Williams," Lowell writes, "My own group, that of Tate and Ransom, was all for the high discipline, for putting on the full armor of the past," and he goes on to concede,

> That time is gone, and now young poets are perhaps more conscious of the burden and hardening of this old formalism. Too many poems have been written to rule. They show off their author's efforts and mind, but little more. . . . And once more, Dr. Williams is a model and liberator.

You see Lowell himself, perhaps prompted by Williams and especially by Williams's poems on his parents, *Adam* and *Eve*, taking off the "full armor of the past" in *Life Studies*, published by Faber here in 1959.

Lowell, and American poets younger than Lowell, saw in Williams a liberator, as he says. Yet one must add to this the fact that Williams, as much as Tate and Ransom, but in a quite different way, stood also for poetic discipline. This had always been so, but particularly during the 1930s when Williams was associated with a group of poets in New York who came to be called the objectivists—a group that also included Louis Zukofsky, George Oppen, and the Englishman Basil Bunting. Oppen— and he is another of my presences who began to impinge on the English scene in the late sixties—has this much in common with Williams. They both adhered to the anti-rhetorical discipline that Ezra Pound had recommended to the Imagists:

> Direct treatment of the "thing" whether subjective or objective. . . . Use either no ornament or good ornament. . . . Don't chop your stuff up into separate iambs. Don't make each line stop dead at the end, and then begin every next line with a heave.

All this had been good enough advice in its day, but the objectivists wanted a verse less haphazard and loose than that free verse into which, according to Williams's account, Imagism "had dribbled off." Williams began to talk of a poem as "a machine made with words." That stress on a constructed object went together with a trust in the primacy of perception—Oppen said that the strength of Imagism had been "its demand that one actually *look*." The direction of the discipline is once more the pull against "artifice . . . only-too-adequate to engulf purpose," as Hill puts it, toward what one is actually perceiving. So in this respect, the examples of

Williams and Oppen are not just liberating; they enjoin upon the poet a discipline, away from self-consciousness, that is extremely demanding. In Oppen's poetry there is a deliberate verbal asceticism more radical than that of Williams. Indeed, it took Oppen another twenty-five years from his 1930s beginnings to perfect his mature style. In 1934 we get his *Discrete Series*, then we hear nothing until *The Materials* of 1962. It is ten years later that he publishes a collection for the first time in England. Only during the sixties did we begin to put together the history of what objectivism had been, and a few of us came to think that from that moment in the 1930s something had emerged which only now was fully revealing itself. It was to achieve perhaps its richest English embodiment in Bunting's *Briggflatts* of 1966. But first Oppen, whose rapidly dwindling private fortune had created the Objectivist Press and made possible the publication in the thirties of Williams's first *Collected Poems* and of *An "Objectivists" Anthology*.

I first picked up Oppen's 1962 volume, *The Materials*, from a pile of books of indifferent poems sent for review. The effect was instantaneous:

### Workman

Leaving the house each dawn I see the hawk
Flagrant over the driveway. In his claws
That dot, that comma
Is the broken animal: the dangling small beast knows
The burden that he is: he has touched
The hawk's drab feathers. But the carpenter's is a culture
Of fitting, of firm dimensions,
Of post and lintel. Quietly the roof lies
That the carpenter has finished. The sea birds circle
The beaches and cry in their own way,
The innumerable sea birds, their beaks and their wings
Over the beaches and the sea's glitter.

This swept world, this confrontation between predatory violence and measure, between life in the raw and art, were presented in poem after poem. The poems involve themselves in the struggle with no backward glance at the artist's personality. The self and its shows are held at a distance: the demands of the living moment on the self occupy Oppen's attention:

### Travelogue

But no screen would show
The light, the volume
Of the moment, or our decisions

In the dugouts, roaring
Downstream with the mud and rainfalls to emergencies
Of village skills and the aboriginal flash

Of handsome paddles among the bright rocks
And channels of the savage country.

Oppen's is a world of delimiting place—beaches, sea, rocks, New York streets. The mind will negotiate with those places and with the situations of history, the depression years, the Second World War, the advent of the bomb. But there is no transcendence:

The innumerable sea birds, their beaks and their wings
Over the beaches and the sea's glitter.

That is as high as we get above our world. There are to be no Eliotic moments out of time. For Oppen, experience is never as with Eliot the interpenetration of the timeless with time. He told me once that he guessed he was a Christian and added, "But with all the heresies." His way at all events was never the mystic's way—the break through "out of time."

Eliot was a poet who counted for much and weighed heavily on my generation. He had long provided an irritant for his fellow Americans. Winters rejected his philosophy of composition. Crane, Stevens, Williams, and Oppen sensed that the success of *The Waste Land* had both stolen their readership and pulled their imaginative territory from under their feet by suggesting that it was *all* a waste land and that only a religious transcendence could give it meaning. So beginning in the New York of the thirties and its very unpromisingness as a soil for poetry, Oppen continued into the sixties and seventies with long poems of meditation that quite consciously sought to face and outface the waste-land experience. So when I say that Eliot counted for much and weighed heavily on my generation, here was one of the attractions of Oppen's work—the typist might not, as in *The Waste Land*, be coming home to an evening of squalid sexual encounter after all; she might be coming home hopeful from her first job in a city grown beautiful under its evening lights:

Phyllis—not neo-classic,
The girl's name is Phyllis—

Coming home from the first job
On the bus in the bare civic interior
Among those people, the small doors
Opening on the night at the curb
Her heart, she told me, suddenly tight with happiness—

> So small a picture,
> A spot of light on the curb, it cannot demean us. . . .

I suppose that, at any given moment of our lives, it is our awareness of contending possibilities that keeps us on our toes. Almost simultaneously with my discovery of Williams and Oppen, I became aware—not altogether consciously at first, but in the way one becomes aware of a vitamin deficiency in one's body—of a certain parsimoniousness toward rhyme in my own work. This, no doubt, was because, like Williams and Oppen, I had my ear on other things. What concerned Williams was the impetus he could get out of "the elements and minims of language" (as Olson called them), out of the syllabic components of verse rather than the clinch and closure of end rhyme. Oppen, too, was drawing attention to the bare architecture of line against line, even warning us of the irrelevance of past art—and, implicitly, rhyme along with it—to present purposes. Learning but also resisting, I found that the work of a very different type of poet—a poet I'd been reading, at Donald Davie's instigation, since the mid-fifties—was now increasingly coming to occupy the forefront of my mind. This was the Irishman Austin Clarke. He was a far cry from objectivists like Williams and Oppen, though less of a far cry from another of the objectivist group, namely, Basil Bunting. He, too, was an intricate and copious rhymer. But first Clarke.

When, a few years ago, Conor Cruise O'Brien declared Seamus Heaney "the most important Irish poet since Yeats," one had the feeling that this handy tag would result in other important Irish poets since Yeats being shunted out of sight. This, I believe, has happened in the case of Clarke. The years 1955 and 1957 saw the publication of two of his strongest books, *Ancient Lights* and *Too Great a Vine*. They became available once more, with earlier work from the late twenties and the thirties that had long been invisible, when Oxford University Press brought out a volume with the misleading title of *Later Poems* in 1961. The splendid *Collected Poems* of 1974 seems to have sunk from sight. *Too Great a Vine* contained a major autobiographical poem, "The Loss of Strength," besides some shorter, often bitter, anticlerical pieces on Irish grievances like "St. Christopher." St. Christopher, it will be remembered, carries a child across a river ford, a burden that, getting heavier and heavier, turns out to be Christ. Here is Clarke's blasphemous variant on the story:

> Child that his strength upbore,
> Knotted as tree trunks, i'the spate,
> Became a giant whose weight
> Unearthed the river from shore

Till saint's bones were a-crack.
Fabulist, can an ill state
Like ours, carry so great
A Church upon its back?

That succession of rhymes from "spate" and "weight" to "state" underlined by "great" awakes the reader to the fact that "state" can be at one and
the same time a political entity and a condition of health. The sound
patterns are even more densely compelling in those earlier poems where
Clarke seeks to reproduce the effect in English of the inner rhymes of old
Irish poetry. In the second stanza of "The Confession of Queen Gormlai,"
the queen recalls her former life, and Clarke in his evocation of that life is
being as intricate as Celtic manuscript-illumination and bringing over into
English, equivalents for Celtic rhyming patterns. This poem is taking
place when the Irish are still fighting the Ostmen, the Vikings, who in the
ninth century founded Dublin, and the passage I have in mind runs as
follows:

With jewels and enamel
Men hammer in black gold,
In halls where feast was trampled
And camps the battle-axe
Had lit, I wore the crimson
My women worked in pattern;
And heard such flattering words,
That I bit to the kernel.

Throughout that passage one has an extraordinary echoic effect in the
rhymes—the e-l sounds and the e-r sounds lacing it all together, the e-l of
"jewels" taken up by the e-l of "enamel," "enamel" itself carried on into
"hammer," the second syllable of "enamel" rhyming, that is, with the first
of "hammer":

With jewels and enamel
Men hammer in black gold,
In halls where feast was trampled
And camps the battle-axe
Had lit. . . .

"Trampled" echoes back to "hammer"; the e-l sound in "trampled" comes
out again in "battle," the bat in "battle" is handed on next through
"pattern" and "flattering," and e-r and e-l weave on through these and
other words in ways that yield themselves to the ear only by meditative
and relished reading.

The lacing-together effect I mentioned in Clarke is something also to be found in Basil Bunting, and both of them imaginatively recur to an era famous for the interwoven patterns of manuscript-illumination. Bunting instances the Lindesfarne Codex (now in the British Museum) and tries to rival its rich visual patterns in sound. Clarke and Bunting are always exploring the sense of an encircling, woven, and plaited reality—in both images and rhyme. Christopher Ricks has commented on this aspect of Clarke in the Dolmen Press *A Tribute to Austin Clarke* of May 1966:

> The delicate and dancing interlacings, the love-knots, are explicitly there in Clarke's poems, 'The silver knots of sleep', 'Chaining and unchaining', 'Curl of her hair, in cluster and ringlet', 'where hands are joined', 'Pleasure is in the round'. Such chains can be affectionately mocked, as in the charming riddling periphrasis for cycling: 'I rode the plain with chain that freed me.'

Clarke is making English verse with an Irish accent, Basil Bunting with a Northumbrian accent. In *Briggflatts* (1966) Bunting sees the twinings of manuscript-illumination as being comparable with the twinings of voices in a madrigal and he hears the Northumbrian river, Rawthey, singing that madrigal as it flows over its pebbles, and the bull in the poem sings (or bellows) a descant to this imagined music:

> Brag, sweet tenor bull
> descant on Rawthey's madrigal
> each pebble its part
> for the fells' late spring.
> Dance tiptoe, bull,
> black against may.
> Ridiculous and lovely
> chase hurdling shadows
> morning into noon.
> May on the bull's hide
> and through the dale
> furrows fill with may,
> paving the slowworm's way.
>
> A mason times his mallet
> to a lark's twitter,
> listening while the marble rests,
> lays his rule
> at a letter's edge,
> fingertips checking,
> till the stone spells a name

naming none,
a man abolished.
Painful lark, labouring to rise!
The solemn mallet says:
In the grave's slot
he lies. We rot.

Decay thrusts the blade,
wheat stands in excrement
trembling. Rawthey trembles.
Tongue stumbles, ears err
for fear of spring. . . .

The best comment I know on this opening of *Briggflatts* comes from a review of the book by Hugh Kenner in *The National Review* for October 31, 1967:

> 'Brag, sweet tenor bull. . . . ' Have those four words ever kept company before? Or any two of them, except perhaps 'sweet tenor'? *Brag, sweet tenor bull.* Five vowel sounds, sharply distinct to the ear because sharp consonants cut syllables. . . .
>
> The short harsh words (have thirty pages ever exhibited so many monosyllables?) are a stark speech reaching back to Eric Bloodaxe; lovingly heard, lovingly set into lines ('laying the tune frankly on the air'), they make a wiry texture of sound, utterly new, that comes with the authority of some lost tradition.
>
> > *Decay thrusts the blade,*
> > *wheat stands in excrement*
> > *trembling. Rawthey trembles.*
> > *Tongue stumbles, ears err*
> > *for fear of spring. . . .*
>
> We are meant to discriminate the sound of four monosyllables, 'ears err for fear,' hear them bracketed by assonantal 'tongue' and 'spring,' and trace the sound of the interposed 'stumbles' back through 'trembles' and 'trembling' to a root in the terminal syllable of 'excrement.' We are meant, that is, to pay attention to the aural identities of simple words, of many such words at once. The patterning of sound is a homage to the words, an affection for the words, an eliciting of their sound on a northern tongue.

And Kenner concludes by saying:

> It is Bunting's unique distinction that he has opened, in his seventh decade, a new career, after being in his forties the most accomplished school-of-Pound poet alive. It's ultimately Pound's

lesson he is now rethinking in local conditions, the speech of the places of his boyhood, the here-and-now he spent a lifetime leaving behind him.

Pound's basic lesson to the poet (one learned also by Williams) is, I take it, a consciousness of the role of the syllable in composition—to adopt Davie's formulation in his book on Pound: "slowing down the surge from one line into the next in such a way that smaller components within the line (down to the very syllables) can recover weight and value." Clarke's pseudo-Celtic rhyme-schemes and Bunting's Northumbrian clarities ("Southrons would maul the music . . . ," he says) have in common with Poundian and Williamsite modernism this desire to recover the expressive weight of the heard syllable. Unlike either Williams or Oppen, they often bring this about through the distinctions of rhyme and assonance used in dazzling profusion.

When I reviewed Bunting's *Briggflatts* just after its appearance in 1966, I imagined that the cleanliness of its artistry would appeal to my old friend, the author of *Purity of Diction in English Verse*. I had some difficulty at first in persuading him that the poem was as good as I said it was, and as he had never warmed much to my regard for Williams either, I let the matter drop.[1] I didn't despair, however, since Oppen had ultimately appealed to us both. When, slightly over a decade later, in October 1977, Davie published in *Poetry Nation Review* an article entitled "English and American in *Briggflatts*," I was pleased to see that the message had got through. I think part of the message was this: that Bunting—who had been (so to speak) underground when *Purity of Diction* was published, his *Poems* of 1950 meagerly available from The Cleaners Press, Galveston, Texas—of all obscured poets had written a masterpiece which, surely, now mopped up any remaining rhetorical tendencies to write like

> By waste seas where the white bear quoted Virgil
> And sirens singing from our lady's sea-straw

or like

> Cast in a dice of bones I see the geese of Europe
> Gabble a skeleton jigsaw. . . .

---

1. Despite a sympathetic account of Williams's prose book *In the American Grain* ("The Legacy of Fenimore Cooper," *Essays in Criticism* 9, no. 3 [1959]), Davie remains adamant about most of the verse (see "A Demurral," *The New Republic*, April 20, 1987).

A further part of the message was that Bunting's lessons as a poet had been learned in association with men like Pound, Zukofsky, Williams, and Oppen and in the New York of objectivism. Perhaps the overriding lesson of the objectivists was that it is the poem and not the poet merits the reader's attention. Davie—and I relish the way he takes up one of my old grumbles about John Berryman—puts it like this:

> Teachers in English classrooms have for decades now persuaded school-children and students to conceive of the reading of a poem as a matter of responding to nudges that the poet, on this showing a debased rhetorician, is supposedly at every point administering to them. And accordingly English readers have taken to their bosoms a poet like the late John Berryman who though an American and at times a very affecting writer indeed, does nudge and cajole and coax his readers, in a way that one can be sure Americans such as Oppen and Zukofsky are offended and incensed by.

And Davie reaches out to include Bunting in this refusal of self-regard when he speaks of "a conviction that is wholesome, which the English reader needs to hear about even more than the American does: the conviction that a poem is a transaction between the poet and his subject more than it is a transaction between the poet and his readers." This Davie applies to Bunting's insistence in print and in interviews on the poem as artefact.

In coming back to the point at which I began, namely, to the author of *Purity of Diction*, I have been trying to register certain possibilities that accrued for the poet in the postwar years—years when that book suggested some of these possibilities, and years when a fresh approach to American poetry became possible. In a trajectory like this, one of the things that stands out for somebody who has lived through it all is how quickly it seems to have happened, yet how slowly in fact the essential news has been in travelling and how soon it can be forgotten. The sixties were an era when American poetry was excitingly re-available to us as readers and poets, and it was a time when what happened in New York in the thirties was finally brought to bear in an English poem of length, Bunting's *Briggflatts*. I wonder whether the sense of all that is perhaps growing a little faint now and is in danger of passing out of the memory along with the sparse obituaries of Oppen and Bunting in 1985. I hope that what I have written here may have helped to suggest the outlines of this past era and to keep in mind a few of the names that made it poetically memorable.

# Donald Davie:
# Self-Portraits in Verse

## *Helen Vendler**

THE TRENCHANT and pugnacious self visible in Donald Davie's prose is not quite the self we find portrayed in his lyrics. The self-portrait in the lyrics is a truer, more vexing, and more distressing one than the prose portrait of a sturdy dissenter. Of course the two portraits overlap, not only in intelligence and depth, but in a common style—one that prefers a "horizontal" conversational force to a "vertical" address upward, one that emphasizes the urbane over the romantic, one that insists on the precise and the rational (even in religious matters) over the ecstatic. In the prose and poetry alike, these "sane" and "civil" aspects of style resemble the proverbial figleaf; they are adopted by Davie to hide the primordial shame of rage, pain, cruelty, and doubt. (I hasten to add that Davie's poetry not only admits this shame, but makes it the substance of his finest poems.)

In the prose, intellect is called to the bar to justify the air of truculence; the sinner's sin, not Davie's secret pleasure in condemnation, is indicted. When Davie says, for instance, of Hopkins, "He has no respect for the language, but gives it Sandow-exercises until it is a muscle-bound monstrosity,"[1] we read the remark for a view of Hopkins. Here, I choose to read it for a view of Davie, as I also read the offense he takes at Galway Kinnell:

> What a fearsome responsibility for the poet, to lead his readers into bestiality . . . a challenge worthy of a titan! So Charles Manson may have thought. Will Galway Kinnell choose to be a titan, or a human being? [Davie's ellipsis].[2]

*My essay is reprinted here from my collection *The Music of What Happens* (Cambridge, Mass., 1988).

1. *Purity of Diction in English Verse* (New York, 1953), 175; hereafter cited as *PD*.
2. *The Poet in the Imaginary Museum*, ed. Barry Alpert (Manchester, 1977), 284; hereafter cited as *PIM*.

The extraordinary animus in these quotations (examples could be multiplied) suggests that the wish to denounce may be Davie's strongest emotion, that his most burning desire is to be that societal outlaw, the prophet, calling "Woe unto you" to his society. He is not above voicing such a desire:

> The fact that American poets can now cast themselves as the
> dissident conscience of their nation, just as Russian and Polish and
> Hungarian poets have consistently done, ought to bring home to
> the English reader how remote from our current ways of thinking is
> any such conception of what being a poet means. As for the
> English poet, he may find himself wishing that the acute but
> muffled tensions between himself and his society might build up to
> the point of strain where he too might be able, without stridency or
> falseness, to speak for the honour of his nation.[3]

However, in recoil from these prophetic and denunciatory impulses in himself, Davie draws a distinction—the single most important for his poetry—between being a prophet and being a poet. He draws it in the context of a discussion of poetic control, criticizing "a dishevelled poetry [where] the poem and the experience behind the poem are . . . manifestly out of [the poet's] control." The passage is a long one, but central to Davie's life and poetic:

> To be sure, 'control' is a word that may easily be misunderstood.
> Yet I think we need it in order to acknowledge how much of the
> poetic activity in the act of composition can be summed up in
> words like 'judgement' and 'prudence'. For I should maintain, in
> the teeth of Kenneth Rexroth, that, as for *prophetic* poetry (which
> may be, but need not be, confessional poetry also), it is necessarily
> an inferior poetry. . . . The prophet is above being fair-minded—
> judiciousness he leaves to someone else. But the poet will absolve
> himself from none of the responsibilities of being human, he will
> leave none of those responsibilities to 'someone else'; and being
> human involves the responsibility of being judicious and fair-
> minded. In this way the poet supports the intellectual venture of
> humankind, taking his place along with (though *above*, yet also
> along with) the scholar and the statesman and the learned divine.
> His poetry supports and nourishes and helps to shape *culture*; the
> prophet, however, is outside culture and, really, at war with it. He
> exists on sufferance; he is on society's expense-account, part of
> what society can sometimes afford. Not so the poet; he is what
> society cannot dispense with.[4]

3. Ibid., 149.
4. Ibid., 146.

Davie's prizing of the judicious and the fair-minded accounts for part of his lifelong quarrel with Pound, the poet whose "sculptural" aim in verse he most admires. The quarrel stems also from Pound's abolition of syntax—the very factor (by contrast to perception, which is phrasal and atomistic) that enacts in verse, as Davie sees it, the presence of intellect and law:

> [Pound] pins his faith on individual words, grunts, broken phrases, half-uttered exclamations (as we find them in the Cantos), on speech atomized, all syllogistic and syntactical forms broken down. Hence his own esteem of the definite lands him at least in yawning vagueness. . . .
> It would be too much to say that this is the logical end of abandoning prose syntax. But at least the development from imagism in poetry to fascism in politics is clear and unbroken. . . . It is impossible not to trace a connection between the laws of syntax and the laws of society, between tearing a word from its context and choosing a leader out of the ruck. One could almost say, on this showing, that to dislocate syntax in poetry is to threaten the rule of law in the civilized community.[5]

Davie's fondness for quarrelsome apodictic statement of this sort—so pervasively characteristic of his essays—might be expected to reappear in his verse. And so, in a way, it does; but what is apodictically stated there is the prevalence—indeed, the inescapability—of moral and intellectual error. This disarming paradox, whereby stormy assertion of the truth of the prevalence of error saves both prophecy and peccancy, is to me the strongest guarantee of Davie's believability as a poet. The particular torment in which rigidity meets errancy is the hallmark of his verse. And because this torment is most visible in his memorable self-portraits (some phrased in the third person but still visibly self-portraits), I want to direct this essay toward a few of these, early and late.

The Davie self-portrait is simplest when stiff resolve and chagrined change of heart are enacted in separate poems, as they are in two poems dealing with Ireland. Davie, with ties to Ireland stemming from his period of teaching at Trinity College in the fifties, vows in 1969 never again to return to "Ireland of the Bombers." The word to notice in the poem of that name is not the word of offended British patriotism, "innocents," but the two inserted words of self-knowledge, "stiffly" and "empty," and the decisive word "home":

> Dublin, young manhood's ground,
> Never more I'll roam;

5. *PD*, 99.

Stiffly I call my strayed
Affections home.

Blackbird of Derrycairn,
Irish song, farewell.
Bombed innocents could not
Sing half so well.

Green Leinster, do not weep
For me, since we must part;
Dry eyes I pledge to thee,
And empty heart.[6]

Eight years later, returning on invitation to Ireland, Davie reproaches himself for inconsistency:

"Green Leinster, never weep
For me, since we must part.
Dry eyes I pledge to thee,
And empty heart."

Travelling by train
—For I am a travelling man—
Across fields that I laid
Under this private ban,

I thought: a travelling man
Will come and go, here now
And gone tomorrow, and
He cannot keep a vow.

Forsworn, coming to Sligo
To mend my battered past,
I thought: it must be true;
The solder cannot last.

But, dear friends, I could weep.
Is it the bombs have made
Old lesions knit, old chills
Warm, and old ghosts be laid?

Atrociously, such changes!
The winning gentleness
Gentler still, and even
The poets not so reckless.

6. *Selected Poems* (Manchester, 1985), 117–18; hereafter cited as *SP.*

> Twenty-five years at least
> Higher up the slope
> That England plunges down:
> That much ground for hope.

After the expression of these hopes and fears, the "stranger," as Davie calls himself, leaves Ireland. He had called his strayed affections home to England in 1969, but now "home" has a different meaning:

> Easy pronouncements from
> The stranger, as he leaves!
> The truth is, he was home
> —Or so he half-believes.[7]

The poem ends in temporariness and temporizing, with a home in Ireland as well as in England.

When the stiff man melts, one sees "the life that is fluent in even the wintriest bronze" (Stevens). Something in Davie is reluctant to manifest that fluent life, because for him it is allied with the treacherous and the slippery. And yet life, as it offers itself to inspection, always betrays that mobility. Davie's chief statement on the subject appears in *Thomas Hardy and British Poetry:*

> Those cast bronzes which Gautier and Pound respond to so eagerly, as showing how art can be durable and rigid, in fact are fashioned out of the most fluid material; the molten bronze is *poured* into the mould. The rigidity and hardness of the end product are in direct proportion to the fluid malleability in the process of production. Most exegesis of Pound's *Cantos* is wide of the mark because by its very nature exegesis pursues what is said, at the expense of *how* it is said; and this means that the exegetes lead us into a world of continual flux and change which does not at all correspond to our experience as readers, of responding to the hard bright surfaces which Pound's language, when he is in control, presents to us as a sequence of images, each sharp-edged and distinct. The exegetes are necessarily concerned with the process, not with the product; with the bronze while it is still molten, not with the rigid surfaces of the finished bust. . . . [The individual psyche] is, as we experience it by introspection, a realm above all protean and malleable, a world of metamorphosis, of merging and self-transforming shapes and fluid contours. Not in those subterranean wynds and galleries, nor in the kneaded wax and the poured bronze which seem their natural concomitant, shall we find what

---

7. Ibid., 118–19.

some of us will always want more than anything else—the resistant
and persisting, the rigid and the hard, everything that poets have
yearned for naïvely in the image of the stone that resists the chisel
and confronts the sunlight.[8]

As exegete, I indeed want to glance at the fluid self in Davie's verse,
but I am equally interested in the moulds into which he pours it. The Irish
poems that I have quoted make a childlike and archaic choice of the ballad,
a deliberate simplification of form in the service of the single vow made
and broken, but it is evident that the vow made fits the ballad form, while
the vow transgressed—except for the "pure" moments of hail and farewell—fits uneasily into the ballad lilt, and in fact, since Davie is true to the
tenor of his own complication, he wrests the form from ballad stanza to
intellectual quatrain by the middle of the poem.

It is a sign of Davie's intentness as a poet that he has found a large
supply of more complex forms into which to cast his anguish of self-
contradiction. In the most accomplished of his religious poems, a recent
one called "Advent," the formal equivalent for his mutinous bluster (his
own admirable phrase) is a harsh Anglo-Saxon emphatic alliteration:
sooner/settled, fearless/flinging, loosed/leash, maunders/mutinous, bet-
ter/blusters, bustles/business. The formal equivalent of the predictability
of his contrariness is strict repetition: no sooner/no sooner/no sooner. The
formal equivalent of his absence of social decorum is the irregularity of his
seven-line stanza rhyming unexpectedly and willfully aslant. In spite of
the ostentatiousness of these traits of language, they do not outshine the
bitterly acute self-portrait of a contradictory man, despising both stability
and restlessness, impatient with domesticity while requiring it, arrogant
in indecorum, self-important even in the light of God's advent, and finally
terrified and rebellious at once, an impotent creature tamed at the last not
by Christ's power but by Christ's need of him, as Christ "prevents" him,
in St. Paul's idiom, "in charity." Here is the whole of "Advent," a spec-
tacular poem of self-knowledge.

Advent

Some I perceive, content
And stable in themselves
And in their place, on whom
One that I know casts doubt;
Knowing himself of those

8. *Thomas Hardy and British Poetry* (London, 1973), 176–77; hereafter cited as *TH*.

No sooner settled in
Than itching to get out.

I hear and partly know
Of others, fearless and
Flinging out, whom one
I know tries to despise;
Knowing himself of those
No sooner loosed than they
Weeping sue for the leash.

Some I see live snug,
Embosomed. One I know
Maunders, is mutinous,
Is never loved enough;
Being of those who are
No sooner safely lodged
They chafe at cherishing.

Some I know who seem
Always in keeping, whom
One I know better blusters
He will not emulate;
Being of those who keep
At Advent, Whitsuntide,
And Harvest Home in Lent.

Some who are his kin
Have strewn the expectant floor
With rushes, long before
The striding shadow grows
And grows above them; he,
The deeper the hush settles,
Bustles about more business.

The eclipse draws near as he
Scuttles from patch to shrinking
Patch of the wintry light,
Chattering, gnashing, not
Oh not to be forced to his knees
By One who, turned to, brings
All quietness and ease.

Self-contradictions, I
Have heard, do not bewilder
That providential care.

Switch and reverse as he
Will, this one I know,
One whose need meets his
Prevents him everywhere.[9]

Davie may reproach us for remembering the pitiable scuttling, chattering, and gnashing of content in this poem more than the stability and firmness of its verse, and his rebuke to exegetes for their emphasis on the psychological has of course its virtue: were the scuttling and the gnashing not poised and balanced in art they could not register as their furtive selves.

Even in an elegy for a friend, Davie will insist on the conscious element in the making of poetry. Unless the "smell of death" undergoes an aestheticizing process, the poet's words of grief will not become a poem. Because for Davie aestheticizing means "sculpting" (as it did not for, say, Keats), a taste accustomed to Keatsian "warmth" may see Davie in his minimalist moments as cold, remote, or scant of feeling. Here is Davie's apologia, his self-portrait as elegist:

### July, 1964

I smell a smell of death.
Roethke, who died last year
with whom I drank in London,
wrote the book I am reading;
a friend, of a firm mind,
has died or is dying now,
a telegram informs me;
the wife of a neighbour died
in three quick months of cancer.

Love and art I practise;
they seem to be worth no more
and no less than they were.
The firm mind practised neither.
It practised charity
vocationally and
yet for the most part truly.
Roethke, who practised both,
was slack in his art by the end.

The practice of an art
is to convert all terms
into the terms of art.

9. *SP*, 120–21.

> By the end of the third stanza
> death is a smell no longer;
> it is a problem of style.
> A man who ought to know me
> wrote in a review
> my emotional life was meagre.[10]

Is there anything to be said for this as a poem? It seems stinting and bare—almost an instance of the reviewer's quoted accusation of meagerness. If we are not to agree with the reviewer that a stinted style is the sign of a stunted soul, we must look into its propriety, seeking in it signs of that excess or redundancy which, in however hidden a way, is the mark of every art, even a "sculpted" one. (Davie himself says in an early poem that in art "all is patent, and a latency / Is manifest or nothing.")[11] The redundancy of the first stanza of the elegy is that of the repetition of the fact of death and of its verb: not "Roethke is dead, as are my firm-minded friend and my neighbour's wife," but "I smell a smell of death. / Roethke . . . died . . . ; / a friend . . . / has died or is dying . . . ; / the wife of a neighbour died." The redundancy of the second stanza is that of the verb "to practise": "Love and art I practise; / . . . The firm mind practised neither. / It practised charity. . . . / Roethke . . . practised both." The extreme dryness of this double redundancy should not blind us to its deliberateness as it sets death against various practices of life. The conundrum of the middle of the poem seems like an extended syllogism with some mysterious missing terms:

> I practise love and art;
> My friend practised neither love nor art;
> My friend practised charity
>    vocationally and yet truly;
> Roethke practised love and art
>    and yet his art went slack;
> Practice does not make perfect;
> ?[I do not practise charity;]
> Death seems neither to increase nor decrease
>    the value of love and art.
> ?[I will die whether or not I practise
>    love or art or charity.]
> The relation of art, love, and charity to
>    death is?

10. Ibid., 59.
11. Ibid., 22.

The third stanza elucidates one hidden proposition, claiming that art dissolves the problem of death by turning it into a problem of style. The reflexive aphorism that "solves" the conundrum partakes of the arid excess of the rest of this harsh elegy:

> The practice of an art
> is to convert all terms
> into the terms of art.

There are moments when aesthetic practice, like religious practice, is habitual, almost (one might say) mechanical, or at least stoic. It can be particularly so in elegy, where a complaisance in "sympathy" or "pity" hides voyeuristic dangers, where a too ready "emotional life," eager not to seem "meagre," is both an aesthetic and a personal betrayal.

At the same time, there is something alleviating, something of the solacing and assuaging power of art, visible in Davie's clenched stanzas. Two features soften his lines here: first, the recurrent feminine endings, composing a quick mini-poem within the whole ("London, informs me, cancer, practise, neither, truly, stanza, longer, know me, meagre"): second, the extra syllables lightening the verse. The poem would sound very different with strict lines and masculine endings. We would then hear a stiffer, less grieving voice, something like the following (if I may be forgiven a rewriting):

> By the end of the verse
> death is a smell no more;
> it is a problem of style.
> A man who knows my work
> wrote in a review
> my emotional life was cold.

The "emotional" Davie lurks in the feminine endings and the reluctant syllabic excess supervening over the "dry" repetitions and the "cold" aphorism.

"We could stand the world if it were hard all over," Davie remarks in "Across the Bay";[12] but no poem can be "hard all over." What Davie calls, in the same poem, "the venomous soft jelly, the undersides," must (for all his sculpting) show through, be represented, have its voice. When he is not being spiteful toward the soft underside, the merely human, Davie can relent toward it. A child of the stony Yorkshire hills, he finds himself at a loss when he must live in the flat wet Cambridgeshire fens:

12. Ibid., 50.

> Tedium, a poison,
> Swells in the sac for the hillborn, dwelling in the flat. . . .
> But a beauty there is, noble, dependent, unshrinking
> In being at somebody's mercy, wide and alone.
> I imagine a hillborn sculptor suddenly thinking
> One could live well in a country short of stone.[13]

For all Davie's insistence in prose on the sturdy "dissentient voice" of his dissenting forebears, it is clear that what draws him to Christianity is precisely the meekness of it—"noble, dependent, unshrinking, . . . being at somebody's mercy," the defenselessness of the sacrificial victim. An art of this meek sort finally appeals to Davie less than the art of the fortress; but in some of his self-portraits he does recognize an aspect of his poetry that is unplanned, "gracious" rather than consciously formed, revelatory rather than sought after. He says of poetry:

> This is the assessor whose word
> Can always be relied on;
> It tells you when has occurred
> Any change you decide on.
>
> More preciously still, it tells
> Of growth not groped towards,
> In the seaway a sound of bells
> From a landfall not on the cards.[14]

However, Davie's more usual self-portrait, especially in the earlier poems, is that of a man and poet at once "disciplined" and obstinate, the archetypal nonconformist, rebellious except in the stern bonds of verse and dissenting Christianity:

> The Nonconformist
>
> X, whom society's most mild command,
> For instance evening dress, infuriates,
> In art is seen confusingly to stand
> For disciplined conformity, with Yeats.
>
> Taxed to explain what this resentment is
> He feels for small proprieties, it comes,
> He likes to think, from old enormities
> And keeps the faith with famous martyrdoms.

13. Ibid., 45.
14. Ibid., 43.

> Yet it is likely, if indeed the crimes
> His fathers suffered rankle in his blood,
> That he finds least excusable the times
> When they acceded, not when they withstood.
>
> How else explain this bloody-minded bent
> To kick against the prickings of the norm;
> When to conform is easy, to dissent;
> And when it is most difficult, conform?[15]

The formal symmetry of "The Nonconformist" (perfect rhymes; no unrhymed lines; each quatrain a sentence; a syntax processional and epigrammatic) is at war with its disruptive lexicon: "infuriates," "confusingly," "resentment," "enormities," "martyrdoms," "crimes," "rankle," "bloody-minded," "kick," "dissent," "difficult." The poem resists our wish to call its resenting and bloody-minded lexicon Davie's soul, its strict quatrains his intellect, by reminding us that his soul too has its desire for conformity. But Davie here renders the "emotional life" of resentment more vividly, I think, than the emotional life of "disciplined conformity." That is (to use the language of the Russian formalists), the lexicon is "foregrounded" (by the mere rarity in lyric of such truculent words) over the form (the common rhymed pentameter quatrain). Davie, a conscious artist if there ever was one, would not be unaware of this difficulty, and in fact brings it boldly to the fore (without solving it) by repeating, in "Method. For Ronald Gaskell," Gaskell's critique of the combination of violent matter and ordered verse:

> For such a theme (atrocities) you find
> My style, you say, too neat and self-possessed.
> I ought to show a more disordered mind.[16]

Davie's retort, in this early poem, maintained his position:

> An even tenor's sensitive to shock,
> And stains spread furthest where the floor's not cracked.

Davie did not foresee the cracking of the floor, and the unevenness of the tenor, in his two most ambitious later self-portraits, "In the Stopping Train" and "The Gardens of the Savoy," the poems with which I will close this essay. But already, in "Life Encompassed," he had faced squarely the loss of earlier certainties, both of "method" and of feeling:

15. Ibid., 30–31.
16. Ibid., 18.

How often I have said,
"This will never do,"
Of ways of feeling that now
I trust in, and pursue!

Do traverses tramped in the past,
My own, criss-crossed as I forge
Across from another quarter
Speak of a life encompassed?

Well, life is not research.
No one asks you to map the terrain,
Only to get across it
In new ways, time and again.

How many such, even now,
I dismiss out of hand
As not to my purpose, not
Unknown, just unexamined.[17]

Later, "Oak Openings" (another poem in the same stiff trimeters Davie
has so made his own) justified a change of style without itself embodying
one:

It is not as if the attention
Steadily encroaches
Upon the encircling dark;
The circle about the torch is
Moving, it opens new
Glades by obscuring old ones.

Twigs crack under foot, as the tread
Changes. The forge-ahead style
Of our earliest ventures flags;
It becomes, as mile follows mile
Inexhaustibly, an exhausted
Wavering trudge, the explorer's.[18]

Here tread changes to trudge, forging ahead to flagging, inexhaust-
ibleness to exhaustion; and are we obscuring, wavering, or exploring? All
three, the poem suggests; and the tentativeness of all three verbs is new in
Davie. Nonetheless, the poem moves with a martial and Roman tread,
rather than enacting its sense of poetry as exhausted wavering, as flagging

17. Ibid., 43.
18. Ibid., 72.

exploring. The writing retains the old style, but the content questions Davie's simpler division of human possibility into "action" and "reaction," with which he had armed a more intolerant poem of self-exposure, "Revulsion":

> My strongest feeling all
> My life has been
> I recognize, revulsion
> From the obscene;
> That more than anything
> My life-consuming passion.
>
> That so much more reaction
> Than action should have swayed
> My life and rhymes
> Must be the heaviest charge
> That can be brought against
> Me, or my times.[19]

The final witty turn against the time out of joint cannot entirely deflect Davie's morose delectation in his own capacity for revulsion (however he may condemn it). Here self-condemnation, it seems to me, does not entirely escape complacency; and one doubts that a man of Davie's harsh temperament could have found any previous era more to his liking. (It is true that Davie has created, in his recent *Dissentient Voice*, a picture of eighteenth-century Dissent as "a vector of Enlightenment," which [however historians finally may judge his argument] serves him as a paradigm of a better era; but inventing or scanning such a paradigm is an imaginative exercise, different from having lived in another era and found it good.)

In the asperities of his earlier verse, Davie could hardly have foreseen the day when he could imagine himself in a comic self-portrait, mocking his own dependencies (alcohol, tobacco, coffee) as much as his own vaunted Rationality:

>                         (I think
>
> Either I need, so early, the day's first drink or
> This is what a sense of sin amounts to. . . . )
> Prosopopoeia everywhere: Stout Labour
> Gets up with his pipe in his mouth or lighting
> The day's first *Gauloise-filtre*; then stout
> Caffeine like a fierce masseur

19. Ibid., 71.

> Rams him abreast of the day; stout Sin
> Is properly a-tremble. . . .
>                                         and stout
> Love gets up out of rumpled sheets and goes singing
> Under his breath to the supermarket, the classroom,
> The briskly unhooded
> Bureaucratic typewriter. . . .
>
> And that mob of ideas? Don't knock them. The sick
>      pell-mell
> Goes by the handsome Olympian name of Reason.[20]

Charming as this ascent into geniality (and self-forgiveness) is, it is less than typical of Davie.

But the nine bitter poems composing the stunning sequence "In the Stopping Train" will, it seems to me, stand as "Davie" in many future anthologies. The lyric sequence, as many poets besides Davie have discovered, enables the contradictions and eddyings of personality to lie side by side without mutual repression. In embarking on this personal sequence, in allowing for an aspectual, "fluid" form of mental and psychological life, Davie must, it seems to me, abandon an essential part of his earlier sculptural "method." It could be objected that a "sculptural" aesthetic allows for the aspectual in the way that one might walk round a statue, seeing its volumes differently each time. But Davie's sculptural aesthetic was formulated from the point of view of the sculptor, not the beholder. The bronze is poured; a rigid mass is created, and stands still. Not for that method the halting metaphor of the "local" (as we in America would call it) or the "stopping" train. The stopping train is a metaphor representing an intolerable prolongation in Time, not a serene extension in Space, and is therefore, for the spatial and sculptural Davie, a figure for unmitigated suffering.

The opening poem of the sequence is unnerving in its explicitness concerning punishment, justice, and torment:

> I have got into the slow train
> again. I made the mistake
> knowing what I was doing,
> knowing who had to be punished.
>
> I know who has to be punished:
> the man going mad inside me;

20. Ibid., 98–99.

whether I am fleeing
from him or towards him.

This journey will punish the bastard:
he'll have his flowering gardens
to stare at through the hot window;
words like "laurel" won't help.

He abhors his fellows,
especially children; let there
not for pity's sake
be a crying child in the carriage.

So much for pity's sake.
The rest for the sake of justice:
torment him with his hatreds
and love of fictions.

The punishing slow pace
punishes also places along the line
for having, some of them, Norman
or Hanoverian stone-work:

his old familiars, his
exclusive prophylactics.
He'll stare his fill at their
emptiness on this journey. . . .

Torment him with his hatreds,
torment him with his false
loves. Torment him with time
that has disclosed their falsehood.

Time, the exquisite torment!
His future is a slow
and stopping train through places
whose names used to have virtue.[21]

Superb in this beginning, the sequence nevertheless ends badly, it seems to me, with the introduction of a red herring in the form of a bearded hippie who takes "some weird girl off to a weird / commune, clutching at youth"—as though that were the only visible alternative to an abhorrence of humanity. Though Davie cannot explain why he "abhors his fellows," one suspects that he does so first of all because he abhors himself. It is with a fascinated interest that one watches the spectacle of an

21. Ibid., 91–92.

author being so hard on himself, lacking even the lyric exaltation and musicality of Dostoevskian abjectness:

> The things he has been spared . . .
> "Gross egotist!" Why don't
> his wife, his daughter, shrill
> that in his face?
>
> Love and pity seem
> the likeliest explanations;
> another occurs to him—
> despair too would be quiet.[22]

When one's family despairs of cure, and sinks from expostulation to silence, even God, it might be thought, would give up on the sinner. Of the nine poems in the sequence, this, the fifth and central one, is the only one wholly devoid of ornament. It exists as a bald and awful axis on which the rest turn.

To the poet in the stopping train, his underdeveloped senses are a source of anguish, especially in comparison with his monstrous inner overdevelopment of language:

> Flowers, it seems are important.
> And he can name them all,
> identify hardly any.[23]

The doppelgänger the speaker meets in the train, all eye and no feeling, becomes a Kafkaesque self-portrait:

> Apologies won't help him:
> his spectacles flared like paired
> lamps as he turned his head.
>
> I knew they had been ranging,
> paired eyes like mine,
> igniting and occluding.[24]

And language, far from existing in sculptural form (or even in the measured dance of Eliot's *Quartets*), becomes instead the compelled agony of the tarantella. Words, poisoned by self-venom, move in a dreadful jig, symbolized for Davie by the irrepressible tendency of language toward polyvalence, manifest in the pun. The passenger in the interminable

22. Ibid., 94–95.
23. Ibid., 94.
24. Ibid., 96.

stopping train of ennui feels the word "pain" seeping into the "pane" of his metaphor, and as he does so, there occurs the last collapse of his early "sculptural" language:

> The dance of words
> is a circling prison, thought
> the passenger staring through
> the hot unmoving pane
> of boredom. It is not
> thank God a dancing pain,
> he thought, though it starts to jig
> now. (The train is moving.) "This,"
> he thought in a rising panic
> (Sit down! Sit down!)
> "this much I can command,
> exclude. Dulled words, keep still!
> Be the inadequate, cloddish
> despair of me!" No good:
> they danced, as the smiling land
> fled past the pane, the pun's
> galvanized *tarantelle*.[25]

"In the Stopping Train" is Davie's masterpiece of self-portraiture. In it, forms of relenting (toward pity, toward flowers, toward courage, toward sociability, even toward despair) cohabit with forms of stubbornness in self-torment; placidity, aimed at, coincides with panic undergone; and stony reiteration (an old resource) goes hand in hand with baffled invention. The poem has for me the stability of ten years' acquaintance, and the power of the unforgettable.

And yet, I am at the moment under the spell of Davie's latest, not entirely successful, but grimmest, piece of self-portraiture, the sequence "The Gardens of the Savoy."[26] There is an explanatory note to the gardens of the title: "In London, between the Strand and the Embankment, frequented by winos and worse." "Come back," calls this new two-part invention (as if echoing the end of "In the Stopping Train"), "to the point of pain." Against the social evils of war ("There are no righteous wars"), racism (the Ku Klux Klan, race wars in Africa), and technology (missiles and rockets; Challenger; the poet's grandchildren bearing home to England a toy moon-buggy), Davie sets worship ("our first and last mission"), aesthetic ambition (for "brilliance"), and poetic alienation. He

25. Ibid.
26. Printed in *Parnassus* 13 (Spring-Summer 1986): 43–52.

is, he perceives, to take instruction in his sixties not only from the aubade of birds ("birdbrains"), but also from those derelicts and drunkards that haunt the gardens of the Savoy, figures for the "upside-down *elite*" who become artists:

> I am to learn from them,
>     from layabouts
> feeding from garbage in the Savoy gardens? . . .
>
> I am, I am; and let the time show how. . . .
>
> A logic not for the many,
>     for the upside-down *elite*,
>     for the self-chosen, cropping
> plastic and mineral fruit
> of the garbage of the Savoy,
> Proserpine's hell-side gardens;
> not Nature, Art.

This is a Swinburnian moment:

> No growth of moor or coppice,
>     No heather-flower or vine,
> But bloomless buds of poppies,
>     Green grapes of Proserpine,
> Pale beds of blowing rushes
> Where no leaf blooms or blushes
> Save this whereout she crushes
>     For dead men deadly wine. . . .
>
> Pale, beyond porch and portal,
>     Crowned with calm leaves, she stands
> Who gathers all things mortal
>     With cold immortal hands. . . .
>         ("The Garden of Proserpine")

That the stout dissenter should, in his sixties, place himself with Swinburne and the derelicts of the gardens of the Savoy means perhaps, in the Yeatsian sense, that "he completes his partial mind." But there are formal changes to be remarked as well. The ghost of Pound, whose fanaticism ruined his poetry, haunts Davie both as mentor and as warning, in "the grand or great / bankruptcy of the *Cantos*." Pound (the derelict, the reprobate) had at his best (according to this poem) "deeps in him . . . unemphatic," and the word "unemphatic," introduced as a *leitmotiv*, grows to become here the aesthetic word *par excellence*—a strange word for the decisive dissenter to end on, unforeseeable entirely

in his early years. The poetic line is to be not epigrammatic, not authoritative, not sententious, but to be "light as a feather," to "fall floatingly," to
have "the lightness of . . . release." "The gift: non-emphasis":

> Drunk, *in ecstasis*
> however artificially,
> a man is reaching
> for the ultimate
> lack of emphasis: "Gods
>     or it may be one God moves
> about us in bright air."
>
> . . . . . . . . . . . . . . . . . . . . . . . . . .
>
> Brilliance is known in
> what the tired wing, though
> it never so crookedly towers,
> wins at last into: air
> diamond-clear, unemphatic.

As the passage I have just quoted reveals, Davie has worked to find a
verse that will not display the tight, repetitive, alliterative, patterned beats
of his earlier "emphatic" style. The tense trimeters, however, wait always
in the wings; as I began by saying, the wish to assert apodictically the
absence of certainty hovers always behind, and in, Davie's writing. That
wish reaches perhaps its most absurd and exploded expression at the end
of "The Gardens of the Savoy," in the closing trimeters:

> "Can you tell the down from the up?"
> The unthinkable answer: No.

Are we to understand that the answer is "No," and that that is unthinkable? or that it is unthinkable that one should give "No" as an answer? I
am not, myself, sure.

     Our trochaic and alliterative British poet—Dón-ald Dá-vie—be-
trays, in this most recent self-portrait, his affinity with American modernist verse. He has argued, in *Thomas Hardy and British Poetry*, that "for many
years now British poetry and American poetry haven't been on speaking
terms. But the truth is rather that they haven't been on *hearing* terms—the
American reader can't hear the British poet, neither his rhythms nor his
tone of voice."[27] If Davie is hearable by an American listener, it is in part
because he has listened, more closely than most British poets, to Amer-

27. *TH*, 184.

ican rhythms and tones. It is true, as he says in "Poetry and the Other Modern Arts,"[28] that "poetry forces us back inside the iron cage of being of a certain race speaking a certain language" (all of us Pisan captives), but it is also true, as he adds, that English is more than most an international tongue. He has become in it an international poet. And though he says of the poet, "It is certain that he does *not* need a critic!"[29] he may, in his person as a poet, at least tolerate our praise. Among his subjects— political, religious, domestic, and historical—not the least is his thorny, restless, dissatisfied, and seeking self. That we end by knowing that self so well—in the way we know the increasingly perturbed, vexed, and resigned face of Rembrandt—is a testimony to Davie's exploratory, stern, and ceaselessly revised art of the self-portrait.

28. *PIM*, 162.
29. Ibid., 163.

# Contributors

VEREEN BELL, Professor of English at Vanderbilt University, is the author of *Robert Lowell: Nihilist as Hero* and *The Achievement of Cormac McCarthy.*

BERNARD BERGONZI is Professor of English at the University of Warwick. His many publications on modern literature include *Hero's Twilight, The Myth of Modernism & Twentieth Century Literature,* and *The Turn of a Century.*

THOM GUNN, English poet long resident in California, has taught at Berkeley. His many books of poetry include *The Sense of Movement, Moly, My Sad Captains,* and more recently *The Passages of Joy.*

ROBERT VON HALLBERG, Professor of English at the University of Chicago, is the author of *Charles Olson: The Scholar's Art* and *American Poetry & Culture.*

GEORGE MILLS HARPER, R. O. Lawton Distinguished Professor at Florida State University, has written mostly on Yeats and Blake and the Platonist tradition. His books include *The Neoplatonism of William Blake* and *Yeats' Golden Dawn.*

SEAMUS HEANEY, Irish poet teaching at Harvard, has published eight volumes of poetry (most recently *Station Island*) and a collection of critical essays, *Preoccupations.*

MARK JARMAN teaches writing and modern poetry at Vanderbilt. He is co-editor of *The Reaper* and has published three volumes of poetry, *North Sea, The Rope Walker,* and *Far Away.*

GABRIEL JOSIPOVICI, novelist, dramatist, and critic, is Professor of English at the University of Sussex. His critical works include *The World and the Book, The Lessons of Modernism,* and, forthcoming, *The Book of God: An Essay on the Bible.*

JAMES KILROY, formerly Professor of English at Vanderbilt, is now Dean of the College of Arts and Sciences at Tulane. He has written mostly on Irish literature, including a study of *The Irish Short Story* and (with Robert Hogan) *The Modern Irish Drama: A Documentary History.*

LAURENCE LERNER, formerly of the University of Sussex, is now William R. Kenan Professor of English at Vanderbilt. The most recent of his eight volumes of poetry is *Rembrandt's Mirror;* his critical books include *Love & Marriage, The Literary Imagination,* and *The Frontiers of Literature.*

255

ALASDAIR MACINTYRE is W. Alton Jones Distinguished Professor of Philosophy at Vanderbilt. His many books on moral and political philosophy include *Marxism & Christianity, Against the Self-Images of the Age,* and *After Virtue.*

WILLIAM PRATT, Professor of English at Miami University, is the author of *The Imagist Poem: Modern Poetry in Miniature* and many articles on modern poetry.

CLAUDE RAWSON, formerly of the University of Warwick, is now Professor of English at Yale. He writes mainly on the eighteenth century and on modern poetry. As well as studies of Swift and Fielding, he has written *Order from Confusion Sprung: Studies in 18th Century Literature.*

C. K. STEAD is better known in New Zealand as a poet and novelist, and in Europe and America as a critic of modern poetry. His books include *The New Poetic* and *Pound, Yeats, Eliot and the Modernist Movement.*

CHARLES TOMLINSON is Professor of Poetry at Bristol University. His many volumes of poetry began with *Seeing is Believing* and include, among the most recent, *The Flood* and *Notes from New York.* His *Collected Poems* was published in 1985.

HELEN VENDLER is William R. Kenan, Jr., Professor of English and American Literature and Language at Harvard University, and poetry critic of *The New Yorker.* She has written books on Yeats, Stevens, Keats, and Herbert, and has edited *The Harvard Book of Contemporary American Poetry.*